Radical Center:
The Heart of Gestalt Therapy

Selected Writings of
Erving and Miriam Polster

Edited and with an Introduction
by Arthur Roberts

The Gestalt Institute of Cleveland Press

Titles From GICPress

ORGANIZATIONAL CONSULTING: A GESTALT APPROACH
Edwin C. Nevis
GESTALT RECONSIDERED: A NEW APPROACH TO CONTACT AND RESISTANCE
Gordon Wheeler
THE NEUROTIC BEHAVIOR OF ORGANIZATIONS
Uri Merry and George I. Brown
GESTALT THERAPY: PERSPECTIVES AND APPLICATIONS
Edwin C. Nevis
THE COLLECTIVE SILENCE: GERMAN IDENTITY AND THE LEGACY OF SHAME
Barbara Heimannsberg and Christopher J. Schmidt
COMMUNITY AND CONFLUENCE: UNDOING THE CLINCH OF OPPRESSION
Philip Lichtenberg
BECOMING A STEPFAMILY
Patricia Papernow
ON INTIMATE GROUND: A GESTALT APPROACH TO WORKING WITH COUPLES
Gordon Wheeler and Stephanie Backman
BODY PROCESS: WORKING WITH THE BODY IN PSYCHOTHERAPY
James I. Kepner
HERE, NOW, NEXT: PAUL GOODMAN AND THE ORIGINS OF GESTALT THERAPY
Taylor Stoehr
CRAZY HOPE & FINITE EXPERIENCE
Paul Goodman and Taylor Stoehr
IN SEARCH OF GOOD FORM: GESTALT THERAPY WITH COUPLES AND FAMILIES
Joseph C. Zinker
THE VOICE OF SHAME: SILENCE AND CONNECTION IN PSYCHOTHERAPY
Robert G. Lee and Gordon Wheeler
HEALING TASKS: PSYCHOTHERAPY WITH ADULT SURIVIVORS OF CHILDHOOD ABUSE
James I. Kepner
ADOLESCENCE: PSYCHOTHERAPY AND THE EMERGENT SELF
Mark McConville
GETTING BEYOND SOBRIETY: CLINICAL APPROACHES TO LONG-TERM RECOVERY
Michael Craig Clemmens
INTENTIONAL REVOLUTIONS: A SEVEN-POINT STRATEGY FOR TRANSFORMING ORGANIZATIONS
Edwin C. Nevis, Joan Lancourt and Helen G. Vassallo
IN SEARCH OF SELF: BEYOND INDIVIDUALISM IN WORKING WITH PEOPLE
Gordon Wheeler
THE HEART OF DEVELOPMENT: GESTALT APPROACHES TO WORKING WITH CHILDREN, ADOLESCENTS, AND THEIR WORLDS (2 Volumes)
Mark McConville and Gordon Wheeler
BACK TO THE BEANSTALK: ENCHANTMENT & REALITY FOR COUPLES
Judith R. Brown
THE DREAMER AND THE DREAM: ESSAYS AND REFLECTIONS ON GESTALT THERAPY
Rainette Eden Fantz and Arthur Roberts
A WELL-LIVED LIFE
Sylvia Fleming Crocker
THE UNFOLDING SELF
Jean-Marie Robine

From the Radical Center:
The Heart of Gestalt Therapy

Selected Writings of
Erving and Miriam Polster

Edited and with and Introduction by
Arthur Roberts

COPYRIGHT © 1999
by GICPress

Women in Gestalt Therapy appears here by permission of Brunner/Mazel
Gestalt Therapy: Evolution and Application appears here by permission of Brunner/Mazel
Therapy Without Resistance appears here by permission of Brunner/Mazel
Escape From the Present appears here by permission of Jossey-Bass
Tight Therapeutic Sequences appears here by permission of Brunner/Mazel
Every Person's Life is Worth a Novel appears here by permission of W.W. Norton & Co.
The Therapeutic Power of Attention appears here by permission of Brunner/Mazel
The Self in Action appears here by permission of Brunner/Mazel
Encounter in Community appears here by permission of Jossey-Bass
Eve's Daughters appears here by permission of Brunner/Mazel
Beyond One to One appears here by permission of Brunner/Mazel
A Contemporary Psychotherapy first appeared in Psychotherapy: Theory, Research and Practice, Volume 3, Number 1.
Sensory Functioning in Psychotherapy first appeared in Gestalt Therapy Now, Harper & Rowe

All rights reserved

Published by GICPress, Cambridge, MA

Gestalt Institute of Cleveland: 1588 Hazel Drive, Cleveland, OH, 44106

Distributed by The Analytic Press, Inc., Hillsdale, NJ

ISBN 0-88163-315-1

Cover Design by Karen Pfautz

DEDICATION

To our students over these many years. You have been stimulating participants in the evolution of our points of view. This dedication is one more loving connection.

ACKNOWLEDGMENTS

Many influences have contributed to this collection of writings, written over a span of 33 years under a number of different stimulations. We would especially like to thank Gordon Wheeler for thinking these scattered writings were worth gathering together into a book and having the editorial savvy to pull it off. His associate, Arch Roberts, has guided us in our day-to-day contact and we are grateful for his acuity, energy, wisdom and good spirit, as we knocked around ideas about how to put these writings together.

We wish to acknowledge the faculty of the Gestalt Institute of Cleveland, where we taught for many years. The faculty of those years helped make our early work a special pleasure. It was marvelous to be so closely involved with them, people who combined laughter, intelligence, friendship and open-mindedness to form an exciting community.

We wish also to acknowledge our current faculty, a group dear to us, with whom the exchange of ideas and friendship go continuingly hand in hand. They are: Sharon Grodner, Rich Hycner, John Reis, Roy Resnikoff and Anna Walden. Joined with them and us is George Sargent, who recently died too young.

Kathryn Conklin has been our secretary for many years and now is about to go off on her career in psychology. She is a sunny and bright addition to our lives, as well as making our office function

CONTENTS

Introduction *by Arthur Roberts* 13
Prologue 20

Part I : Setting the Stage

A Contemporary Psychotherapy 42
The Language of Experience 55
Sensory Functioning in Psychotherapy 65
Women in Therapy: a Gestalt Therapist's View 75
Gestalt Therapy: Evolution and Application 96

Part II : Transformation of Principles

Therapy Without Resistance: Gestalt Therapy 118
Escape from the Present 143
Tight Therapeutic Sequences 164
Every Person's Life is Worth a Novel 179
The Therapeutic Power of Attention 202
The Self in Action: A Gestalt Outlook 219
Translating Theory into Practice: Martin Heidegger and Gestalt Therapy 238
Commonality and Diversity in Gestalt Therapy 260
In Memory of Carl Rogers: Great Men Cast Great Shadows 277

Part III : The Role of Community

Encounter in Community 286
Eve's Daughters: The Forbidden Heroism of Women 312
Individuality and Communality 332
Beyond One to One 339
It's Only the Most Recent Year of the Woman 356

Coda

What's New? 364

References

The Dialectical-Synthetic Mode in Gestalt Therapy:
An Introduction to the Contributions of Erving and Miriam Polster

Arthur Roberts

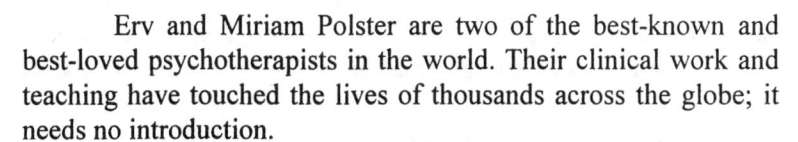

Erv and Miriam Polster are two of the best-known and best-loved psychotherapists in the world. Their clinical work and teaching have touched the lives of thousands across the globe; it needs no introduction.

A collection of their written work such as this one, however, does call for an introduction. The Polsters' professional writing spans 4 decades in the history of Gestalt therapy and is so broad in scope and profound in implication that no single book can do it justice. But certain themes which speak to and from the heart of Gestalt therapy can be seen to recur over the course of their long career. In this book, we at GICPress have tried to present these central themes—culled from the larger body of their work—in one volume.

The outstanding hallmark of the Polsters' thought is this: they refuse to oversimplify. Their thinking is clear, clean, straightforward. It lays bare the ripples in our theory; each involution is explored and surveyed in all its native complexity. This tight focus paradoxically leads to theoretical expansiveness, for as the Polsters encourage us to look more and more closely at the minutiae of Gestalt theory, we discover—quite concretely—that each point implies an equally valid counterpoint (what they

INTRODUCTION

call the *point-counterpoint relationship*). And as they illuminate the importance of each side of this relationship, even the most partisan among us find ourselves nodding in recognition. Their work speaks to every kind of reader. Intellectuals are lured by the rich references to such figures as Tillich, Berlin, Graves, Kozinski; the artistically inclined revel in hints of Proust and James, Dreiser and Eliot; historically-minded readers delight in archival excursions into Gestalt therapy's theoretical origins, as well as reminiscences of working in the flesh with such names as Perls, Goodman, From, and Weisz; and clinicians relish the frequent, candid reflection on actual cases. With such range and experience at their command, the Polsters have put forth an original body of work which distinguishes itself not only by its theoretical bravado, but by its intention to include and acknowledge a great variety of dissonant perspectives within Gestalt therapy. The energy resulting from their effort leaps off the page.

The reader of this collection may also notice that the themes with which the Polsters began to grapple—presciently—4 decades ago, are today at the very center of discourse on psychotherapeutic theory: ideas relating to such contemporary notions as intersubjectivity, plurality, continuity and discontinuity, neo-pragmatism, narrative, paradox, experiential reality, the implicit "nextness" or "praegnanz" or "forward-movement" of experience, and more. While such ideas are now hotly debated in the contemporary literature and at professional gatherings, Erv and Miriam Polster have been exploring this territory for decades, steadily working away at the countours of theory and practice.

*   *   *

One of the distinguishing features of the Polsters' work is that it consistently embraces a dialectical-*synthetic* mode. History shows that one idea often emerges as a corrective to an earlier one, and the two ideas then face one another across what seems like an un-bridgeable theoretical divide. This is the beginning of the dialectical process. Unfortunately, in the brief history of psychotherapy, it is also usually the end. But unlike so much psychological thinking put forward in the last century, the lines of thought which the Polsters pursue do not seek to explain definitively; they do not tend to converge on a predetermined point. Instead they fan outward, expansively, toward the horizon—toward more possibilities and greater complexity. Instead of ending a dialogue, the Polsters work seeks to start one, or to keep another alive; it always points toward the *next step* of the dialectical process: synthesis. One of the reasons their work continues to enliven our field is that they do not leave synthesis out. They *aim* for it.

The Polsters ideas have an immediate impact on real lives and real work. This happy result is due to their intuitive understanding that, without synthesis, dialectics is not much more than an intellectual exercise. In their view, Gestalt therapy's richness and depth come from the fact that its basic principles describe a dialectical process whereby whatever we need is integrated organically *as we embrace novelty*—as we release ourselves into contact. For them, the *sine qua non* of Gestalt therapy theory is that it articulates a natural process by which we assimilate and transform (*synthesize*) new figures as they emerge; what at first seems to be "Not-I" is absorbed and assimilated if we do not break contact prematurely. If we do break contact, we prevent new theoretical figures from emerging. Such a failure to carry the process forward to completion is a failure at the level of synthesis; it spells the end of dialogue and the beginning of dogma. This is one of the Polster's core convictions, and not only does it distinguish them among Gestalt theorists, but it has led them to a prolific body of work which is both theoretically robust and immediately practical.

The expansiveness of that work is due to their willingness to *approach* new ideas where other theorists turn away. This is the integrative tendency beneath the surface of the Polsters' thought; it is always working in this direction, always weaving together, always drawing toward, always moving into the culminating act of synthesis—which starts the cycle afresh.

This bent of thought shows itself time and again in the present collection, especially in their canny grasp of the way that human minds tends to gravitate toward one particular pole of what is actually a totality—toward an emphasis, for example, on "raw experience" as opposed to "meaning," or "process" as opposed to "content," or "figure" as opposed to "ground." While some Gestalt therapists focus almost exclusively on figure-formation and others on the structure of ground, the Polsters point out that neither position is supportable by itself. They avoid the trap of these false dichotomies by doggedly shining a light on *both* poles of the dialectic—not for argument's sake, but to encourage us to do the same. Their work suggests that it is only when one *maintains* the tension between opposing poles that the critical step of synthesis can take place. Jung called this final step the "transcendent function" of the psyche—the function by which thesis and antithesis merge and are transformed into a new whole. The Polsters insist that it is by admitting of the complexity and diversity of dissonant experience—by hearing every inner and outer voice—that we are able to transcend limiting stances which reflect only one fixed perspective of a larger complex reality.

The Polsters want the kind of sustained, well-differentiated contact that makes such synthesis possible. In their work, they make their convictions clear: they not only speak *for* inclusion, they speak *against* exclusion. They continually point to the perils of taking up an exclusionary stance—of supporting one fixed doctrine or another—and warn that submitting to *any* theoretical dogma can weaken a clinician; it can result in a rigidity which limits the person's ability to act in accordance with the aesthetic demand of a given situation. Instead, the Polsters encourage a more complex, more arduous effort: they ask us to get to know *both* poles of a "point-counterpoint" relationship—they

INTRODUCTION

encourage us, for example, to become adept at working with content *as well as* process, with meaning-making *as well as* "raw experience." They propose that we sit with the tension of seemingly incompatible polarities—knowing that the polarities are incompatible only in theory, not in life. Logic can be contradicted, but experience cannot. The Polsters staunchly insist upon each therapist's right (and responsibility) to continually rediscover the dynamic balance—between any two poles—which best fits a given situation.

By discouraging exclusion and encouraging inclusion, the Polsters urge us to turn *towards* one another, and *towards* the field of which we are a part. By doing this, by opening ourselves to new ideas and new experiences, we amplify the creative tension between what is known and what is unknown—we create the field conditions in which there is the possibility of an integration between the two. Creating these field conditions is all we can do, and, in the end, it is all we need to do. The synthetic function operates autonomously when its field conditions are met; and when it occurs, its coming solution is given to us in experience. When this process goes well, we do not "create" the coming solution, it "comes to us"—*it* creates *us*.

But volition, effort, will—these play a crucial part in the process, and the Polsters do not shy away from this fact. They expect us to use our volition wisely. The will can be directed toward *including* a feeling or idea instead of staving it off; it can be harnessed in service of *hearing* an other instead of shutting her out. This intention to open oneself to something other—to include another perspective alongside one's own—helps make a coming synthesis possible. As volition is by definition something over which we have some control, it is here that the Polsters intervene, urging us towards a voluntary ethos of inclusion—and their theoretical writing to the Gestalt community has been their longest running intervention.

Their belief in the transformative power of inclusion is infectious, and the special quality found in their written work arises in part because of their dedication to this ideal. It is not merely that they "believe" in theoretical inclusion—many believe in that—but that they devote themselves to it. If there is any conviction implicit in the Polsters' work, it is that our lives (and our theories) move forward when we actively make room for every aspect of our experience and our differences—it is even important to make room for that part of ourselves which does not want to make any more room. This conviction leaps off nearly every page of their work: that it is far better to turn towards and respond—to engage in dialogue and risk change—than to retrench and settle into an enduring stuckness. The enormous creative output of their careers is a testament to the power of this conviction.

Another result of their dedication to this belief is the flexibility the Polsters show in their work with patients. The clinical interventions described in this book reflect the spontaneity and skill of therapists who are refreshingly unimpeded by introjected doctrine of any sort. They are remarkably *free*. Each somehow manages to incorporate all the clinically relevant ideas, angles, intuitions and perspectives, and transform them into a an elegant intervention which supports the patient in moving beyond his or her stuckness, into what comes next.

But at the same time, the Polsters advocate for clinical freedom within a framework of theoretical knowledge and discipline. They see the constricting effect which introjected rules have upon therapists—how they limit options, diminish awareness, and dull therapeutic creativity—and they also see the necessity and value of theoretical structure. It is in this spirit that they have always struggled to extend the boundaries of Gestalt therapy theory—not out of ideological fervor, but out of a deep-rooted belief that the therapist's individuality is at least as important as the particular theoretical axioms to which he or she is admonished to cling. They intuitively understand that it is only a living theory that can serve living people—it is only by continually extending the boundaries of a theory that we can make

INTRODUCTION

room for the always-greater complexity of the individuals who employ that theory. The vicissitudes of experience are ever beyond the reach of our theories, and the best way to begin to approach the complexity of our lives is to continually expand, refresh and renew our ideas.

And the Polsters live this creed. In this book, the reader can see how their work has evolved continually; they never cease from exploration. There is a joyous vitality and progression to their writing, a flow which carries thought and thinkers through decades of study, practicing, teaching and living. And there is more still to come, as they continue to write and contribute their energy to the community they've nourished for so long. We have much to be grateful for, and more to look forward to.

But for now there is this—both a treasury and a celebration. We hope you enjoy.

Arthur Roberts
Providence, Rhode Island
Summer, 1999

PROLOGUE

ERVING AND MIRIAM POLSTER

Looking with nostalgia over this collection of papers, we wondered what the thematic relationship might be between the early and later writings. In reading the first paper, *A Contemporary Psychotherapy*, 32 years later, it is surprising to see the persistence of key themes. It is as though Erv was unwittingly drawing up a prologue for future theoretical focus. Subsequent writings have taken many new turns but they remain rooted to the original theoretical premises. Perhaps people generically compose their lives like that, moving ahead from an early sensibility which is re-cycled, sometimes unrecognizably, never repeated, but always with a kaleidoscopic re-arrangement of what they already care about.

That is not to say that the past *causes* the present but rather that they are *interconnected*, a holistic theme which insinuates itself throughout these writings. As we look around with one brain, two eyes and a billion neurons, we take for granted the astonishing accomplishment of pulling an infinity of events together into a unified experience. This happens naturally in all of us, thanks to a configurational reflex which connects these experiences. But the success of this reflex is never assured. We are thrown off balance, always challenged by innumerable disconnecting behavioral and emotional options.

Gestalt therapy was born out of just such a challenge, integrating the works of seemingly incompatible thinkers, including a stellar array of psychoanalytic dissidents, gestalt learning theorists and existentialists, all held to be unassimilable within Freudian psychoanalysis. This integration created coherence out of a heterogeneity of positions and also set the tone for the theory of Gestalt therapy itself, which established a fundamental hospitality to dissonant or opposing forces. From this background, it is not surprising that Gestalt therapy theory would include the concept of *splitting* as a key to recognizing the neurotic effects of disunity and calling for the identification and synthesis of alienated parts of the person (Perls, Hefferline and Goodman, 1951, p. 240).

THE RADICAL CENTER

The concept of the Radical Center is a take-off point for the coordination of unity and diversity. The term Radical Center is not as oxymoronic as it sounds. On the contrary, dictionaries tell us not only that the word, radical, points to the root or fundamental of an issue but also that it refers to *being at the center* (*Webster's Dictionary*, Second Edition). In common connotation, however, radical does mean extreme and is contrasted with a moderate and accommodating center. The inference of contradiction between radical and center is troublesome because it stems from the mistaken expectation that energy, novelty, progress and creativity, so often associated with radicalism, reside in extreme positions. The center is often wrongfully seen as a lesser source of vitality, often merely a compromise, and even sometimes even a resignation to the influence of warring extremes.

Gestalt therapy took an extreme position, opposed to psychoanalysis, when it ratcheted up attention to raw experience, trying to replace excesses of emphasis on meaning. Yet it should also be understood that, in spite of countering psychoanalysis, Gestalt therapy from its beginnings became a work from the radical center when Perls took Friedlander's creative indifference as a prime orientation. From this position, Perls said

Every event is related to a zero-point from which a differentiation into opposites takes place. These *opposites* show *in their specific context* a great affinity to each other. *By remaining alert in the center*, we can acquire a creative ability of seeing both sides of an occurrence and completing an incomplete half. (second italics ours) (Perls, 1947, p.15)

Extreme positions contribute greatly by feeding new perspective into the system of which they are a part. But they are always a part of the system, indivisible even while individuated. To create wholeness one must find a way selectively to incorporate inconvenient dissonances into the existing system, where the center is a magnate to the swirling variety of ideas circling around it. From this position, where the indivisibility of one principle from another is more clearly apparent, one may more readily reconstitute the struggle among unruly conceptual relationships. T.S. Eliot famously enunciated this indivisibility when he joined past and future at the "still point of the turning world...neither from nor towards; at the still point, there the dance is" (Eliot, 1943, p.15). The "dance" as the pivotal force of the center was given a kindred meaning also by Heidegger, one of Gestalt therapy's forebears. He implied, it seems to us, that the center was a source of both being and caring when he said, "both the 'ends' and their 'between' are in the only way which is possible...as care" (Heidegger, 1962, p.426). Nietzsche, the great hero of free spirit, said, "art is the joyous hope that the spell of individuation may be broken in augury of a restored oneness" (Nietzsche, 1967, p.73). He further said, "In what strange simplification and falsification man lives...How have we made everything around us clear and free and easy and simple...and will continue to talk of opposites where there are only subtleties of gradation" (Nietzsche, 1989, p.35) Eliot's "dance", Heidegger's "care" and Nietzsche's "joy" are vitalizing commentary, reflecting the energy which emanates from a center pulling for oneness. From this position, Gestalt therapy would never be rightfully identified by any single element of a dialectical complexity. Rather than identify it as a process therapy, for example, it would be recognized as a process/content therapy, interweaving the two, welcoming these indivisible facets of personal experience. This interweaving seems so obvious where process and content are concerned. But the common avoidance of such obvious indivisibility only highlights the existence of a *simplification reflex*. This reflex compels people to value clarity even at the cost of breadth and proportion. The resulting split between the basic need for simple theoretical positions and the equally compelling need for *interconnections* among diverse positions is a hazard for all theorists seeking a coherent communication of the breadth of the theory. The magnetics of simplicity—brightness, clarity, assuredness, easy connections with like-minded people, a sense of being all there—tantalize people into favoring one or another particular principle. This highly focused selectivity counters the mind's ravenous accumulation of experience. Every theory must contend with the consequences of this struggle, because listeners gravitate toward single resonant points and other points are cast into the shadows.

Freud was the most famous beneficiary and victim of this process. Many psychologists see Freud as the apostle of rationalism even though his work was the major agent in all of history for appreciating the emotional undercurrents of human existence. This paradoxical phenomenon is evident also in the work of Carl Rogers, whose image was long based on his therapeutic techniques of reflection and clarification, too often mechanically applied. But he was actually the major theoretical advocate for *empathy*. Many of us will identify Aaron Beck exclusively with a focus on thought processes, but he is also sensitive to emotional components, as well as to the power of experience *qua* experience. He said, "the experiential approach exposes the patient to *experiences which in themselves are powerful enough to change misconceptions*" (Beck, 1979, p.214) (emphasis ours). He was also an advocate of "therapeutic eclecticism" (Beck, 1991).

So also was Perls' breadth distorted. Through his own aphoristic indulgences, as well as the simplification reflexes of others, he has been identified with the here-and-now while his actual therapeutic foundation was an effervescent relationship of figure and ground, the indivisibility of organism and environment and the undoing of unfinished business. Not only are stereotypes of each of these therapeutic masters held by those who know them only glancingly, but they are often held by their devoted adherents.

The estrangements created by the multiple facets of any theory have often led to misunderstanding, territoriality, denominationalism, and jettisoning what cannot be easily unified. However, increasing the flexibility and broadening the range of principles is also risky business because it threatens the cohesion of any theory and the accompanying clarity of principle and discipline. Fertility of ideas may indeed create an unacceptable overgrowth. Yet, *artful* pruning and *creative* evolution of principle based on the struggle with contradiction will take care not to prematurely discard principles that just don't fit easily. When Freud made just such exclusions, expressing concern for the integrity of his psychoanalytic system, he set a tone of orthodoxy and formalism from which psychoanalysis is only recently recovering. This recovery has come after re-visiting therapeutic principles which had been kept alive by the followers of the original psychoanalytic dissidents. In recent years we see a flowering of neo-psychoanalysis into a respect for face value experience and the interpersonal imperative which impacts all therapy. The fact that Gestalt therapy has been one of the key forces keeping alive the contributions of the analysts who either left Freud or were excluded is noteworthy but not widely recognized.

SEARCH FOR THEORETICAL UNITY

Three basic factors expand the theoretical diversity of Gestalt therapy while retaining theoretical unity. They are: 1) point/counterpoint relationships, 2) dimensionalism and 3) personal style and repertoire.

1) The point/counterpoint phenomenon refers to the coexistence of *alternating theoretical options*. These options are most often recognized in pairs, as, for example, in the relationship between self-support and environmental support. These alternating options are always indivisible even though one may receive greater focus than the other at any particular time. When self-support is receiving focus, environmental support moves to the background but it must be flipped into ascendancy as new interest impels a shift in focus. This versatility retains the breadth of theory as it offers continuous reverberation among alternating focuses. Therefore, the successful management of this impulse toward point/counterpoint unity will affect how well integrated any theory may remain. The open mindedness required by point counterpoint reverberations will help its practitioners and theorists to discover variations on early theoretical themes and unforseen gaps in the application of the techniques spawned by the theory.

2) Dimensionalism refers to the position any therapist may stake out between the extremes represented by any pair of theoretical facets. Not only is the *alternating* of focus on self-support and environmental support an option, but the therapist is also free to lean toward one or the other. Some therapists will give more attention to their patients' development of self support while others would be more likely to help them to explore prospects for environmental support. Whether a therapist is faithful to Gestalt therapy theory will depend not on *where* she stands on this dimension, but whether she is *informed* by this dimension, as well

as a number of other dimensions, some of which we will soon describe as vital to Gestalt therapy theory.

3) The repertoire and style of any practitioner are key factors in the fresh application of any theoretical system. Style encompasses how a therapist idiosyncratically carries out his procedures while repertoire would be represented by the range of procedures, themselves. While there are some clear differentiations between style and repertoire, they are so closely interrelated that they are sometimes indistinguishable.

What would be clearly *stylistic* would be such characteristics as verbal facility, toughness, pacing, sentimentality, humor, dominance, and permissiveness. Some people are more quick than others, some more cynical, some more inspirational, some more informed, some more kindly, some are concerned with broad areas of a person's life, others with the finest details. What would represent therapeutic *repertoire* would be the range of procedural options, such as the variety of experiments with which one is familiar, the technique of tightening sequences, intra-personal dialogue, simple conversation, focusing on the body, the use of visual fantasies, the use of hypnotic techniques, offering advice, self disclosure, etc. Some gestalt therapists will do extensive dream work; others will do it hardly at all. Some are primarily concerned with their patients' awarenesses; others are primarily concerned with the quality of their patients' contact. Some will do experiments in every session; others will hardly ever do them.

Since we are saying that procedural and theoretical openness is a basic attribute of the Gestalt therapy system, it becomes necessary to distinguish it from eclecticism. There are indeed theoretical principles which underlie everything gestalt therapists do, even though the theory doesn't precisely say what to do, when to do it, with whom to do it or in what proportion to do it. But this theoretical identity must be achieved through struggle among unruly principles, not cheaply through emphasis on those which are narrowly selected. Any narrow perspective, easy though it may be to identify with, will reduce options which the principles of point/counterpoint reconciliation, dimensional choice and pluralistic repertoire and style may foster. Fortunately, such freedoms are built into the fundamentals of the gestalt system, which was formed from the inclusion of many voices. What we are proposing is that Gestalt therapy offers the advantages of an integrative perspective, incorporating diverse stylistic and procedural options which can be incorporated within its principles. This point of view fits well with the early Perls who said

> At present there are many 'Psychologies', and every school is, at least in part, right. But alas, every school is also righteous. The tolerant professor of Psychology in most cases takes the different schools out of their respective pigeon holes, discusses them, shows his preference for one or two of them, but how little he does towards their integration! I have attempted to show that something of this nature *can* be done, if one throws bridges across the gaps... (Perls, 1947, p.5)

EVOLUTION OF PRINCIPLE

In the writings selected for this book, we have discerned ten dimensions of Gestalt therapy, each of which encompasses a pair of opposing theoretical perspectives. Some of these perspectives are elaborated in a number of these writings while others form the central theme of a particular article. These dimensions do not, of course, cover the range of all possible dimensions, but they show how we have reformulated some basic Gestalt therapy positions:

1) Here and now vs. concentration—*Troubled by the narrowing effect of Gestalt therapy's here-and-now orientation, we have tried to retain the sharp focus it fostered while providing a more explicit sense of the full dimension of time and space we*

live in. The present is only one moment, so mercurial that when you point your finger at it, it is already gone. Nevertheless, in spite of this evanescence, the illusion of the present as the home of all personal experience has been a powerful therapeutic vehicle, not for its excision of time but because it has stimulated sharply directed attention, the *concentration* which Perls originally proposed as a fundamental of psychotherapy. As Erv has said

> A most powerful instrument, one which helped shape the history of psychotherapy, was Frederick Perls' advocacy of therapeutic pointedness by heightening the concentration on one's own experience and heightening the contact with other people. The accompanying emphasis on focal experience was a hypnotic-like innovation and served as a breakthrough into therapeutic simplicity. Though this emphasis was not faithful to the broader principles of Gestalt therapy, which stressed the importance of context and contradiction, it nevertheless served as a bright spotlight on any experience when the experience was freed from the often paralyzing complexities of existence. The excision of much of the ordinary spread of personal concerns, the there-and-then, opened many eyes to the satori-like psychological power of highly focussed simplicity. This specialized attention was more than an evasion of a larger reality; it was a resounding entry into restricted regions of the mind. Clarity of perception, empowerment in action, and openness to previously disabling fears were among the benefits generated by pointedness and the narrowing of life context. (Polster, 1990)

However, this accentuation of directed attention should not amputate the events of the past and future, from which our lives are composed. In spite of the proviso that present experience includes remembering and planning, the connotations of the concept of here- and-now, wrongly taken, have steered too many people away from the future and the past. The time has come, it seems to us, to give up the bromide about here-and-now as the source point of experience and replace it with well directed attention along a broad range of events. Erv's description of the attention triad is especially apropos (Cf. Polster, E. *A Population of Selves*, 1995, pp.63-81).

2) Storyline vs. "aboutism"—*We have revisited the wariness with which Gestalt therapy has often viewed the content of living, which Perls called* aboutism. Giving renewed recognition to the event-fullness of life helps to recover a sense of continuity and restores connections among the range of events we all live through, creating a sense of personal coherence. A good story also fleshes out the abstractions which may otherwise narrowly define a person's life (Cf. Polster, E. *Every Person's Life is Worth a Novel*, 1987). Though abstractions are valuable as introductions or summaries of large arcs of experience, they leave out much that matters. They are the mind's housing for stories. But, if there are no stories within those abstractions, you have an empty house.

3) Configurational reflex vs. gestalt formation—*The configurational reflex is our way of looking at the concept of gestalt formation.* The usual image of gestalt formation is that the world of experience is given to us in wholes. The configurational emphasis we have proposed takes account more explicitly of the relationship between wholes and parts. It portrays a creative act which reflexively organizes an infinite number of ingredients. The well being of each person will depend greatly on his successful management of this challenge to create a sense of wholeness out of a huge range of disparate experiences.

This recognition of the inter-relationship of the whole and its parts seems quite obvious to the perceiving person. To psychologists, however, the question of this inter-relationship has historically created great schisms. For example, gestalt learning theory—which emphasized the wholeness of an experience rather than its parts—was dichotomized from associationist learning theory, which was based on the relationship between one and another experimentally observed event. When gestalt therapists came onto the psychological scene, we postulated wholeness as fundamental not only to perception but to all personal experience, distinguishing this perspective from the analysis of what single event went with what other event, more nearly characteristic of psychoanalysis. The rigidity of dichotomization fixed both parties into position and created a large burden for the configurational process, which seeks unity out of a world that does not readily fall into place. As we have said, Perls addressed this challenge by calling for "differential thinking" (Perls, 1947, p.13). This means that people live with contrasting phenomena and that these contrasts provide proportion and meaning. Day gets its meaning from its relationship to night, disappointment from its relationship to satisfaction, *whole from its relationship to parts.*

4) Self as classification vs. self as fluid experience—*We have revised the concept of self so that it can include those classifications of self which evolve from a native configurational process.* Gestalt therapy was a contributor to the phenomenological reaction against the classification of events, giving increased attention to the fluidity of experience. Instead of feeling confined by the social implications of membership in such classes as gender, race, personality type, occupation, etc. people began to open up the boundedness of options and they became more optimistic about carving out their own lives.

In a good cause, Gestalt therapy went too far. Our current proposals about self-formation attempt to retain phenomenological fluidity without sacrificing the personal benefits of classification. One might well say that classifications of self are a manifestation of gestalt formation and are therefore as generic to living as fluidity of self. People seek both. Classifications of self, such as an altruistic self or a judgmental self are complementary to fluidity, often offering dependable *identity.* People seek to know who and what they are, a major source of personal unity, carved out of the infinity of events they live through. Our concept of the self is therefore rooted in the configurational process which creates *clusters* of characteristics (Cf. Polster, E. *A Population of Selves*). The accompanying task of therapy, therefore, is to identify, name and reconstitute these clusters of characteristics, which have a continuing and recognizable place in each person's life. When the appropriate clusters are re-integrated the person may feel whole again, answering to the sense of his personal identity.

5) Tight therapeutic sequences vs. here and now—*The concept of tight therapeutic sequences represents a change in focus from the here-and-now to transition and movement.* The person never resides in the present but always leans ahead, connecting to whatever is *next*. Since this process is always vulnerable to interruptive and distorting forces, therapy is called upon to restore the connections between moments of experience. Tightening up these sequences means that the experience of any moment will have *immediate* consequence. If a person is sad in one moment, the next moment will carry that sadness forward, perhaps in telling about the sadness, perhaps in crying, perhaps in vowing never to be so involved again, perhaps anything which fits the particular person with a particular sadness, fitting a particular set of circumstances, etc. A therapeutically empowered by-product of tightening these sequences is that restoring this continuity fosters an "of course" frame of mind, which, as momentum grows, will make it seem natural to take a previously blocked next step. Connectedness through these moment to moment transitions becomes one of the pillars of personal wholeness—it restores fluidity and a trust in future experience.

The concept of tight therapeutic sequences evolves from our earlier attempt to clarify the struggle between the concept of resistance and the concept of raw experience. While accentuating raw experience we have abandoned the concept of resistance altogether. In Perls, Hefferline and Goodman's *Gestalt Therapy*, the writers objected to therapy's then common *attack* on resistances. They proposed instead the concept of *creative*

Prologue

resistance, saying that behaviors commonly viewed as mere resistance must be taken as "active expressions of vitality...Rather than being liquidated, they are accepted at face value" (Perls, Hefferline and Goodman, 1951, p.25). What was creative about the "resistance" was that the child forged personal solutions against difficult odds, deriving unforseen benefits which offset the pain. Blocked in crying, for example, the person could develop a determination never to be beaten down or she could develop empathy for a mother who could not tolerate crying or she might discover how much sadness her body could contain without requiring release, etc. In the context of such spunk, resistance lost its pejorative implications and therapists gained an appreciation for the formative and valorous powers of troubled people.

What this meant functionally was a greater empathy for the patient and the therapist became less likely to explain away belligerance, apathy, distortion or other obstructions of the therapist's own view of the necessary therapeutic pathways. Instead, she became responsive to behavior at face value, dealing with belligerance, apathy, distortion, etc. with curiosity, apology, reminiscence, advice, support, silence or whatever fitting response her range and skill in responsiveness calls forth. Nevertheless, in spite of the momentous correction represented by the concept of creative resistance, we believe the concept of resistance, creative or not, has too much of the baggage of historically unilateral appraisal by the therapist of what is the right therapeutic behavior.

The concept of resistance has long been a primary source for understanding the pitfalls of hidden meanings and obscurely obstructional experience. What we offer in its place are concepts which address meaning and obstruction but are less likely to eclipse actual experience. We have introduced a distinction between vertical meaning and horizontal meaning. Vertical meaning occurs when one cuts into the surface of experience and sees what *underlies* the experience. This is a valid way to understand any experience but it tempts intellectual virtuosity and is often overdone or untimely, overshadowing the experience itself, offering a hollow abstraction.

The other pathway to meaning, the horizontal, is represented in the evolution of meaning through a *sequence* of experiences. Meaning is the understanding of the interrelationship of events. It may be achieved through the restoration of connections between experiences as they evolve from moment to moment. These meanings may seem to fall short of the "deeper" meanings commonly sought, as in seeing a connection between a current fear of social relations with a traumatic isolation by a first grade teacher, but this depth comes also through horizontal development. For us to dismiss the concept of "resistance" is not to skip over meaning or to ignore the variety of obstructional behaviors which interfere with any person's continuity. Rather, we take gaps in meaning as well as interferences with continuity to be natural aspects of complex behavior. By fleshing out these gaps through the horizontal restoration of moment to moment continuity, the recovery of such simple connections becomes a vehicle for restoring meaning and continuity to the minds of those people who may have lost meaning or who may live choppy lives.

6) Contact vs. empathy and merger—*Contact is what happens at the boundary where self and other meet. We must, however, also take account of contact's indivisible relationship with empathy and merger, which we have described as a "contact triad."* This union was often disregarded during the years when individuality was emphasized. Empathy was suspect because one person might unilaterally and mistakenly assume feelings that others may not actually feel. I might, for example, empathize with your supposedly sad feelings about losing your job when you may actually feel relieved. Merger was suspect for similar reasons, not so much for mistaken assumptions but because a union of two individuals' purposes could result in a blurring of either person's own identity. When, however, we join contact, empathy and merger as a contact triad, the concept develops a deeper and more strongly felt sense of relationship.

Surprisingly, in introducing the concept of contact Gestalt therapy did not take explicit account of relationship, any more than it was explicit about contact's relationship with empathy and merger. What was not sufficiently addressed was the fact that one could, after all, be in perfectly good contact with another person without much of a relationship. In our book, *Gestalt Therapy Integrated*, we proposed *contact episodes* as a concept which would take contact beyond a particular moment by enunciating certain stages through which contact evolves. Even so, that concept is limited to a particular unit of contact and falls short of addressing personal relationship.

Adding further to the contact triad as a step toward increased attention to the larger aspects of relationship is the *merger triad*. There are three gestalt concepts subsumed within the merger function: introjection, confluence and synthesis. Each of these concepts contributes to the sense of personal indivisibility from other people. Introjection, for one, is widely thought to *contrast* with contact while we see it as *coordinated* with contact. As Erv has said

> So close in touch is the contacting person (that he is) a lubricant for the intojective process because it opens the person to receptivity. (Polster, E., 1995, p.32-33)

Introjection is therefore best seen, we believe, as spontaneous receptivity, unimpeded by the deliberative faculties of the mind. For us, the introjective process includes good quality contact, as well as successful configuration and reflexive tailoring (Ibid, pp.29-40). As such it is generically a healthy function, which unfortunately may go haywire, much as do other generically healthy functions, such as breathing and heartbeat. As breathing brings air in and as heartbeat regulates blood flow, introjection serves as a generic source of learning. To accept introjection as a fertilizing process is far-reaching in terms of the therapist's freedom to relate influentially with patients; it recognizes that a patient yielding to the therapist's beliefs or implied suggestion may not always be merely gullible but may also be allowing a sensible entry into new experience. This openness to union with the therapist, as well as others, risky though it may be to one's powers of self-determination, also has great leverage for the formation of new self images, as well as an acceptance of salutary communal experience.

Without going into detail here about confluence and synthesis, the other members of the merger triad, we may observe that they offer the same spirit of mutuality which is represented in introjection. Confluence establishes a common ground among people and supports the coordination of individual interests. Synthesis serves well in creating a sense of wholeness out of both the harmonious and dissonant variety of life experiences. Such expansion of theoretical recognition of the broad parameters of human relationship leads to greater emphasis also on the concepts of belonging, identity and community. As Erv has said

> In our highly individualized society, it is easier to neglect people's basic need to belong...Therapists generally expect that if a patient's individuality is restored, she will find a way of belonging.. However, in point/counterpoint relationships, as we have seen before, when one side is taken for granted, the other backgrounded side becomes diminished. If we want to handle the paradoxical needs for individuality and belonging, we have to take account of both (Ibid, p.179)

7) Content vs. process—*Gestalt therapy recognized the importance of the "how" of experience, which diverted attention from the "what".* Of course, there is no escaping the *what*. But when the content is merely taken for granted, process observations may take the therapy over. Focus on language, musculature, and frame of mind may then become primary while the telling of actual events fades into the background. Questions like, what are you doing, feeling, wanting, may emphasize process, but also

express a wish to know *what* that the person is actually doing, feeling and wanting. Excessive attention to process, in our observation, tends to make the therapy more mechanical than when content is proportionally emphasized. When focus on content is restored, the story becomes a prime source of feeling whole and self-confirmed (Cf. Polster, E. *Every Person's Life is Worth a Novel*).

8) Awareness vs. action—*We described the* "synaptic experience," *as a heightening of experience through the union of awareness and action. This union parallels the sensory-motor nature of existence.* When this union of awareness and action is called into full play the high focus increases the chances for the necessary *registration* of experience. This registration is a powerful force, often engendering large experiences in the patient; perhaps of crying or anger, perhaps of amplified excitement, perhaps of appreciation of another's love, perhaps a realization of new possibilities, perhaps of feeling all-together because of the successful interweaving of the disparate modes of awareness and action. Further, the effects of the union of awareness and action become part of the heightened contact between therapist and patient—and it may also propel the patient forward into stories of a lifetime of experience. The interweaving of action, awareness and contact—especially when it creates relationship—is basic to therapeutic illumination.

9) Humanity vs. technology—We recognize that technique is vital to therapy. But we also believe that ordinary language and relationship are the grounding for technical work. As Erv has said

> Since common contact is more recognizable as a 'natural' engagement, available at any time in everyday life, it would be important for therapy to include some easily recognizable contact qualities. Among them are kindness, curiosity, colorful and clear language, radiance of attention, endurance, gentle strong-mindedness, and many

other interpersonal considerations that people seek in their everyday lives. (Polster, E., 1995, p.142)

The interweaving of ordinary human engagement with the technicalities of psychotherapy always goes on, but the proportion of one or the other varies according to the particular therapist. With some therapists, it will always be very clear that every move is technically directed while with others, at certain moments, one could easily mistake the session to be no different from any two people listening and talking.

A corollary to the key role of good quality contact in the humanizing of psychotherapy is an *attention triad*, which combines the processes of concentration, fascination and curiosity. These components propel the therapist to be responsive and caring. Further, through our emphasis on the evocation of the patient's storyline, we also give added recognition to the drama of a person's life and the personal intimacy engendered by the therapeutic engagement.

10) Field theory vs. systems theory—*A key plank for many gestalt therapists is the belief that Gestalt therapy is a field theory. Others believe that the holistic perspective of Gestalt therapy, featuring the interconnectedness of events, would qualify it also as a systems theory.* Both positions are complex, and we hold no allegiance to either except for the insights they offer about holism and interconnectedness. One question that has been asked in trying to differentiate field and systems theories is whether wholes are primary, then differentiated or whether parts are primary, then integrated. Stated in human terms, the question is: which comes first, *we*—differentiated into *me* and *thee*—or vice versa. For us, that is a chicken and egg question, intriguing but not definitive about our understanding of Gestalt therapy. What the theory of Gestalt therapy helps us to see is the perpetual effervescence between wholes and parts, irrespective of which comes first. Furthermore, context will define wholes and parts. We see this in recognizing that a nose is a whole entity while

being part of a whole face, which is part of a whole person, which is a part of a whole family, etc. ad infinitum.

The second factor which is said to differentiate field and systems theory is the contrast between linear and non-linear language. But that contrast doesn't hold up well either since either theory must deal with both. Intuition, for example, supposedly non-linear, may be communicated in clearly recognizable sequences or it may be only understood through later experiences and with surprising flashes of recognition. Furthermore, there are extremes of linearity and non-linearity, as represented on one side by surrealistic writers whose sequential connections are not readily evident to the reader and scientific writers who insist on strict sequences of ideas. However, the surrealistic writer may be very clear in what she is communicating, irrespective of strange connections, and scientific writers may be muddy in their syntactical purity. We see no good basis for demonizing or hallowing either category. But what we think *does* count is the need for adherents of either position to get across in communicating to patients and to be open to the surprising connections among the patient's experiences.

There are other differentiations to be made, more than we can address here. But whatever holistic guidance any Gestalt therapist may receive from either field or systems theory, a key consequence of both is the realization of the vital role of community in the life of any person, a discussion of which appears in several of the papers selected for this book. The obvious reason the community is important to therapeutic process is that all people receive their major pleasures or pain from the way they and their communities relate to each other. Therapeutic pay-off comes to patients from transforming what they learn in therapy to their engagement with the community.

It is very clear nowadays that both individual and group therapy fall woefully short of the societal need. Therapeutic work arose originally out of the recognition of suppressed individual need, too long ignored by religion and other societal institutions.

The pendulum swings, though, and now we recognize the need for a reciprocal relationship between the individual and his community, each contributing to the other. This reciprocity has a functional character which may be addressed therapeutically on two fronts. One is helping the person to become more and more alert in his everyday life to create this reciprocity by finding a community which nourishes his individuality. The other is for psychotherapy to construct opportunities for such reciprocity by utilizing large groups as an instrument of therapeutic process. These may foster life focus during an ongoing process in a communal atmosphere rather than only fostering the resolution of particular life disturbances.

CONCLUSION

We believe Gestalt therapy derives its primary identity from such integrations of opposing principles as these ten dimensions represent. There are other dimensions and the struggles for synthesis which they introduce are also crucial to the identity of Gestalt therapy. These are the ones which are most prominent in this selection of our writings.

The fertility of any theory springs from its central principles. But in maintaining wholeness, theories must take account of conceptual areas the principles don't cover or the contradictions they throw off. Fresh perspective and application are rooted in just such struggles between clear theoretical identity and unruly growth of principles. Piece by piece we move to implications originally invisible. This happens partly because the requirements of learning any complex method are prodigious and there isn't much room left over for questioning it—especially when the questioning is experienced by key theorists as a threat to the system. After a while though, one may become more confident in the system—sufficiently so that it no longer appears to be unduly threatened by inroads into its sanctity.

Part I: Setting the Stage

A Contemporary Psychotherapy

Erving Polster

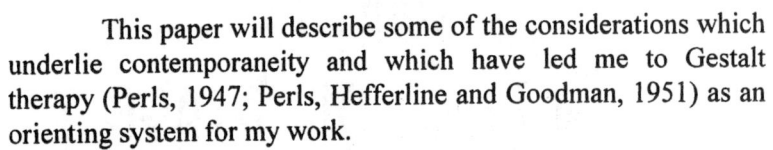

This paper will describe some of the considerations which underlie contemporaneity and which have led me to Gestalt therapy (Perls, 1947; Perls, Hefferline and Goodman, 1951) as an orienting system for my work.

Usually, words like "contemporary" or "modern" are applied only to the arts, such as architecture, painting, and music, rather than to science. Yet science, and certainly psychotherapy, must also think in terms of the contemporary. Even truths which weave in and out of the generations make new marks every time.

Where new discoveries are made, or old ones reformulated, there is a cultural lag during which the discovery is understood only by a few and seems relevant only to a small portion of the population. Thus, the application of the new principles is delayed. During the time of lag the innovators of the new position, painfully confronted with the resistant or disbelieving society, need to devote considerable energy to managing this resistance so that the principles may become realized. During this period the protagonists become enamored of their own positions, and what begins as a justifiable manipulation on its own merit is inflated and labeled ultimate or universal. This exaggerated impact provides the adherents of the new view with the time, support, and continuity they need to gather acceptance for the application of their ideas. Then, however, more new discoveries are made, which in turn, face difficulties in becoming understood and in having their appropriate effect. At this point battles begin between the old-new and the new-new because the old has not had its chance to go all the way with its program.

Freudian psychoanalysis has been in this position for a good many years. Now that society has begun to understand its principles, many professionals have moved on, learning from the early masters, but changing according to the contemporary challenge and new discoveries. These facts of change and lag have especially confused those who see their work to be only a science, and thus presumably to have universal beliefs, which must be defended *against* others. These workers forget that we view nature from only one perspective at a time. Only as long as we retain that perspective do we see nature as we do. If we shift, we see the world differently. Such shifting is necessary and lively and lies at the heart of contemporaneity.

Today, the psychotherapist must integrate old insights into these new perspectives. He must distill a system unique for himself, consistent with prior formulations, yet not merely a static reenactment of what has gone before.

THEORETICAL CHANGES

Since we creatively advance processes begun in the past, the first requirement for contemporaneity is that we allow past accomplishments to illuminate our path. Only sometimes do we proceed from scientific discovery. More often, we make artful choices based on having been touched by a huge range of effectors. Some of our greatest contributors have offered us only intuitive judgements. There were no proofs from Freud, nor from Jung or Adler, yet obviously, many of our great methodological and philosophical riches come from them.

Looking further, since Freud there have been some great procedural inventors. Ferenczi required patients to *do* that which they feared, thereby bringing action into rhythm with the previous exclusively introspective methods in psychoanalysis. His work was a forerunner of the techniques of experimenting with life now so prominent, for example, in psychodrama and operant conditioning. Wilhelm Reich, going deeper than Ferenczi and meeting greater resistance, developed character analysis. His techniques concerning the body and his interpretation of details of the patient's behavior were important precursors to the contemporary interest among existential therapists in phenomenology and the deep self-experience.

Franz Alexander and Otto Rank were also important proceduralists, each in his own way making deep alterations in the core concept of transference. Alexander emphasized the importance of non-therapy experiences and broadened the interpretation of the transference phenomenon to include relationships outside the analytic office. This broadening was a tacit recognition of the therapeutic efficacy of day to day human relationships. Rank brought the human relationship directly into his office. He influenced analysts to take seriously the actual present interaction between therapist and patient, rather than to maintain the fixed, distant, "as though" relationship which had given previous analysts an emotional buffer for examining the intensities of therapeutic sensation and wish. Rank's contributions opened the way for *encounter* to become accepted as a deep therapeutic agent.

Also important historically is the advent of the here-and-now experience in psychotherapy. The here-and-now became important in four distinct movements before it was given crucial emphasis by the existentialists. These movements were: 1) psychodrama, which fostered growth through action, placing the individual into experimental scenes where he could face with relative safety those aspects of the world which would not ordinarily be so safely available; 2) the general semantics movement, which treated language as a culminating life event, taken seriously for its own characterological nature; 3) Rogerian psychotherapy, whose techniques of reflection and clarification served to accentuate presently existing conditions in the patient;

4) group dynamics activities emerging from Lewin's theories about how people perceive and communicate with each other in groups. Thus existentialism and existential psychotherapy had the road already paved when they came to prominence in the United States in the early 1950's. The new view of the primacy of preset events in therapy was and is being assimilated by a constantly more receptive profession and public. In addition, these pre-existentialists expanded the relevance of therapy beyond those who were sick to people interested in their own growth and fulfillment, and they broadened professional practice beyond the limits of the psychoanalytic or psychiatric fraternities. In the light of obvious social need, these may prove to be two of the most energizing innovations.

The existentialist philosophers supported a change in tone. They owed less to the Freudian system and could offer a new configuration for the splinters shooting off the Freudian mass. New bases for holism appeared.

First, cause and effect were no longer broken into two separate pieces. They came to have an interactive unity, not the disunity brought on by blaming the present ₀effect on the past cause.

Second, symbols were no longer mere fronts for specific referents, but appreciated for their impact as creative representations. It was recognized that symbols do not hide a separated referent but bring it into unity now, an indissoluble ingredient of the manifest moment.

A third holistic factor was the union of therapist and patient as participants in a two-way encounter, not in the separations previously enunciated by special dispensations to the therapist. By now, the verity of each actual experience can be taken seriously for its own sake, not just as an intermediate circumstance standing between now and cure. The implicit faith is that good present experience has intrinsic healing power and need not be explained away.

SOCIAL NEEDS

The second requirement for contemporaneity in a psychotherapy is that it face the social needs of the day. There are many social needs, for example those reflected in such present issues as interracial tension, delinquency, international mistrust, the poor quality of sexuality, psychologically sterile education, and the concern for authenticity in religious experience. The implications of psychotherapy theory for the solution of these social problems are profound and must be explored much further than they have been.

Let me consider one of these issues: the social need for new religious experience. By religious, I mean not what is conventionally intended by that word, but rather man's concern with his self-experience, and his quest for coherence, unity, support, direction, creativity, microcosm. Man has always sought for these. In our time this search is impelled by the psychotherapeutic process, discovered through work with patients, but too relevant beyond pathological need to remain isolated from public concern.

Psychotherapy has often been described as a counterforce emerging from repressive religious principles. Freud denied the reality of God and described the obsessional nature of religious practices. He propelled man into a new view of his own true nature and rejuvenated his potency for facing it head-on. But the Judeo-Christian society, thus threatened, tried to isolate the new force he represented. Nevertheless, Freud raided the grand social unit and enfolded many of its members, one by one, in the most painstaking, prolonged, and devoted explorations of individual people in history.

But his early methods were not suitable as a community-wide process. First, the rituals, such as free association and lying on a couch were too private. Second, the generation was preoccupied with explanations, and although Freud and psychoanalysts generally knew the dangers of overintellectualizing, their attitudes, times and techniques were over-susceptible to it. Third, the theory and methods were socially non-activist and unconcerned with fostering good encounter among members of a group.

The need for arranged opportunities for this encounter is widespread. Witness the current expansion of group psychotherapy and related group processes as indicated in the reports of Hunt, Mowrer, and Corsini. Hunt traces therapeutic progress from the early one-to-one transference of psychoanalysis to concern for "enrichment" in interpersonal relations, and ultimately to an authentic place for group psychotherapy in the concerns of social psychology (Hunt, 1964). Corsini documents the increasing impact of group psychotherapy by reporting that the number of publications on the subject has increased from 15 in the decade of the 1920's, to 1,879 in the decade of the 1950's (Corsini, 1957). Mowrer in his recent book *The New Group Psychotherapy*, reports a proliferation of so-called self-help groups, another sign of the undercurrent needs of the day (Mowrer, 1964). Although his views suffer from an overemphasis on confession, he is, nevertheless, an eloquent spokesman for psychotherapy in communion with others rather than only as a private, professional engagement.

The need for microcosm, a world set apart, which is basic to religion, exists also in psychotherapy. What cannot be done in the large society may be done in small communities. One seeks opportunities for new encounters unburdened by the anachronistic demands of a production system geared to achievements and leaving little room for simple being and growth. One needs to step off the conveyor belt where indiscriminate obedience, secrecy, stereotyped language, and currying favor may be given up, without inviting loss of job or friendship. As one patient said of her group meetings, "It is a time out of the week." Indeed, the therapy group provides an opportunity to say, "Stop the world. I want to get *on*."

Thus a group therapy with a unifying and liberating view can be a strong force for the development of good community, creating opportunities for self-renewal as well as chances to try out a new morality, permitting new ways of being together which are currently unsafe in the large society. Community, self-renewal and morality are and always have been fundamental human concerns. In our culture, these factors have been most fully appreciated by the Judeo-Christian system, but they are now growing in relevance for the psychotherapy process.

Psychotherapy also offers the possibility of satisfying the important human need to symbolize. Symbolizing, inherent in religious experience, is fundamental in the psychotherapeutic process. Symbolizing serves man's need to condense and synthesize his inner processes by means of expressing, in one stroke, related, diverse details of his existence.

Community, self-renewal, morality, microcosm, and symbolizing are such lasting and compelling human needs that a respect for them permits even fruitless religious anachronisms to exist beyond their rightful day. Psychotherapy's rightful day is now. It must satisfy these lasting needs in today's way.

LANGUAGE

What language is most useful and best understood? The early psychoanalysts had a language of their own which was impactful in its day. They had to create new words because their concepts were new. Some of them are: oedipus complex, libido, ego, id, superego, etc. Sometimes it was hard to tell whether the concepts were symbolic or concrete. There were arguments, for example, as to whether the id, ego, and superego were actual parts of the body or whether they were only abstracted convenient pictorial representations. Such arguments were no accident, since Freud used words which bridged the gap between science and religion and had both literal and symbolic qualities. Confusion was inevitable.

There are no longer the same demands for a language of psychotherapy. First, it is now possible to be less figurative and more concrete in descriptions of personality. Second, psychotherapists are beyond communicating only to the technically and theoretically sophisticated. They are moving into the society and want to be understood by a greatly widened range of interested people. While Freud's words were classificatory, albeit dynamic, the current words tend to be more descriptive of *process*. The existential mode of therapy looks less for essence and tries to deal more with each individual actuality as it occurs. In Gestalt therapy, which emerges from the existential scene, some of the key words are: awareness, contact, experience, excitement, encounter, emergency, clarity, present, etc. These words are closer to everyday language and deal with those aspects of living which are the foreground concerns of people. This kind of language invites experience rather than explanation to be the core of living.

Pinning our nature down to categorical words such as neurosis, diagnosis, profession, repression, cause, patient, etc., results in deification of transitory lingual conveniences. All of these have an indispensable place in history, but they are only scaffolds. When we say someone has a neurosis or someone is a psychologist, we do say something important, but such technical terms usually communicate too readily, leading frequently to smugness and semi-understanding.

Common words are bothersome because they are not inherently or reliably "understood." Nevertheless, psychotherapy is composed of commonalities, and technical language all too often obscures real meaning. A person wants to tell about how softly his mother stroked his hair when he was crying, not about his oedipus complex. He searches for joy, perspective, effervescence, faith, vigor, scintillation, flexibility, delight, etc., not greater ego strength. Descriptions of process, appreciation of function, and awareness of self offer a framework for new sensitivity to that which is uniquely immediate.

STYLE AND REPERTOIRE

The fourth requirement is freedom for the psychotherapist to function in a manner suitable to himself using formulations which will permit him to develop a personal style and a ranging repertoire of procedures.

By style is meant the therapist's organization of personal characteristics, behavior, and taste which identify him as a unique practitioner. For one to have a desirable style is to be predictable in general character and also consistently surprising and fresh, both to one's patients and oneself.

Some people are more kind than others, some more verbal, some more permissive. Some make broad strokes, describing grand life processes and stimulating patients to awareness of large sections of their natures such as fear of death, gross lechery, noble generosity. Others may face tiny details of existence such as the way a patient uses the word "wish" rather than "want" in asking for a promotion or the way a particular position of his musculature affects his expressiveness. Clearly, variations in style must exist, theory notwithstanding.

A person must find a theory which is sympathetic to his best talents, whether they be interpretive, poetic, directive or such. If he doesn't do so, he will be inept, or more likely, phony. Each style has its advantages and disadvantages, and one must learn what particular problems are the consequences of his own style. One may know, for example, under what circumstances one is likely to make speeches to patients or laugh with them or refuse to answer questions. If one makes speeches, one may have to deal with resulting awe or fear or dependence. If one laughs readily, one must face possibilities of the patient's taking the process too lightly or making inconvenient buddy-buddy demands. If one refuses to answer questions, one may face resentments or feelings of abandonment. The primary question about the "rightness" of a style is whether one accepts responsibility for the consequences he evokes and is skillful in facing them.

Style and repertoire are closely related. Repertoire is the range of procedures from which the therapist may draw, depending for his choice on his sense of the immediate need and his intuitive guess as to the procedure most likely to be effective. Thus, the psychotherapist may at one time use such techniques as interpretation of dreams, productions of fantasies, free association, various introspective exercises. On other occasions alternative possibilities are available: use of body language, role-playing, visual contact, voice integration, reports of experience, directed behavior, and patient-therapist contact.

Certainly, psychotherapists should be aware of the unlikelihood of discovering *the* single technique of psychotherapy. There are no such purified factors as "rationalism" in therapy or "operant conditioning" or "interpretation of dreams". These methods and others have been successful, but to put them on a competitive basis in terms of which is the *right* one is absurd.

Psychotherapists are people trying to find a way to work and some do better with some styles or procedures than with others. Systems of therapy which forget this become travesties. For instance, there is the story of the two psychoanalysts who were discussing a failure and saying that it happened because the patient was not required to lie on the couch in the first session. Such totemic sterility is widespread, and it is especially pronounced when the repertoire is so rigidly circumscribed as to prevent individual expression. Carl Rogers' early work was filled with such restrictive procedures, although his later existential orientation has expanded the range. His own depth of inner experience and sensitivity to his patients flowed within his early system of procedures, and this has been true also for many of his followers, certainly the effective ones. For many, though, such restrictions would have interfered with the fruitfulness of function.

However, the alternative to such limitations is not a dilettante eclecticism. The former is absurdly competitive and doomed to stereotypy; the latter is an empty shell, sterile even in knowledge. Variations in style and repertoire must cohere in a larger whole within which the psychotherapeutic exploration makes sense.

INTEGRATIVE PRINCIPLES

The fifth requirement of a contemporary psychotherapy is for integrative principles which bind previous historical directions together and orient the psychotherapist in what he is doing now.

Gestalt therapy has such unifying characteristics, integrating existential and psychoanalytic insights with procedural inventiveness. It deals with three primary therapeutic devices: 1) encounter 2) awareness and 3) experiment. Although these require extensive description, here is a brief sketch of each.

First is encounter, the interaction between patient and therapist, each of whom is in the present moment a culmination of a life's experiences. They may engage simply, saying and doing those things which are pertinent to their needs, the therapist offering a new range of possibility to the patient through his willingness to know the truth and to be an authentic person. Ideally this would be enough. It is curative for both to speak freshly, arouse warmth, and encounter wisdom. Contact of this nature may develop without self-consciousness or interpretation. But, of course, the resistances are great. Therefore, the encounter factors, potent as they are, usually require augmentation from the other two sources of therapy.

Second is awareness of bodily sensations and of the higher orders of self-experience such as emotions and values. Awareness is necessary for recovering liveliness, inventiveness, congruence, and the courage to do that which needs doing. Until one can accept strong inner sensations and feelings, one's expressions, verbal or physical, of anger, affection, disappointment, grief or the like will have little effect. Reduced living is the inevitable result of blocking internal self-experience. In Gestalt therapy self-awareness is fostered through techniques requiring phenomenological articulations of self-experience. An inward look is required, one which goes beyond taking life for granted. This look encompasses the breathing process, tightness of sphincters, awareness of movement and an infinite number of similar details ranging from small and physical aspects to larger awarenesses like expectancy, dread, excitement, relief, etc. All of these are directed toward rediscovering one's actual existence based on concrete experience rather than on logical deductions, like, "of course I'm breathing or I wouldn't be alive." In *Gestalt Therapy* by Perls, Hefferline, and Goodman there is an example of a young man exploring his own process of chewing food. He discovered a previously unknown feeling of disgust for food and noticed the way he desensitized his taste experience in order to avoid this feeling. The phenomenological discoveries one makes during such explorations grow into meaningful wholes. For example, a person may discover that his voice sounds weak when talking about his job or that he feels warmer inside than anybody realizes or that his neck tightens up frighteningly when he is surprised. He may discover a feeling of bewilderment during silence or embarrassment about saying goodbye.

  The third therapeutic force is the experiment, a device which creates new opportunities for acting in a safely structured situation. Included are suggestions for trying one's self out in a manner not readily feasible in everyday life. For example, a progressive minister—calm, intelligent, and permissive—knows he does not reach his parishioners. Upon relating his hatred for the hellfire and brimstone style, and his own terror of it while growing up, his over-reaction to such a minister became apparent. He was asked to imitate such a sermon but to say what he himself might want to say to *his* people. After some resistance, the result was an electrifying sermon with deep impact, yet sensible and consistent with his own character. The experiment provides this opportunity for trying out varieties of behavior for which one may not be ready in everyday life. A safe emergency is created where, with the immediate help of the therapist, it may be more readily resolved. These experiments, if sensitively arranged, are graded in difficulty so as to be within the range of possibility but challenging enough to arouse resistances which may be faced and, hopefully, dissolved.

Out of these three interlocking areas, a large diversity of specific techniques emerges, bound into a broad but delineated frame of reference. There is support for authenticity of personal experience for both therapist and patient. There is encouragement for inventiveness in technique. There is integration of action as well as introspection into the therapy process. And, finally, there is a return to the primary experience of self, the generic foundation of our existence.

The Language of Experience

Miriam Polster

I've been impressed lately by the number of articles, books, commentaries of various types, which deal with the language of psychotherapy. They are beginning to find ways to caricature us and, as with all good caricatures, many of them are right. As I considered what they were saying, I began to wonder about the language of experience. What do we know about it? And how does it relate to our work as psychotherapists?

Within Gestalt therapy we have come through a period when many people believed it was difficult, even destructive, to talk about ourselves and our experiences. We were trying to get past the stultifying consequences of the exclusively verbal therapies we had inherited. But in our correction for the deadening influence of too much talking, we frequently have gone to the opposite extreme and enshrined inarticulateness, as if inarticulateness might be more authentic than being able to use words effectively and well. Somewhere in this yin and yang of fashion in language, we may begin now to pick our way forward to suggest some principles of the relationship between language and experience. Let me start by talking about a familiar principle and one which is basic to Gestalt therapy; the principle of figure/ground formation.

In Gestalt therapy we've tried to define what healthy function is. One definition is that healthy function consists in a sense of life lived with a succession of figure/ground formations

(Polster and Polster, 1973). My experience centers around a figure of current interest that attracts me, that keeps me with it, that engages me, that provides me with new and welcome material, new detail, new richness, freely and generously; to which I respond and which I am interested until, at some point, I experience a sense of completion and I move on to another figure of interest without feeling guilty or precipitous about leaving.

Now, if you and I are fortunate, our lives contain a great deal of this kind of experience. We engage freshly with the events in our lives. We continue to find in each new experience something that will animate us, enliven us, make us curious, puzzle us, satisfy us. A healthy engagement with the environment has a sense of fluidity and what you might almost call a lively lack of prejudice. Boredom is prejudice in action. When I am bored, it is because there is something I am unwilling to see, something I am unwilling to recognize, or something I am unwilling to do. That prejudice withdraws the sense of vital engagement with my experience and results in stale interaction, which translates into boredom.

I propose that, since you and I are verbal animals, our language can support this figure/ground phenomenon in a number of ways.

Paul Goodman says

> Much of our experience is silent perception, both of body and environment, and much is wordless action in the environment. Speech can latch onto almost all experience, including what is silently perceived and wordlessly acted, creating a vast domain of verbalized experience... (Goodman, 1971)

Now, he's saying that language can attach itself to our experience, much of it non-verbal, in a way that can perform some kind of function on it—that there is mutual and reciprocal influence. Since we are verbal creatures, our verbalistic gift affects our perception of our experience.

Goodman also observes

> Normal speech is always a concrete coping with the real situation; and the real situation may, of course, include remembered, stored concepts as the second nature of both speaker and hearer. (Goodman, 1971)

In this statement he is describing figure and ground. The figure is the present situation and the relevant "coping" speech, and the ground for this present experience is provided (probably unspoken) by the "remembered, stored concepts" of both speaker and hearer. Here, very clearly, we can sense the rhythmic and constant dance between figure and ground and the part that speech plays in that dance.

Thinking has long been recognized as sub-vocal talking to ourselves, and we know that you and I are engaged in this much of the time. Those of us who have tried to meditate know what it takes to still the chatter that goes on endlessly in our minds. Sometimes we don't still it so much as we distract ourselves from it with a mantra. If you and I are talking to ourselves all the time, this speech can either enhance our experience or it can blunt and distort it. It can either add to the clarity and vivacity of experience or it can dull and muddy it.

What are some of the characteristics of good language?

It's fresh, it's specific, it's accurate, it carries the weight of the moment. In short, to paraphrase Joyce Cary, it conveys both "the fact and the feeling about the fact" (Cary, 1961). It supports us in defining present experience clearly and satisfyingly.

Let's consider the word "definition" in two possible meanings. First, there is the standard dictionary sense, which provides a description of the import that is intended and which may offer synonyms and examples of how the word can be used. There is also another meaning of the word "definition." This meaning refers to the way a photographer uses the word when he or she speaks of clear definition, of an image that is well-defined, a form that is perceived clearly and with rich detail. One of the most important functions that good language serves is to permit our experience to be well defined in both senses of the word. Good definition supports sharp awareness and richly perceived events. Good definition of experience, then, is one of the most important functions of language.

Another function that language performs is a more troublesome one. That is, the capacity to abstract. We are familiar with the cautions against abstraction as a way of separating ourselves from experience, from actuality, but let's not confuse the abuse with some very genuine gains that the ability to abstract provides. Kurt Goldstein chronicled only too well what the loss of this ability meant to the brain-damaged soldiers he observed. It was a frightful loss to them and, more generally, to all those who dismiss useful abstractions too cheaply.

Abstractions and generalizations afford us the chance to achieve a perspective on our present experience. This is necessary. We need this, you and I, because if we are forever and inescapably embedded in our experience, and only in that, we are often dealing with more than we can comfortably handle. We need some time off. We need to be able to back away, if not physically, then symbolically, and to place our present experience back into the continuity of our lives.

F. Perls once observed (in a filmed therapy demonstration) that meaning is the relationship of figure to ground. The ability to abstract is one of the abilities basic to establishing meaning. By abstracting we form useful and fitting categories and classificatory schemes. With these, an individual can compare present experience with previous experience. With useful comparisons, a sense of the continuity of life is encouraged and restored. I can reassure myself about my ability to deal with or to withstand what may presently feel like an overpoweringly intense situation. I can make comparisons between this present circumstance and other similar ones; how deep the pain may be, perhaps, or how long such feelings or reactions may last, or the simple reminder that I did weather something that time and probably can now. This capacity is invaluable for survival; we are not buffeted about by our experiences but instead move through them perceptively and self-supportedly. Our life is less, then, "full of sound and fury, signifying nothing." We spin out the sense of meaning in our lives, then, woven from the threads of our experience. Language is one such thread.

Finally, the language of experience allows for the recoverability of memories when they are relevant. It does this by accurately summarizing and describing present experience, either to another person or through my internal monologue, and by promoting the sense of completion. The right word does this because it may be absorbed in recoverable form. In this manner, language enriches my present experience and will in the future allow me to engage with current experience while past experience supports and adds perspective if needed.

Goodman talked about how language can fail the speaker, how it cannot convey what he wants to say; he calls this, rightly but perhaps incompletely, a form of aphasia. Usually aphasia is an organically related failure of language which might take one of several forms. Two are relevant here. An aphasic person may have no language at all; may be unable to produce a word, just sputters. All you see is the vehemence and the energy with no word to drain it, to express it. Or the aphasic may have lots of words but they do not fit the action or the objects he or she is trying to describe. So he or she says, "glasses" and points to a typewriter.

Goodman suggests a non-organic kind of aphasia. We could call it learned aphasia, or acquired aphasia, or perhaps selective aphasia. It has some of the same characteristics of the physiologically based disorder.

One form of acquired aphasia occurs at those times when people cannot put into words what they may be experiencing. They have no words, as in the first form of aphasia, with which to capture or describe or communicate their condition or feelings. They have no discriminative word to say what is happening with them. There's another kind of acquired aphasia where the words are there, but they have no connection to the specifics of the experience. The word is not attached to the experiential reality. So there are lots of words, but they have nothing to do with the emotion or the circumstances they are supposedly concerned with.

How does this happen? How does one become aphasic?

As an individual grows up, there are experiences that he cannot or is not permitted to have. As a result of the environment in which these experiences are denied or punished or covered over or given different names, there will not be words for them. In a world where it never snows, you will not have a word for snow. If you live in a place where no one is permitted to express anger, there will not be words for anger. It doesn't mean that anger will not be there. It means that there will not be the language to express it adequately and to deal with it effectively.

The important people in the child's environment might not permit him or her to have the experience or to name it accurately; so you have a situation where you are not supposed to argue, you're not supposed to hit, you're not supposed to criticize, you're not supposed to feel sad, you're not supposed to brag, you're not supposed to get too excited. Little by little the words for expressing these states begin to wither, just as any kind of growing thing (and language is a growing thing, after all) withers when it is not given the conditions it needs.

In other instances, the child cannot support the emotion and then gets into trouble. Behavior which occurs in an inexperienced or immature little person and is then punished, is likely to die out. So, there is a child who is dying of excitement, jumping up and down and practically quivering all over and lo! the child wets her pants and is severely punished or derided for it. This punishment is accompanied by words which call the behavior bad. Now, what is bad, the excitement or the pants-wetting or the jumping up and down? This non-discriminative lumping together blurs over the specific event and impoverishes the language that might clarify. All the child knows now is that too much excitement equals catastrophe.

THE LANGUAGE OF EXPERIENCE

Still another way to produce aphasia is to mislabel the emotion, to call it by another name or to deny it altogether. Mother loves you dear, but right now she's busy. So: loving and business are somehow related, and busy is more important. Or: I'm not fussy, you're just too dirty to touch me right now. Not fussy? Dirty? Or the best example, frequently used in the doctor's office; "Now, that didn't hurt, did it?"

Another way to make an aphasic (a group project) is to deal in what our critics are beginning to call "psychobabble," to deal in jargon, slogans, formulae and pat phrases. I read an article called "Marin County" language or "hot tub" language or "encounter group" language. Here you find lots of words, few of which convey much and most of which gloss over contactful interaction. Paul Goodman (1971) had something to say about this: "What kills language is dull, stereotyped, lazy or correct speech. There is a tendency of mass speech to deteriorate."

Now if this non-organic aphasic never has an experience which taxes the limits of her language, she can manage in a limited but perhaps tolerable way. If it never rains, you do not need a word for umbrella. But into each life some rain must fall, and the chances of such a stable and routinized life are pretty slim. What is more probable is that, when the inexpressible experience occurs, the individual is either threatened by the experience and has no words to release or communicate the resulting anxiety or has no recoverable "remembered, stored concepts" to create a useful perspective. So she either blanks out or turns stupid as a way of escaping the anxiety, or diminishes the anxiety by impulsive, inappropriate, or even possibly injurious action.

I want to give some examples of dysfunctional language, language that robs present experience of the vitality and clarity which we would consider essential to healthy function.

First, there is non-discriminative language, a collection of all-purpose words. These words are stereotyped and common, they're not much effort and they depend a lot on the implicit and often mistaken grasp of the listener. Jargon falls into this category.

An example would be the phrase, "That bugs me." Let me give you some ways in which it has been used: "My boss just told me I gotta work this week, and that bugs me." "My dog got run over last night and that really bugs me." "I talked to my mother the other day and she says that she and my father are getting a divorce and that really bugs me." "They're out of hot fudge and that really bugs me." Another type of non-discriminative language is when you ask someone whom you are working with what they feel about something they may have just told you and they say, "Okay..." or, "Good..." or, and this is probably more truthful, "I don't know..."

Language which has a large proportion of nouns instead of verbs is also dysfunctional. Nouns are classifying words and they classify experience making is seem immutable and unchangeable. Furthermore, they do not provide support for action. An example: a person who says, "I want to be a writer," instead of saying, "I want to write." When you think about it, it is easier to write than "to be a writer." Recently, in a workshop, a woman was talking about herself, and she was dealing almost wholly in nouns. One of the things she said was, "I'm a mother" and as she said it she was sitting cross-legged on the floor. I asked her to make that into a verb and when she said, "I mother" her arms moved into a broad expansive gesture and she raised herself up off the floor. Using a verb translated her statement into movement, into possibilities for action into the world. The noun, mother, had kept her static and immutable, coming out perhaps only on Mother's Day to get her flowers and then going back and putting on her shawl.

Still another form of acquired aphasia is the poor use of referents. Someone says something vague and global, a recital of a whole large lump of his life and ends by saying, "...that's what makes me feel so bad." In addition to the passive voice of the language there is a chaotic sense of trying to unwind a ball of yarn. What is the "that" about which he feels so bad? The referent is muddy. The jumble of the language expresses the sense of jumble in that individual's life. When experience is cloudy, it is hard to get a grasp on the difficulty and hard to know where to begin in order to move toward resolution. There's this huge "that" which is ill-defined and feels eternal precisely because there seems to be no way to know what it actually is.

Finally, there is the kind of acquired aphasia which consists of using words as objects. This is a consequence of the mislabeling of experiences. One learns to throw out words and to retreat behind them, hoping that somewhere in all these words there will be one or two that meet the requirement of the situation; words used as objects, pushed around, put in front, not really penetrating nor reflecting the nature of the experience. Very often these words are impersonally stated. I remember one woman's customary mode of reply when I would ask her how she felt about an event she just mentioned; she would give me an inventory. She would say, "Well, I feel the loneliness, the rejection, the pain, the discouragement..." just like checking it off at a physical exam, "Did you have measles, mumps, whooping cough...?" I am not making fun of her experience. I am deploring the fact that her language doesn't move me. The situation between us is such that I might be affected or touched by her story and I'm not. Now that's aphasic interaction with her world; her language is not working well for her.

There is another form of (not dysfunctional) buried richness in a person's language: personal metaphors. Very often these are a connection to live experience. Attending to the metaphor heightens this connection. An example: a man was deeply sad, genuinely and profoundly sad, because of all the leave-takings in his life. He was leaving a profession that had once inspired him and that he had fulfilled with great idealism much of his life, and he was ending a marriage that had lasted a long time. In describing his sadness he said a phrase that to me was magical. He said, "I guess I'll have to pick up my baggage and leave." I said to him, "It sounds to me as if you are not leaving empty-handed." This was something that had not occurred to him but had a great deal of significance for him. He became aware of what it was that he was leaving with at the end of this long period of his life. It was not just full stop, goodbye, with no relationship between this one phase of his life and the next.

Goodman summed up his belief in the centrality of good language and its relation to experience: "Personality consists (largely) of one's speech habits—learned because they have worked in spontaneous acts of speech on many occasions." (Goodman, 1971). Laura Perls has written "I work with speech patterns and the particular idiosyncratic uses of language." (Perls, 1976). She is working, among other things, with how that individual is talking to him/herself and how the language is shaping and structuring his/her experience.

What are the implications this has for therapy? In the article I just quoted, Laura Perls talked about the influence of past and future on the present engagement and she wrote

> The past exists now as memory, nostalgia, regret, resentment, phantasy, legend, history. The future exists here and now in the actual present as anticipation, planning, rehearsal, expectations and hope, or dread and dispair. (Perls, 1976)

This is an example of how the ability of a therapist to make fine discriminations, to capture the subtle shadings of emotion are the very instrumentality of her working with her patients to sharpen the nature of their own lived experience. This is what we are working for, the sharpness and savor of experience. To the extent that you and I have the language to make these discriminations, to the extent that we can inspire and support people to close the gap between their experience and their ability to express it richly and satisfyingly, to that extent we have enhanced the nature of their being-in-the-world.

Goodman says, "Meaning...is speaker and hearer making sense to one another in a situation." I propose to you that often contact is speaker and hearer making sense to one another in a situation.

Sensory Functioning in Psychotherapy

Erving Polster

I would like to show how psychotherapy can help close the gap between a person's basic sensations and the higher experiences derived from these sensations. Identifying these basic sensations has become difficult for people because of the complexities of our society. A person may eat not only because he is hungry but also because certain tastes delight him, because it is mealtime, because he likes the company, or because he doesn't want to feel depressed or angry. His sensations are often only obscurely related to each other. What he does about the resulting muddle contributes to our current, frequently described crisis of identity because in order to know who we are, we must at least know what we feel. For example, knowing the difference between being hungry, angry, or sexually aroused surely is a lengthy step toward knowing what to do. In this interplay between feeling and doing lies the crux of our search for good living.

As conceptual background for identifying and activating sensation, I would like to introduce the concept of *synaptic experience*. The synaptic experience is an experience of union between awareness and expression. You may feel this union if you become aware, for example, of breathing while talking, of the flexibility of your body while dancing, or your excitement while painting. At times of union between intensified awareness and expression, profound feelings of presence, clarity of perception, vibrancy of inner experience, and wholeness of personality are common.

The term *synapse* is derived from the Greek word meaning conjunction or union. Physiologically, the synapse is the area of conjunction between nerve fibers, where they form a union with one another. The synaptic arc facilitates union between sensory and motor nerves, bridging the gap between these neural structures by special, though not altogether understood, energy transmissions. The metaphoric use of the synapse focuses our attention on united sensori-motor function as represented by awareness and expression.

Various therapies differ as to their methods for bringing expression and awareness together, but most, if not all, do share in calling attention to the individual's inner processes, sometimes including sensation as well as expression. Some therapies do not acknowledge any concern with inner process (the operant-conditioning people are among them), yet they repeatedly inquire about how the patient experiences anxiety. Most therapists would agree that if a patient were, for example, to tell about his feelings of love when his mother sang him to sleep, his story would have a greater effect both for him and his listener if he were aware of his feeling. The patient, if given timely direction, may become aware of many sensory phenomena as he speaks. His body may be moist, warm, flexible, tingly, etc. The emergence of these sensations increases the restorative powers of the story because through the resulting unity of feelings and words it becomes a more nearly incontrovertible confirmation of a past love experience.

Exploring sensations is, of course, not new to psychology. Wilhelm Wundt foresaw sensory experience as the root support from which all higher feeling emerged, but his research and that of many others never had the humanistic flavor that attracts the psychotherapist. However. there are many recent humanistic views that do herald a new recognition of the power of sensation. Schachtel (1959) for one, has shown the commonality of the infant and the adult in their experience of primitive, primary, and raw sensation. He says,

> If the adult does not make use of his capacity to distinguish . . . the pleasurable feeling of warmth [from] perceiving that this is the warmth of air or the warmth of water . . . but instead gives himself over to the pure sensation itself, then he experiences a fusion of pleasure and sensory quality which probably approximates the infantile experience. . . . The emphasis is not on any object but entirely on feeling or sensation. (Schachtel, p.125)

The child's sensation tone is the paradigm for the purity of sensory experience. Although sensations do become cluttered over the years, early experiences need not be merely infantile. In our quest for fulfillment, many of our energies are directed toward the recovery of early existential possibilities. The early innocence of sensation has been neutralized by social forces that dichotomize the child and the adult into altogether separate creatures. However, the adult is not merely a replacement for the child. Rather he is the result of accretions which need not make the character of childhood irrelevant. A child-like sense may orient and vitalize us even in the face of newly developing realities. As Perls, Hefferline, and Goodman (1951) have said about the recovery of past memories,

> the content of the recovered scene is unimportant but the childish feeling and attitude that lived that scene are of the utmost importance. The childish feelings are important not as a past that must be undone, but as some of the most beautiful powers of adult life that must be recovered: spontaneity, imagination, directness of awareness, and manipulation. (PHG, p.297)

Reports of LSD users also extoll the primacy of sensation. Alan Watts (1964) says that while on LSD he is aware of changes in his perception of such ordinary things as "sunlight on the floor, the grain in wood, the texture of linen, or the sound of voices across the street. My own experience," he adds,

> ...has never been of a distortion of those perceptions as in looking at one's self in a concave mirror. It is rather that every perception becomes—to use a metaphor—more resonant. The chemical seems to provide consciousness with a sounding box... for all the senses, so that sight, touch, taste, smell, and imagination are intensified like the voice of someone singing in the bathtub. (Watts, p.120)

In our own way, we psychotherapists may also provide a sounding box for resonance, as I shall now describe.

We may start by dividing the whole range of human experience into *culminative experiences* and *ingredient experiences*. The culminative experience exists in a composite form. It is a total and united event of primary relevance to the individual. As I write these words, for example, the act of writing is the culmination of a lifetime of experiences leading to this moment and forming a part of the composite structure of writing. Furthermore, each movement of my finger, each breath I take, each tangential thought, each variation in attention, confidence, zest, and clarity join together to form the composite experience I-am-writing. As elements in the composite unit, however, each of these is an ingredient experience. These ingredient experiences frequently go unattended, but when one does explore their existence and discovers their relationship to the culminative event, one may develop a heightened experience. The gourmet does this as he tastes a sauce. Hopefully, he encounters the quality of that taste in totality, as an integrated experience. However, he also examines his experience more pointedly so that he may identify the ingredients that make up the sauce. He may identify certain herbs, a familiar wine, proportions of butter, etc. This awareness enriches him, leading him to a new dimension of taste experience. The analysis and re-synthesis create a rhythm between destruction of the composite taste and re-creation of it. This reverberation between destruction and re-creation occurs over and over, helping to intensify the vibrant taste. So also, when we explore our inner sensations, we may identify the ingredients of the everyday experiences which form the substance of our lives. Enrichment occurs when there is maximal possibility for the emergence of underlying or component parts into the foreground of our knowledge. The adventure of unlimited accessibility of experience and the fluctuations between a synthesized experience and the elemental parts of our existence provide a dynamic and continually self-renewing excitement.

The recovery of this dynamic process frequently requires close attention, much as relearning to walk after a illness. Concentration is one technique for the recovery of sensation. It is well known that one must concentrate to do good work, but instructions to do so usually sound vague. moralistic, and general. Yet, concentration can be a specific mode of operation that involves giving close regard to the specific object of one's interest. It must be pointed and single-minded. When these conditions are satisfied and one's concentration is brought to bear on internal sensations, events may occur that are remarkably comparable to events arising out of hypnosis, drugs, sensory deprivation, heroic eruptions, and other conditions that take the individual out of his accustomed frame of reference. Although not usually as potent as these other conditions, a great advantage of concentration for heightening experience is that one may readily return to ordinary events and ordinary communications. Thus, one may move in and out of other modes of interaction such as talking, role-playing, fantasy, dream work, etc., which makes it easier to accept the experience as relevant to everyday consciousness.

Moving now to the therapeutic situation itself, I shall describe the role of sensations with three therapeutic purposes in mind. They are: (I) the accentuation of fulfillment, (2) the facilitation of the working-through process, and (3) the recovery of old experiences.

First, with respect to fulfillment, there seem to be two kinds of people, the action-oriented and the awareness-oriented. Both can live rich lives if one orientation does not exclude the other. The action-oriented person who has no deep barrier to the awareness of experience will, through his actions, arouse his experience of self. The swimmer, for example, may discover many powerful inner sensations, as may the business executive who won leadership of a new company. The individual who is oriented toward awareness will find that so long as he does not exclude action, his awarenesses will direct him to action. The psychologist may write a book or create an organization, the restless person may move to another city, and the sexually aroused person may have intercourse. Psychological troubles result when the rhythm between awareness and expression is faulty.

To illustrate, an action-oriented person, a successful businessman, came to therapy because he was not experiencing fulfillment in life. Unusually vital and active, he needed to make every second count and became impatient with any moment of nonproductivity. He could not accept the accumulation of sensation, keeping always ahead of himself by prematurely discharging sensation either through action or through planning action. Consequently he was having great difficulty knowing "who I am." During the first ten sessions we talked a great deal and made some introductory explorations into his inner experience. These included certain awareness experiments and breathing exercises. Then, one day when I asked him to close his eyes and concentrate on his inner experience, he began to feel a quietness in himself and to experience a feeling of union with the birds singing outside the window. Many other sensations followed. He kept them to himself, as he told me later, because to describe them would have meant interrupting himself, a wise but atypical appreciation for feeling rather than productivity. At one point, seeing that his abdomen was not integrated into his breathing, I asked him to use his abdomen more fully, which he was readily able to do. When he did, he began to feel a new ease of breathing, accompanied by an easy strength as distinct from the impatient strength with which he was familiar. He could really tell the difference between the two kinds of strength. He said he felt like a car that had been perfectly tuned. He then left, saying he was recovering a missing link in his life. He felt as though he had *experienced* time rather than having *wasted* it.

We may illustrate our second therapeutic purpose, the facilitation of the working-through process, by the story of a woman who recently became an executive in a toy factory. Her secretary had been in her department for years, but was a disorganized and controlling person. My patient became aware that this secretary was the root of many of the previous departmental troubles and confronted her with certain departmental requirements. This was a great blow to the secretary, who suddenly looked "like a waif." My patient felt as though she were now sitting face-to-face with another part of herself. She and her brother had grown up in an impoverished section of New York and had indeed been waifs. However, since she had always nurtured her younger brother, she only saw him as a waif, not herself. In her life she had alternately supported waifs and played the waif herself.

In our talk, she realized she didn't want to be a waif any more and knew that in this confrontation with her secretary she had accepted the chance to get rid of the waif in herself and become a woman in her own right. As she told me about this, a new look came over her face, a mixture of absorption, alert introspection, and yielding to puzzlement. When I asked her what she felt, she said in surprise that she felt a tightness in her breathing and in her legs. She concentrated on these sensations and after a few moments of silence looked surprised again and said she felt a tightness in her vagina. I asked her to attend to this sensation, which she did. Again, after a few moments of concentration a brightness arose in her face, and she said the tightness was leaving. Then she seemed startled and suddenly had a deep sensation that she didn't describe but instead burst into paroxysms of crying, calling out the name of a man she loves and with whom she has for the first time had a relationship of mutuality and strength. When she looked up, there was great beauty and wholeness apparent in her. As we spoke further, she realized the importance of her confrontation with her secretary, whom she subsequently fired, and the rediscovery of her feelings about waifs. But she knew that her deepest breakthrough came with the discovery of the sensation in her vagina. The subsequent awakening of her palpable feelings of womanhood gave substance and therefore primal resolution to problems which might otherwise only be verbalized.

Finally, a third purpose served by the recovery of sensation is the recovery of old events. The unfinished situation moves naturally into completion when barriers are dissolved and when new inner stimulation propels one toward completing the unfinished business. Psychoanalysis although differing from Gestalt therapy in many details of conceptualization and technique, has made the return of the old and forgotten a familiar expectation in psychotherapy. Although many words about the' past have been spoken in therapy, these are frequently without the accompaniment of deep sensations. The next situation illustrates how sensations rather than mere words may lead the way to an old event.

A woman whose husband had died about ten years previously, had spoken about her relationship with him but had never gotten across sense of the profundity of their experience together. In one session, series of awarenesses evolved, including the experience of her tongue tingling, a burning feeling around her eyes, teneseness in her back and shoulders, and then dampness around her eyes. Following a lengthy sequence of these experiences, she caught a deep breath and realized that she felt like crying. There was a sense of tears in her eyes and a sensation in her throat that she could not describe. After a very long pause, she felt an itch, which she concentrated on at some length. It should be said that with each new sensation, the silence and inner concentration was lengthy, frequently lasting for minutes. Silence when joined with focused concentration has the effect of building up the intensity of feeling. Soon she began to feel itchy in many places. She found it difficult to stay with these sensations without scratching, but she did. She was feeling somewhat amused about the surprising spread of her itching sensation, but she also began to feel frustrated and sad again, as though she might cry. She talked about a irritating experience she had had the night before at the home of her parents where she had not been able to show her irritation. Then she felt lump in her throat, and after a period of concentrating on the lump, palpitation appeared in her chest. Her heart started beating rapidly and this made her quite anxious. She verbalized the *pump, pump, pump* sounds, then became aware of a sharp pain in her upper back. She paused at great length to concentrate on the pain in her back, then said under considerable stress, "Now I remember that horrible night that my first husband had a heart attack." Another lengthy pause followed where she appeared under great tension and absorption. Then she said in a hushed tone that she was aware again of the pain, the anxiety, and the whole experience of that night. At this point she gave in to deep, heartfelt cry which lasted about a minute. When she finished she looked up and said, "I guess I still miss him." Now the vagueness was gone and I could experience the reality and wholeness of her relationship with her husband. The clear transformation from superficiality to depth was apparently brought on by the buildup in sensation through self-awareness and concentration, letting her own sensations lead the way rather than her ideas or explanations.

To summarize, the concept of synaptic experience provides a background for the relevance of sensation for good living and accentuates the importance of the rhythm between one's awareness and one's expression. Although it represents only part of the total therapeutic methodology, the individual's discovery of his sensations, where it becomes relevant, may lead him to an experience of fulfillment, may complete the working-through process, and may stimulate the recovery of old events.

Women in Therapy: A Gestalt Therapist's View

Miriam Polster

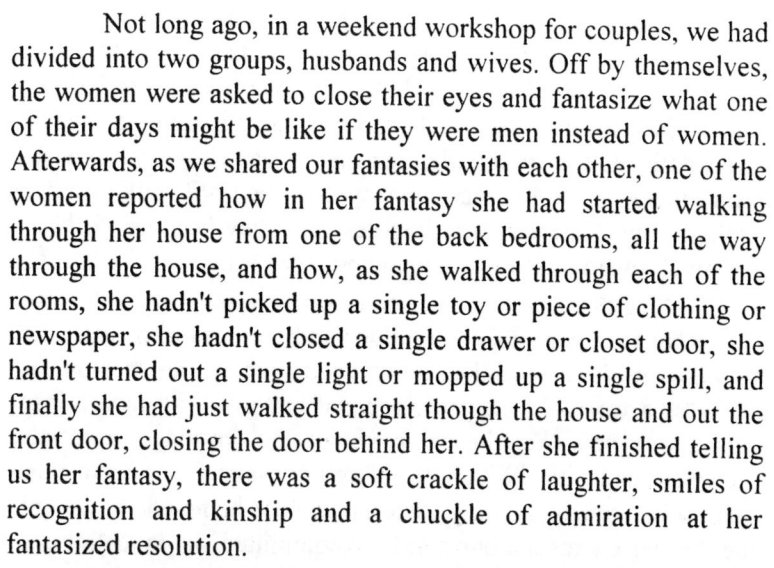

Not long ago, in a weekend workshop for couples, we had divided into two groups, husbands and wives. Off by themselves, the women were asked to close their eyes and fantasize what one of their days might be like if they were men instead of women. Afterwards, as we shared our fantasies with each other, one of the women reported how in her fantasy she had started walking through her house from one of the back bedrooms, all the way through the house, and how, as she walked through each of the rooms, she hadn't picked up a single toy or piece of clothing or newspaper, she hadn't closed a single drawer or closet door, she hadn't turned out a single light or mopped up a single spill, and finally she had just walked straight though the house and out the front door, closing the door behind her. After she finished telling us her fantasy, there was a soft crackle of laughter, smiles of recognition and kinship and a chuckle of admiration at her fantasized resolution.

Now I had met the husbands of these women. They were not brutes, bullies or martinets who insisted that household duties be performed with militaristic timeliness and dispatch. But these women didn't seem to need that, anyhow. They had arrived at the point where they felt compelled to do things they didn't really want to do and which they could get out of doing only by special effort, like fantasizing, or under special conditions, like illness. Somehow, they had constructed for themselves standards of behavior that they felt obliged to live up to and which often bore only slight resemblance to the actual pattern of their own personal needs.

A double thread runs through the stories of many of the women I see, married or unmarried. On the one hand, they feel trapped in a round of commitment and activities which keeps them busy but leaves them feeling unsatisfied, frantic and unfulfilled. On the other hand, adding insult to injury, they do not even experience themselves as having a hand in making many of the decisions about how they are to live. They feel locked into a situation—a career decision, a relationship or a life-style— which they didn't elect or which has turned out to have hidden consequences they didn't foresee, but which they feel powerless to change or to abandon. They bottle up the feelings and desires which they believe they can't express, either because expressing them will cause more trouble than they already have or because it won't make any difference anyway and they will only wind up feeling more frustrated and impotent. So they become skillful at learning how to dance when somebody else leads.

The difficulties any person experiences in life will reflect his or her own particular limitations and these, in turn, will relate to the prohibitions and limitations which society imposes on each of us. If a woman is married, societal patterns will have a lot to say about how her husband views the marriage and what expectations he has brought to the relationship. Her own personal bent will, correspondingly, determine how hemmed in she may feel by these expectations and how committed she is to living up to them, whether she finds them compatible or not with her own needs. Single or married, at work she will encounter the expectations her colleagues carry in with their lunch pails or briefcases, and her response to built-in expectations also pervades her experiences as a woman at school, within her family and among her friends.

It is a major piece of work for a woman to integrate all of these inclinations and influences and to come up with a harmonious personal sense of herself where no experience need be discriminated against as inadmissible or unworthy.

As a child, all of her experience was viewed freshly and uncritically. She made her own standards for what she wanted to do and what she didn't want to do, spinning them out of the shining thread of her own sensations and values. She could play as happily with shit as she could with mud. Only gradually did she begin to learn that some things that made her happy weren't supposed to, and some things which weren't so pleasing to her were, nevertheless, better regarded and were to be more highly valued. She began to distrust knowledge based primarily on her own experience and to introject, to swallow whole with the same lack of criticism, the precepts of other stronger and wiser people around her. She began to exchange pure joy for secondhand wisdom. In doing this she had her first exercise in learning how to deny or disapprove of some of the most beautiful parts of her own experience.

But these denied or disowned parts of herself did not just meekly disappear. The imprint of firsthand living is not so easily erased. The taste of honey lingers somewhere in one's insides and sends up vague traces of something better than the present watered-down experience which is only an inadequate substitute. Somewhere underground, her original knowledge of joy sits uneasy and only too ready to contradict or sabotage the surface confluence agreed upon by her shrewder and more politic socialized self which denies the primal zest and richness that she knows can underlie her actions.

Eventually, these antithetical characteristics freeze into postures of mutual alienation and standoff; this is the genesis of her own personal polarities, those internal contradictions which nourish ambivalence and fatigue. Perls (1969) formulated the concept of polarities into the basic characters of topdog versus underdog, but there is more diversity than this in the cast of polarities making up the composite which is any particular woman. Topdog and underdog imply merely that in these polar struggles one of the opponents appears to be winning or to have the upper hand. However, any characteristic aspect of a woman can spawn its own polar counterpart. So, contests can rage on internally between a woman's ruthlessness and her tenderness, between her conventional self and her rebel, between her meekness and her arrogance. Any woman is a composite of many Dr. Jekylls and Ms. Hydes.

To the extent that a woman keeps herself out of touch with one of the polarities engaged in her personal conflicts, she is ensuring her own immobility and impotence. Rooted in her submerged and disowned underdog are the seeds of change and movement. Like all the disenfranchised, her underdog has little to lose and everything to gain from change. When she remains out of touch with this unacknowledged part of herself, she is, in effect, silencing her own protest against the *status quo*. The parts of herself which she refuses to give ear or voice to remain isolated and unavailable as a support for informed action. They are relegated to underground activities, dissension and sabotage. This is what underlies her sense of being trapped or crammed with unexpressed and inexpressible feelings.

In Gestalt therapy, a central focus of our work is the individual's responsibility for shaping his or her own existence. In spite of how her environment leans on her, a woman, nevertheless, has to know how to engage with it in ways which will be nourishing and zestful, not just successive acts of self-betrayal. She is creating her own life, bit by bit. She needs all her energy and ingenuity to come up with hours, days and years that she feels she has had a hand in shaping. To do this, she has to be able to integrate her awareness of sensations, actions, wants, values, relationships and all the raw material of her life with her own personal willingness and skill in using this awareness as her basis for action.

When her awareness is unprejudiced and unimpeded, when she has no stake in keeping parts of her experience alien and unknown, her actions can spring expressively from naive mobilization. Her sense of her life is that it has flexibility, surprise, enthusiasm and movement. She experiences herself as a free agent, acting from her own needs, making choices from a range of possible alternatives and being free to change whatever she becomes aware of as unsatisfying or toxic.

An example of this is the experience of one woman who came to realize, in her awareness of the tyranny that her family and their rigid upbringing had imposed on her, that she had even furnished her entire house according to their dictates and not at all to her own taste! In addition to standards of interior design, she had also swallowed much of what the family had to say about such virtues as thrift, frugality and conservative behavior. One day we were working with her distaste for her furniture and how angry she was with herself for feeling so stuck with it. She was far from poor and could probably have afforded to chuck it all and simply refurbish. I instructed her to use her anger and give herself a lecture on what she might do with her herd of white elephants. She was a woman of rich imagination and exuberant sense of drama, and she swung into the assignment with energy. Her ideas ranged from burning it and collecting the insurance to giving it all to a charitable organization and claiming it as a tax deduction. But her eventual solution illustrated an important and basic principle in Gestalt work with polarities, in this case her aesthetic self and her practical self. Resolution of a conflict, in its most effective and enduring form, usually involves respecting both parts of the polarity and merging them into a course of action which represents a synthesis or an alliance of these previously disparate parts. Her solution turned out to be a house sale, leaving her house bare, cannily getting top dollar for her unwanted furniture (even selling some of it to her relatives!), and winding up with a healthy bankroll to finance her refurnishing.

Now all of a woman's actions may not be this exciting or have such a sense of turnaround. Life is not so unstintingly generous. But even when a woman performs humdrum tasks, if she experiences herself as not locked into doing them she is free to recognize that she regards these tasks as necessary and *chooses* to do them rather than delegating them to someone else or letting them go undone. She is also free to stop doing them when she senses that the psychological cost to herself has become more than she is willing to pay.

The experience of being stuck, on the contrary, consists of finding one's present status malnourishing, distasteful or even downright poisonous but feeling unable to do anything but hang on to it. A woman may know exactly what it might take to turn her life around, but such changes may frighten or repel her. On the other hand, she may only vaguely want something more or something different than she has right now, and this amorphous discontent scares her, or results in her feeling guilty, despondent or overly demanding.

What a woman finds unwelcome about making changes in her own life is, at least partly, a projection. That is, what scares her or repels her or makes her feel guilty is the unknown or the unacceptable or the reprehensible *in herself*. What she fears about making changes is primarily the re-awakening of aspects of herself, unpredictable, untried, alien, demanding and leading to consequences she is not sure she is willing to permit. Her self-doubt also has an introjective core. It is the accumulation of the judgments and values of other people which she has taken in and adopted as her own and which she feels uneasy about questioning. Unchallenged, these foreign doctrines govern her actions from a position analogous to that of a distant ruler sending out edicts, which are not to be questioned, to the inhabitants of a territory he has conquered. Instead of viewing herself as a population of potential and unrealized capacities which she might explore, she fears rebellion and the overthrow of her established routine and is immobilized by this fear. She keeps herself in check like an uneasy dictator who fears change. This is how she has arrived at her current impasse—unhappy with her present life, but afraid or unwilling to try new behaviors or adopt new values which might lead to resolution. As a way of relieving herself of the responsibility for this situation, she projects outside of herself her own unwillingness to change and decides that she has no effect on an immutable and intransigent world. She is stuck.

One young married woman deplored the boredom of her life with a husband whom she considered dull, unadventuresome, overweight and her social inferior. Some of these things were true about him, but he was also generous with her, listened to her periodic tirades without getting too angry, and had enough emotional resilience to come out of these combats still loving her and not bearing any grudges. He worked at an unskilled job where he was his own boss and dealt with machinery which he loved. He was not a milktoast; he was an easygoing guy with a good sense of humor and a no-nonsense attitude towards himself and the world around him. He was pretty well informed, had some interest in politics, but mostly he liked his job, his family and his friends.

She was filled with the idea that she was really better than all this, too good for such a husband, and wanted to split. Where she wanted to go and what she planned on doing when she arrived were inconsequential details that she couldn't be bothered with. She admitted that she very much liked the financial and material comfort she had with him, and he came in very handy when there were practical issues that demanded attention. She had very little tolerance for handling frustration in a creative way, she would get bogged down in emotional upheavals, and his good-humored patience was indispensable at those times. This was not a very good omen for her independent function without him.

During our work together, interestingly enough, she changed very little. He lost weight, became more active in volunteer political organizations, began to read more and talk to her about what he was reading—but she was still not satisfied. She had a great stake in not recognizing change, since she wanted to retain her picture of herself as a woman burdened with an inferior husband. This freed her of the necessity to do anything about making changes in herself that might move her out of her own boredom. Of her own shortcomings she remained steadfastly unaware, and when her husband confronted her about them on those occasions when he was moved beyond endurance, her response was tears and hysteria.

This elevated picture of herself had been handed to her by her mother, along with the family recipes. But all she had was a vague sense that she was cut out for better things, and there was very little substance behind these feelings. Her first chore was to learn how to make her own life interesting without blaming her boredom on her husband and expecting him to do something about it. We worked at making her more aware of the specific things she wanted from her husband, and she began to give up expecting him to be a mind-reader and divine what she wanted. She began to take a couple of courses at the local university extension program. Not grand actions, surely, but initial steps in shaping her own movement out of boredom.

The need to keep from making changes imposes certain conditions on a woman. She has to keep herself from becoming aware of attractive possibilities for action either within herself or in her environment. She has to keep new directions from becoming fascinating or compelling enough to disturb and arouse her. She has to construct and maintain an equilibrium for herself where she can exercise just enough sensitivity to know that she is unhappy, but not enough to discover or invent what she might do about her unhappiness.

There are several ways she can keep herself in this condition. For the most part, they consist of not allowing her own experience to become sharp enough, figural enough, to articulate clearly what is bothering her. Whenever an individual has a stake in things-as-they-are, she has to do something to obscure the native flux that all living things display. To keep phenomena which *are* changing appearing as if they are not changing at all, she has to prevent herself from seeing them clearly, in rich detail, as well-defined and active figures against the background of her general orientation to her life. In the above example, the young wife had to learn to see change in her husband, as well as work toward changes in herself.

One way of not perceiving clearly is to play dumb or vague by remaining unaware of specifically what she may not like about her present situation. She can't identify what displeases her. Nothing is actually wrong. She has a lovely home, or a good job, or a fine husband, or great kids, or good people to work with, and she can't conceive of how to change anything when nothing is wrong. She blurs her own experience and keeps herself in the dark as a way of short circuiting the excitement and the arousal to action that awareness brings. Awareness calls for responsive and expressive behavior; it tips the balance against inaction.

Take the example of another married woman, beautiful and intelligent, doing well at a job which she found interesting, loving and being loved by her husband, but still feeling that there was something missing. One day she was recounting her experience with one of the administrators in the agency where she worked. It had been an unsatisfactory interview where she had failed to get her point across to the older woman who had brushed aside her questions, giving her only perfunctory answers and hurrying her out of the office. My patient made excuses for her supervisor, saying she was busy, that she had to take other people into consideration and wasn't free to devote herself to just one person's needs. Then she fell silent. I asked her what she was aware of, and she replied that she was holding her breath and clenching her teeth. I instructed her to breathe more deeply and regularly and to attend to what happened when she did this. She observed that her teeth remained clenched, but that now she also noticed some tension at the back of her throat. I asked her to make some sound when she exhaled, incorporating the tension in her throat and the clenching of her teeth. What emerged was a somewhat throttled but unmistakable growl. She looked startled at making such a sound. I asked her whom she felt like growling at, and after a pause she said, "You know, I don't really mean what I said about my supervisor. I think she's giving me lousy supervision and I'm angry at her for not giving me the kind of supervision I need." Another moment's pause, "And I'm mad because *I* made it easy for her! *I* let her get away with it!" This led to a chain of memories of instances when she had made it easy for people to ignore her, or to not take her seriously, or not give her the information she wanted from them. I told her I would play her supervisor, and we would start the interview over again and this time to make sure that she got what she needed and didn't let me squirm off the hook. To do this she had to mobilize more of her own aggressive energy, to the point where, when I began to rise out of my chair as if indicating that the interview was over, she put one forefinger against my chest and pushed me back into the chair saying, "I'm not done with you yet!" When we finished she looked lively and vigorous. Subsequently she became more active in getting what she wanted, not only from her supervisor, but also from doctors and salespeople whom she had previously allowed to intimidate her.

Another way for a woman to avoid moving directly against her predicament is to retroflect, to direct her disapproval of something back against herself in the form of a blanket condemnation. She condemns herself totally as inadequate or unworthy. Other people are stronger, more capable, more knowledgeable or just plain nicer than she is. Other women manage a home and kids and a job and go to school, and *they* aren't worn to a frazzle and shrewish like she is. Or they have special talents or ideas and even though they live under some of the same conditions she does, *they* manage to come up with creative and sparkling answers. *They* are more virtuous, less self-centered, less selfish and they never complain about their troubles. Everyone else seems so happy and competent, why is she the only malcontent? All of her troubles exist because she is so incompetent, and she engages in a constant round of self-accusation and blame.

As an example of this, I remember a young woman who was creative, hardworking, generous and loving to her family with these talents. When she was able to do something that made her happy, she was as radiant as a sunrise, and often the things that made her happy were things that made life better for her husband and kids, too. Often—but not always. There were some things she wanted to do for herself; she wanted to paint, and teach practical nursing, in which she was trained, part-time, and more generally establish an island of personal competence and achievement not rooted in her own home. Her husband gave superficial approval to these ambitions. As long as they didn't interfere with her care of the kids or her maintenance of the house, or her serving as hostess to his family and business associates, and so long as it didn't involve his having to take up the slack in the family living arrangements, it was okay with him.

Her husband was a reliable, conscientious and hard-working young man. He took his responsibilities seriously. He took everything and everyone seriously, too. But what he didn't know about was joy, grace, luminosity and free-flowing love, and he was choking these very qualities right out of his wife. She was ripe for such a bargain, it turned out, because her mother, a conventionally practical woman, had dismissed as trivial her daughter's very real artistic talent and had left her a set-up for anyone who continued the routine. Her husband differed from her mother superficially in that he was indulgent and condescending instead of harsh, but he, too, put her down in his own way. She was so snowed by his good qualities that she believed she was too demanding, and he was a saint even to put up with her. He agreed with her and treated her with a tolerant benevolence that bordered on the ludicrous, except that it had such tragic repercussions. I worked with them as a couple on those few occasions when he was willing to come in. Mostly, he thought it was his wife's problem, an effective defense, and he was generously willing to pay for her treatment. So we worked alone, she and I.

Our sessions focused on her becoming aware of what she wanted and how she might get it without needing anything from her husband. If this sounds like a mixture of subversion and autonomy, for many women it boils down to just such a method. She became an expert, using the proceeds from the sale of several of her paintings to hire someone to do some of the work at home that didn't need her personally. She also got into touch with her own attractiveness, began dressing with more dash and began to hear some of the admiring things that people other than her husband had to say about her. She even considered taking a lover, but decided against it because she really loved her husband, pompous as he was, and reasoned that it would cost her more anguish than she wanted. Her sense of her own worth began to equal her estimate of her husband's worth, and she started to teach him some of the things she needed him to know, like how to make love better. She even realized that in some ways he was more fragile than she, and her loving could more realistically cope with his needs, as well as her own. What she accomplished in therapy was to stop believing exclusively in outside authorities and to look to herself as a person whose experience and authority were at least as valid as theirs. When we terminated, she had a more accurate appraisal of both herself and her husband. She was past the idolatrous worship of him that was the obverse of her own self-condemnation.

Another way that some women paralyze themselves is to make their goals so grandiose or drastic that they can't get started on such vast plans. What they conceive it would take for their own personal improvement is a grand societal reformation, family upheaval, a graduate degree, or an administrative position that would give them prestige and clout. Even if this were true, which in some sense it always is, this is not where she can get started. The trouble with these ambitious plans is that they sound so elegant and far-reaching that they become a substitute for action. A woman asserts that she could run her own advertising agency, but she just can't get someone to stay with the kids while she would be away. Another wants a graduate degree, but hates to do the required reading. This settling for external and obsessive planning with no consummatory action is what Perls called "mindfucking."

One young woman, lethargic and indolent in her sessions with me, would engage in repetitious denunciations of a society where people didn't care about one another and where women were relegated to subservient roles. But she sat for hours in my office expecting all of the action to come from me, and putting nothing into the pot. I was supposed to lay some kind of therapy on her which would change everything while demanding very little action from her. My aim, whenever she tried to engage me in this way, was to do something which would compel her to take over an active role. So, every time she complained about the evils of the society, I would get her to move out of her usual listless protest by engaging the offenders in an imaginary dialogue, or by playing the part of the transgressors defending themselves, or any other means I could come up with to energize her.

One day she began to complain, logically enough, about my not being more active in our session. I asked her to scold me and to tell me what she wanted from me. As she berated me, I directed her to listen to what she was saying. Before long, she became aware that she was assuming a subservient role in our work together, perpetuating right in my office what she had ascribed to society's ill will. Our sessions changed after that, with her assumption of more responsibility for the conduct of her own therapy. Her energy was not so devoted any more to pointless harangues and focused instead on the specifics she wanted to change in her own life; she switched her major at school, selected a new advisor whom she found she could really talk to and joined a couple of activist groups where she began to act on her social grievances in the company of kindred spirits.

In working with a woman who feels stuck, it becomes important to ascertain whether she expends more energy in emphasizing the objections to movement than in supporting her own positive momentum. Many women specialize in throwing roadblocks in their own paths, cluttering up their experience with side issues that obscure and distract from the central concerns, leaving them worn out and with little energy left for the main event. There is usually much for her to be discontented about, but she prevents herself from doing anything about it because she is so hedged in with conditions, precepts, moralisms, projections, contingencies, qualifications, corollaries—*ad infinitum*—all of which must be considered. And considered they are, endlessly, until she begins to sound like a broken record. I recall the fantasy of one woman who was reciting all the contingencies she had to consider before she could do something she wanted to do. I asked her to fantasize that each of these considerations was a bar in a cage that she was making for herself. As she named each one of the objections she was putting up, she was to picture it as one of the bars. She built a marvelous cage for herself; she had enough objections to ring herself in completely.

Growing up a woman in our society leaves a psychological residue that cripples and deforms all but the most exceptional women. It is no comfort to know that the same distortions also pervade growing up a man and with some of the same unhappy consequences. There is also no comfort to be found in the fact that some of the best teachers of these principles are themselves women, who ought to know better from their own experience. Our society reinforces in women dependent, exploitative and defensive behaviors aimed at procuring conventional and stereotyped rewards. For the woman who is disdainful of either the method or the rewards, there is frequently much trouble and meager compensation. No wonder many women give up the fight. For those who persevere in trying to establish an independent sense of their own identity, it is still not without cost in the form of nagging self-doubt, criticism from others and displacement of energy into dealing with side issues and irrelevancies.

For example, one woman was doggedly independent and resented the marginal status of a single woman who couldn't call a man for a date with the same freedom that he could call her. The artifice of sitting at the phone and waiting for him to take the initiative was galling. Many times she wouldn't wait, but even when she called, knowing it was as much her right as his, she felt precarious and unsure of her welcome. In addition to the universal doubt about whether or not someone wants to hear from you when you are the one making the overture, she was worried about the onus of the aggressive female. This kind of defensiveness pervaded many of her actions so that even the simple act of having to put air in her bicycle tires and needing the gas-station attendant to show her how to use the air hose for the first time aroused in her the disgust at looking like another dumb female who didn't understand mechanical contraptions. Our work together was devoted to getting her off the ground and making her strong, assertive energy work for her, rather than against her. She had to learn how to keep her own motor running, how to be as much as she could be and how not to water herself down in order to minimize trouble. She was strong enough to tolerate trouble better than weakness any day. But the fact that she had to work so hard to establish and maintain her own independent function is a black mark against a society that insists on caricatures of women instead of fully dimensional self portraits.

Even for women who appear to accept the traditional roles and outwardly function well, there is still a hidden personal toll. Physical complaints, boredom, feelings of fatigue, problems about their own sexuality are evidence that all is not well with them, either.

One woman came to see me complaining of feeling tired and with head throbbing even when she woke up first thing in the morning. Her doctor had found nothing wrong with her physically and she was desperate. One day, as we worked with her chronic headache, I asked her to attend to her pain and to observe what it felt like. She answered that it felt like a heavy sandbag on top of her, bearing down and oppressing her. I told her to take ownership of the sandbag, to fantasy that *she* was the sandbag and was pressing down on her own throbbing head. She began to speak as the sandbag, "Here I am, right when you wake up and I'm going to stay with you all day, too. I'm going to press down on you and tell you all the things you have to do and I'm going to remind you about all the things you left undone from yesterday..." Tears came to her eyes and she spoke about how she never seemed to let up on herself, even when she was exhausted, always goading herself with lists of chores to be done, always feeling she never did enough. "I do this to my husband, too. I ask him to do something and I don't let up on him, I nag at him until he gets it done and I make him miserable and mad, and then I feel like such a bitch!" I remarked that she didn't have to go on sandbagging herself and her husband if she didn't want to, and asked if she had any ideas about how she might quit this. She continued to talk about how unrealistically high her expectations were from herself and others. As she went on, she evolved a system for herself whereby she would decide which chores she felt were really essential and wanted done right away, and which were less important and could be done whenever someone had the time. She also worked out a motto which she put at the top of her list: "Remember, the sun will rise tomorrow even if I don't pull it up." She was able to stay with this scheme, too, and her headaches went away, along with the discarded sandbag.

Another woman complained she was overly concerned about her bowel habits, worrying about constipation and drinking prune juice whenever she hadn't had a daily bowel movement. She was constipated, but not seriously, and where she had got the idea that she had to have a daily bowel movement she didn't know. She described how attentive she was to both the quantity and quality of her stool—and was usually not very pleased with what she had produced. I asked her to try some homework—not to look at her bowel movements at all, just to shit and then flush the toilet. The very next week she reported that her constipation was gone! Once she stopped evaluating herself and allowed herself just to produce freely, she could just produce shit freely, too. No more prune juice either, nor did the constipation come back for the next year and a half that we saw each other.

I believe that a mode frequently resorted to by women is retroflection, turning back against themselves something they would like to do to someone else or have someone else do to them. It is the recourse of people who have only a minimal expectation of having enough impact on their environment to make it produce what might satisfy them. So they give up their expectation and settle instead for a self-contained action; they do for themselves or to themselves what they would like done for or to them, or what they might like to do to someone else. Often they turn back against themselves their unexpressed feelings of resentment, disappointment, criticism, deprecation and hostility. I remember one woman who, unwilling to criticize her husband who was away a good deal on business trips, made the back of her scalp raw with scabs as she picked at herself instead.

Sexual difficulties in women frequently revolve around a retroflective nucleus of resentment and self-punishment. A fringe benefit, of course, is that in some cases this also permits some punishment of another person as well as herself.

One woman, married for about 12 years with three children, began suddenly to find intercourse with her husband excruciatingly painful. A gynecological examination revealed no physiological explanation for her discomfort. She was a bright, spunky woman with definite opinions of her own and good insight into the problems of other people, but unable to soften up long enough to see when or how she was defeating herself. We did some work focused on getting her to relax the sphincters of her vagina, moving her pelvis more freely and coordinating her breathing with a feeling of openness throughout her body, not just in her nose and mouth. These exercises were successful in freeing her own feelings of sexual want, but when she got close to her husband she was dismayed to find that she stiffened up and couldn't move softly and loosely into the contact that both he and she wanted. One day she was talking about her father, an overbearing, dictatorial and deeply disrespectful man. Most of her early life had been spent in resisting his insistence that she meekly knuckle under to his orders and opinions. I asked her to fantasy that her father was sitting in the empty chair in my office and to express her feelings directly towards him. She told him of her resentment at his steamroller style, how he just ran over people who opposed him and how the only way she had escaped was by just not taking any crap from him. I asked her what she felt as she said this. She replied that she felt tight and tense all over, just short of trembling. I asked if this was how she felt in her vagina, too. She replied that it was. I directed her to intensify her tightness until she felt she was as tense as she could be, to hold it for a moment longer, and then abruptly let go. There was a moment when she let her breath go after holding it while she had tensed up, and her face softened from its grim expression. She began to yield to crying. She shook her head and said through tears that she remembered how she hated her father and that she thought she was all through with that, had settled it long ago. I said that it seemed to me that she had stored up all her resentment and centered it in her vagina, where she was still acting as if she wasn't going to take anything from a man, even if she loved him. She closed her eyes for a minute at the sudden rush of self-recognition and wordlessly nodded her head.

A woman in trouble is frequently a woman whose sense of her own boundaries is both rigid and fragile. Her I-boundary (Polster and Polster 1973), her personal tolerance for permitting awareness to grow and ripen into contactful interaction with her environment, is severely restricted by her inability or reluctance to risk takeover. Her selectivity for contact—which is determined by the I-boundaries she has chosen to maintain for herself—will govern the style of her life, dictating the choice of friends, lovers, husbands, work, geography, fantasy, lovemaking, childrearing and all the other experiences which are psychologically relevant to her life. If she allows herself to become figurally aware of aspects of herself or her life which displease or frustrate her, she risks allowing this growing tide of awareness to surge into a direction which might lead to action. If she is unwilling to risk this, she becomes committed to a policy of unawareness and inaction.

Awareness is a way of keeping up to date with herself and her current experience. It is a preamble to lively engagement and expressive interaction in the present moment. It is an antidote to remaining fixed in past commitments or outgrown values. The woman who is aware of her wants, and can express them, experiences herself as being on target and moving towards a sense of completion and release. With the completion of a cycle of awareness-wanting-action, she is free to continue her contemporary interaction with her own experience rather than becoming mired in incomplete and unfulfilled wanting.

Awareness is no guarantee against pain or unhappiness. It means that she may indeed perceive clearly the dead-end quality of a lifeless relationship, she may recognize that a work scene is sterile, she may acknowledge that something she once wanted is, in actuality, no longer what she wants now. It also means that she must take the responsibility for creating and/or perpetuating this unhappy state of affairs.

But until her sense of responsibility and ownership is acknowledged—and eventually welcomed—there is no therapeutic leverage for movement. She has to learn to cherish her awareness because of the information she can glean from it to guide and orient her in making her own decisions and taking subsequent action. She has to want to know herself well so that she can move with grace and spontaneity, confident enough of her own flexibility so that error or second thought needn't scare her. She has to be able to commit herself to a course of action, *not* in perpetuity but in existential enthusiasm. Awareness is a necessary ingredient in this kind of living.

I have found that my own womanhood is a very important factor in my work as a therapist. With some women it adds an expectation of being understood in a way no man could understand them. This leads to a willingness to be open, to discuss things with me that they might "confess" to a man but that they can "tell" me. It leads also, I believe, to their becoming more confronting, less docile, less cowed by their therapist. Taking me on in an argument makes the odds seem a little more in their favor; I swing enough weight as a therapist, at least I am also a woman. It gives me an advantage in working with women because there is a diminished likelihood that they can brush aside my disagreeable comments or observations as less relevant to them because I "don't really know how it is." I *do* know how it is, I have been there and I am still there. This gives a resonance to our relationship that can amplify what I do and say.

My being a woman also enhances my value as a personification of other possibilities of being-a-woman. It is not unusual for a woman to ask me if I juggled the same set of problems she is trying to keep in the air. How did I deal with the conflict between marriage, children, personal and professional needs? Do I ever have trouble with my kids? Do I ever feel rejected or unsure of myself? Have I ever lost a baby? Do I feel the responsibility dumped on me for aging parents? These questions demonstrate an incontrovertible parallel that she is drawing between herself and me. My answers, when I give them, are surely not intended to provide instructions for imitation. When I can, I answer more about *how* I arrived at an answer, about what my contingencies were, than about the actual solution of a particular problem. That way, she and I can work towards inventing new answers, personally and uniquely applicable to her.

This is not to be taken as a statement that I believe women should be in therapy with other women and men should seek help only from other men. There are important therapeutic rewards, as I know from personal experience, when women work with a male therapist and men work with a female therapist. The basic human dimension of *personhood* is at stake in therapy—moving beyond stereotypes of man or woman into the full articulation and integration of everything any individual can be when all aspects of one's experience are available.

A good woman has pungency, flexibility, suppleness, energy, responsiveness, tenderness, toughness, grace, depth... so does a good man. She doesn't play favorites with these qualities. She needs them all to go about the serious business of creating her own life.

Gestalt Therapy: Evolution and Application

Miriam Polster

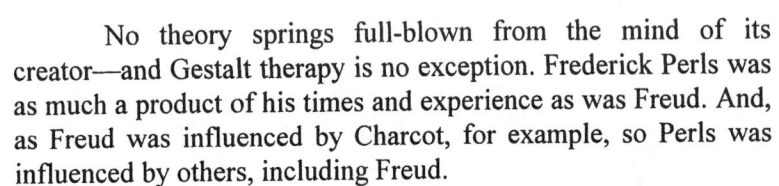

No theory springs full-blown from the mind of its creator—and Gestalt therapy is no exception. Frederick Perls was as much a product of his times and experience as was Freud. And, as Freud was influenced by Charcot, for example, so Perls was influenced by others, including Freud.

I will begin with a short summary of some of the psychological and psychotherapeutic antecedents of Gestalt therapy, in order to illustrate both the impact of these theories and the brilliant ability of Perls and his wife, Laura, to synthesize, uniting disparate parts into a new formulation which reflected the contemporary needs and knowledge of a different generation. Following that, I shall discuss three concepts which are basic to the theory and practice of Gestalt therapy. I will conclude by offering a perspective—consonant with Gestalt theory—which may illuminate certain essential sequences in the course of psychotherapy.

EARLY INFLUENCES AND PERLS' FORMULATIONS

First of all, anyone who does therapy today is hugely indebted to the insights provided by Sigmund Freud. The implications of his assertion that mankind was driven by impulses and motives which were not rational, or even conscious, shocked a generation that prided itself on its capacity to reason, and then to act in conformity with such rational decision. Into this smug society, Freud introduced the suggestion that much behavior which seemed self-crippling was the result of experience and impulse which were *not* under rational control; his therapeutic belief—and one to which Perls also subscribed—was that the cure resides in self-knowledge. Both Freud and Perls conducted "raids" on the unacknowledged and unrecognized determinants of neurotic behavior, trusting that this knowledge was essential to good function. Freud used the illuminating power of insight; the patient agreed to speak freely, to let her thoughts flow unhindered as much as possible, and the analyst facilitated self-discovery by the careful timing of interpretive statements.

The Gestalt equivalent to the analytic sequence of free association-interpretation-insight is the awareness continuum. The patient increasingly concentrates on the simple components of experience and it is this process of awareness, mediated by the patient himself, that culminates in self-knowledge.

Another important influence on Perls' formative experience was Carl Jung. Mystical, almost poetic in his conception of the struggle for individuation, Jung had confidence in the human impulse for expression. He differed from Freud, therefore, in his attitude toward patients' dreams. Freud saw in the dream an attempt of material from the unconscious to escape and dominate. In this struggle of the repressed against censorship, the dream was a battleground of disguise, evasion, and distortion. Jung, on the other hand, viewed the dream as a creative effort wherein the dreamer grappled with contradiction, complexity, and confusion, trying to express these dilemmas as fully as possible. The dream was not an attempt to disguise but rather to express. It was a creative urge, cunningly using symbolic representations of aspects of concern in the dreamer's life. Its aim was resolution and integration. Furthermore, Jung viewed each element in the dream as an aspect of the dreamer, and each person's individuation required a re-incorporation of these projected qualities.

Perls advanced Jung's conception of the dream as projection by having a dreamer play out parts of the dream and, in doing so, reclaim what she previously disowned. In addition to re-owning projected parts of the self, Gestalt therapy also conceives of the dream as a setting for making contact with others (Polster & Polster, 1973).

Another formulation of Jung's which is relevant to Gestalt therapy was his understanding of the polarities inherent in human nature. He cast these dualities in archetypal characters such as anima and animus, or in the concept of the shadow—the obscure but inevitable companion to the public persona. Otto Rank was influenced by Jung's concept of polarities and it was through his work that Perls became interested.

Perls' genius at extending what he learned from others led him to perceive the energy bound in the polar struggle and to devise a methodology—the use of dialogue and of the empty chair—to release this energy and put it at the practical service of the troubled individual. Perls' characterization of topdog/underdog can be seen as a more dynamic restatement of Jung's shadow versus the persona. The struggle between topdog/underdog also often appears similar to the clash between id and superego. Underdog speaks for the resentment, reluctance, and subversive impulse of the disrespected or disregarded aspects of the person. The enlivening addition of the dialogue between these warring parts reveals the ways in which underdog subverts: through confusion, pseudo-stupidity, laziness, or just plain hostility. Through dialogue it is possible to reach a new level of respect and understanding which can resolve the debilitating conflict.

Two gifted and inventive divergences from classic Freudian thought also influenced Perls. Wilhelm Reich (1949) was actively curious about the *how* of human behavior. This resulted in his observations about the body as both the expressor and repository of the problems and experiences of the individual. The body incarnates habitual structures that reveal and record attempts to resolve these conflicts. Reich's view of the body was more real than Freud's, whose autoerotic zones are more concept than flesh and blood and deal primarily with only three bodily areas: the mouth, the anus, and the penis. Reich's theory depicts the sensate nature of the whole body and explores the relation of body armor to character armor. Perls' work advances this attention to the body, finding in gesture and posture relics of past experience, attending to them instead of ignoring them, permitting them to move past petrified habit into adaptive present activity.

Two more aspects of Rank's influence on Perls deserve mention. Rank respected creativity and perceived the creativity contained in the production of what other therapists labeled symptoms. He insisted that this effort deserved to be dealt with more respectfully—not as resistance to be exorcised, but as a creative function which represented an attempt to solve a dilemma. After all, the patient is not trying to create a symptom but an answer to a troublesome situation. This attitude finds its parallel in the Gestalt concept of creative adjustment (Perls, Hefferline, & Goodman, 1951), where the individual creatively balances personal needs and environmental opportunity.

Respect for the creativity of the patient also pervaded Rank's attitude about the nature of the therapeutic relationship. He was one of the early advocates emphasizing the importance of the relationship between therapist and patient. Instead of the distancing concept of transference and analytic neutrality, Rank held that therapeutic leverage depended, in large part, on the person-to-person interaction between therapist and patient. Gestalt therapy's emphasis on contact is a logical extension of this idea; it emphasizes the relationship of organism to environment and of patient to therapist.

Both Kurt Lewin and Kurt Goldstein were acutely aware of the importance of environmental and organismic influences on human behavior. Lewin masterfully explored the impact of the environment on the person. He did this in topographical representations of the individual in a life-space, in classic sociological experiments which investigated approach/avoidance conflicts and the influence of groups and group leadership on individual behavior (Marrow, 1969).

Goldstein (Hall & Lindzey, 1970) studied brain-damaged veterans of World War I and observed how the entire personality of the veteran reorganized itself to accommodate to his diminished capacities in dealing with his surroundings. He identified the *catastrophic reaction* and described some of its sequelae: increased psychological rigidity, greater emphasis on superficial orderliness, and a reduced capacity for abstract thought. All were attempts by the veteran to decrease the likelihood of surprise, of unpredictable or excessive environmental demand. Perls' concept of the *catastrophic expectation* of the neurotic can be seen as an extension of Goldstein's analysis. Here, psychological trauma replaces or accompanies physical trauma—and the incapacity may result from the *unwillingness* to confront troublesome issues in addition to, or instead of, actual inability.

It was from the Gestalt psychologists that Perls learned of the powerful organizational skill underlying human perception. Their most basic principle was the organizing perception of figure and ground. A figure of interest invites the lively response of the viewer, and the background fades, supporting the current figure and offering a source for new figures yet to come. Perls extended this concept beyond purely perceptual behavior and expanded it into an analogy for units of human experience. From these, and other Gestalt principles of learning, Perls applied the activity of Gestalt formation as problem-solving efforts whose interruption springs from neurotic inhibition. A fixed gestalt is a figure which is not surrendered by the perceiver. She insists on perceiving it as static, not risking the inevitable evolution into new figures because of a neurotic attachment to things-as-they-are. In this fashion, the individual's behavior remains archaic because it is not focused on actuality but is dominated by habitual coping with the painful past or the dreaded future.

Gestalt learning theorists also discovered the persistence in memory of experience which feels incomplete or interrupted. From this concept Perls developed his view of unfinished business and how its preservation interferes with present experience. The person is so inhabited by past incompletions that she remains preoccupied with stale concerns. Until these persistent distractions can be resolved, for example, through dialogue, reenactment or fantasy, they will continue to compete for attention and prevent full and satisfying engagement in the present.

BASIC PRINCIPLES IN GESTALT THERAPY

Gestalt therapy evolved from these traditions to an emphasis that insists on the relevance of the environment in any appraisal of individual behavior. In *Gestalt Therapy* (Perls, Hefferline & Goodman, 1951), the book which delineates his theory most completely, Perls et al. state

> There is no single function of any animal that completes itself without objects and environment, whether one thinks of vegetative functions like nourishment and sexuality, or perceptual functions, or motor functions, or feeling or reasoning...every human function is an interacting in an organism/environment field, sociocultural, animal, and physical. (p. 228)

Gestalt therapy proposes that the relationship of the individual to his environment is growthful and exciting, and that the basic element in this relationship is contact. Good function, therefore, can be assessed by the quality of contact, by the ability of the individual to respond flexibly and creatively, with persistence and clarity within an environment that invites interest and is responsive to his needs. Perls et al. (1951) describe this process

> The materials and energy of growth are: the conservative attempt of the organism to remain as it has been, the novel environment, the destruction of previous partial equilibria, and the assimilation of something new. (p. 373)

This sequence is disrupted when there is an overpowering need for the person to perceive a situation as unchanging or containing no novel elements. To foster this illusion, she then inhibits perception and remains stuck in past circumstances, viewing herself as incapable of change or viewing the situation as equally intransigent. This situation is what Perls et al. (1951) called a *chronic low-grade emergency*.

In Gestalt therapy, there are three therapeutic instrumentalities to dislodge the psychological stand-off and to restore momentum and excitement to the stale situation. These are awareness, contact, and experiment.

Awareness

The fluidity of awareness is equivalent to the perceptual flow of figure/ground, where new figures succeed one another in effortless progression and the individual's experience is one of interested participation in a lively and engrossing environment. Ideally, awareness is determined by the individual's needs and moves sequentially between an internally mediated focus and responsive attention to the environment. It is in the nature of the individual to move energetically from experience to experience, reacting to what is novel—be it internal sensation or external event—and engaging with it as long as the interest or need lasts. This process is apparent as we watch any healthy infant. Neurotic interruption occurs when the individual has erroneously diminished faith either in herself or in her environment.

Recovery of the acceptability of awareness—no matter what it may reveal—is a crucial step along the road to the development of new behavior. For one thing, the willingness to be open to new experience, come what may, is already a new level of courage and a step out of the stale habit. It is a return to the fluidity of experience, instead of the *fixed gestalt* that excessive or dysfunctional anxiety commands. This courage initially requires the assistance of the therapist in mobilizing the self-support system of the individual—a sequence which I will describe in greater detail later.

Awareness has three major characteristics. First, it is a continuous means for keeping up-to-date with oneself. It is an ongoing process, readily available when needed. The focus of one's awareness can range through the awareness of sensations, of feelings, of wants, of personal values, and of appraisals or expectations. The therapist can concentrate on these components of experience, staying with them and amplifying them until the patient moves organically into some form of expressive action.

The second characteristic of awareness follows from the first. It produces a buildup in arousal which demands expressive discharge, not merely on a cathartic level, although this is not to be dismissed lightly, but also in order to evoke a responsive echo from something or someone in the world outside. The person is impelled to a sense of mutual interaction in which he moves and is, in turn, moved by an event which includes, but is not limited to, the self.

Awareness has a third attribute. Not only does it lead to expressive and contactful engagement with what is outside the person, but it also caps or completes this sequence by sensing and registering that something did indeed happen. The confirming influence of awareness includes the recognition of success or pleasure, a sense of satisfaction. Completed, and recognized as complete, the individual is free to move into new experience, free to become interested in what comes next. The fixity which was required by the neurotic expectation of catastrophe and the excessive preoccupation with unfinished business is nudged back into movement. The self-imposed stalemate is eased out of familiar but unsatisfying territory, and the client begins to explore fresh experience—which might inspire fresh living. Awareness accompanies this movement; one notes when the dreaded catastrophe did not materialize, or when it does, the person can note that she faced the catastrophe with ingenuity and courage. This cycle may have to be repeated many times in order to lay the unfinished situation to rest. Each time the process must be accompanied by awareness which will make it a vital experience, not just a stale rehash of previous events.

A young woman patient was all practical do's and don'ts. There was hardly a statement in therapy that she didn't immediately make into an order or a recommendation for herself to carry out immediately. One session we spent most of the hour just attending to what she became aware of, reducing her experience to its simple essentials: what she was aware of sitting in her chair; what it was like for her to be in my office; what it was like for her to have her hand on her knee; what it was like to lean forward and move her head; and so on. She surprised herself by not moving immediately from awareness into giving herself orders to "do something" about it. Her delight in being able to notice what simple things were happening, without plaguing herself into making them productive in her accustomed fashion, was a joy to see. For her, it was an entirely new way to move about in her environment.

Contact

It is no news to anyone that life is full of paradox and that much of our energy goes into trying to resolve or, more realistically, to live with inconsistency and contradiction. In Gestalt therapy, paradox is apparent in the relationship between the organism and its environment. Perls et al. (1951) observed that every organism maintains itself in its environment by heightening and remaining acutely aware of its difference. Even so, the human organism is an open system, not at all totally self-sufficient, requiring for survival and growth that it receive sustenance—physical and psychological—from the world outside of itself. Air and food must be taken in, companionship must be provided, so that each human creature can flourish. Growth is therefore best understood as interaction between the organism and its environment, whereby the organism assimilates the environment according to its needs and according to the generosity of environmental conditions.

Awareness is a mediating prerequisite in the sequence, because it is through awareness that the environment is perceived as novel, as worthy of attention. This perception, while heightening the separateness of the perceiver, also draws him toward closer interaction, toward contact with this otherness, whatever it may be—an eclair, a sunset, an easy chair, or another person. This contactful interaction can take many forms: obstacles may be overcome or averted, nourishing objects are taken in and digested, useful information is heard and selectively adopted, dangers are rejected or shunned, appealing people are approached, while toxic or feared people are avoided, and so forth.

The concept of the contact-boundary is Gestalt therapy's formulation, recognizing the paradoxical nature of contact, where the organism maintains its separateness, while at the same time seeking assimilation and union. The contact-boundary is the *organ* (Perls et al., 1951, p. 229) of the meeting between the individual and her milieu, at which, in moments of good contact, there is both a clear sense of oneself and a clear sense of the other. The energy inspired and used in this meeting risks a momentary loss of self in order to make the meeting more poignant. This is not a decision deliberately made, but rather a merging into a surge of the moment when the union between self and other is irresistible. The clear sense of oneself can be risked precisely because, in the healthy individual, it is sensed as reliable and stable, and therefore recoverable. In contact, the energy of the individual is aimed at a satisfying completion of interaction between self and other—completion, but *not* perpetuation (Perls et al., 1951, p. 420).

Contact, then, is the continually renewed and renewing creative adjustment of the individual and her environment. It is through contact that novelty is responded to with interest and reworked into usefulness and relevance. Contact uses and produces excitement as the basic fuel which supports the individual during moments of strong concern. It is the lifeblood of growth, using all the responsive capacity of the individual. In good contact there is always "cooperation of sense and movement (and also feeling)" (Perls et al., 1951, p. 228).

When arousal is unwelcome there will be an attempt to subdue it, by constricted breathing, dulled vision, incomplete hearing, failure to understand, confusion, numbness, and so on. These inhibitions divert energy which could be available for rich contact and keep it bound up in maintaining the state of pseudo nonexcitement that neurotic self-regulation requires for reassurance. This is an artificial and uneasy calm, a stand-off, where the person deadens her responsiveness and devotes her energy to prolonging suppression and minimizing contact.

Every person decides what will be for her the limits of permissible contacts. This I-boundary (Polster & Polster, 1973) determines what psychological territory she is willing to venture into; where to go; whom to be with; what ideas to believe; what wishes to permit; what images to entertain—in short how fully she will participate in those arenas where contact might contain threatening or unpredictable possibilities.

The I-boundary determines the selectivity about contact which governs a style of life—which actions are permissible and which are out of the question. For example, there was the young woman who was reluctant to appear as the stereotyped ninny-about-things-mechanical which she thought all men believed. As a result, she was uncomfortable about going into a service station and asking the attendant how to use the air hose to inflate the tires on her bike. Instead of viewing this as a chance to learn something she wanted to know, she saw it as an indictment of her character, and yet another chapter in her ongoing battle with know-it-all men. Her I-boundary required that she not appear stupid. The irony was that this requirement perpetuated her ignorance.

I-boundaries are the archeological record of experiences of the person as she progresses to the present moment; the experiential background, if you will, for the figural present contact-possibilities. It is at the I-boundary where opportunities for growth are most probable. It is here also that improvisation and courage are often required because the circumstances are more likely to be unfamiliar and one's response is untried and risky. The spirit of improvisation which has been stifled by neurotic self-regulation needs to be activated to support more nourishing interaction between the individual and her world.

Experiment

Experiment is a Gestalt technique aimed at restoring momentum to the stuck points of a person's life. It is one way to recover the connection between deliberation and spontaneity by bringing the possibilities for action right into the therapy room. Through experiment, the patient is mobilized to confront the emergencies of his life by playing out troublesome situations or relationships in the comparative safety of the therapeutic setting. This is a safe emergency. Safety and emergency are actually components whose proportion can be calibrated to reflect the patient's needs at various points in the therapy, incorporating the advances made during the course of therapy and extending them into newer levels of experience. The therapist observes whether the experiment seems too safe or too risky and makes suggestions that change the ratio of safety to emergency. For example, to imagine doing or saying something to the therapist or to another group member is less of an emergency than actually doing it and may unearth some of the same information. Alternately, adding gestures and volume to something that was only muttered softly adds to the sense of daring and emergency.

There are several forms that a Gestalt experiment might take involving the enactment of an important aspect of a person's life: dramatizing the memory of a painful or profound experience; imagining a dreaded encounter; staging a dialogue between the patient and otherwise unavailable, but influential, characters in his life; playing one's father, mother, or some other person who is important to the patient; setting up a dialogue between isolated or disrespected parts of the patient; attending to an otherwise overlooked gesture, grimace, or posture and allowing it to evolve into broader expressive possibilities, and so on.

Dreamwork is another activity which Perls (1969, 1973) explored in his demonstrations and writings. The Gestalt view of dreams as projection, where the dreamer has cast himself into each of the constituents of the dream, is well known. These cast out parts of the dreamer must be re-owned and assimilated as relevant information in the experience of the dreamer. There are other opportunities in dreamwork, however. The dream may contain representations of central people or concerns in the dreamer's life, so dreamwork may focus (through dialogue) on improving the contact between the dreamer and these figures (Polster & Polster, 1973). The dream may be seen as a retroflective act where the dreamer, in a sense, communicates with himself rather than the therapist, and the process can be reversed by addressing the therapist directly (Isadore From, personal communication). The dream may be used as theater where the dreamer can, in a group, cast other members as parts of the dream, and its relevance may extend beyond the dreamer to the significance that the parts they have played may hold for the other participants (Zinker, 1977).

THE INTEGRATION SEQUENCE

The process of growth is usually a fitful one, oscillating between rewarding experience—where advances in therapy are mirrored in successful consequences—and episodes of discouragement—where what has been accomplished in the therapy session appears to work badly or not at all when tried out in everyday circumstances.

It is important to pay attention to this uneven pattern of progress and identify some of the factors which may be at work during the gradual improvement that all therapists seek. I propose an orienting principle that I call *the integration sequence*; this is the sequence of stages that culminates in the integration of new behavior within the I-boundaries of the individual, where it becomes an indistinguishable "given" in the range of permissible experience; where the person feels whole or entire, and the possibilities for fresh, unstereotyped interaction between the individual and his environment are increased.

Discovery

The first part of this three-stage sequence is the phase of *discovery*. It is at this point that something novel occurs—a new realization about oneself, a novel view of a familiar situation or belief, or a new look at another person or event. This realization often comes with a sense of surprise and a temporary absorption in the discovery, which momentarily blots out distracting perceptions and leaves the patient with a heightened sense of figural discovery but with a diminished awareness of context. The discovery is figural and the customary support system of the patient is caught by surprise, unprepared for the rush of excitement—either welcome or unwanted—that arises. This is what Perls et al. (1951) call an *aperiodic* process, occurring irregularly; as contrasted with periodic processes, such as hunger, which occur predictably and with regularity. In this condition the attention of the individual is withdrawn from the environment and focused instead on the body; the therapeutic focus is on the supportive functions that the patient can provide for herself and extends into the possibilities for environmental support of which she may not be aware at the moment.

The personal supports of the patient are threefold. First, the patient's breathing may be constricted or disrupted and therefore does not support the rise of arousal. Regular and rhythmic breathing must be established so that the patient's excitement is not only supported by the better supply of oxygen, but also because regular breathing can help to distribute the excitement throughout the body rather than limiting it to a narrowed and concentrated locus, for example, in the upper chest. This confinement contributes to a sense of strain and is experienced as anxiety. Breathing is also one of the most basic exchanges between the individual and the environment. It reflects a sense that the environment is safe to take in and to use for purposes of self-support. Finally, breathing is a subtly optimistic function. It implies that the person is going to exist a little while longer and it reestablishes momentum, if only for a moment. This is a nonverbal process—a metaphor. The resumption of regular breathing suggests a crisis has been met and is presently being traversed, the situation is in flux, it is not static. The customary stuckness is challenged.

Second, the patient needs to experience the support that her skeletal and muscular system can provide: to feel the support of her legs and pelvis, if standing; to feel his or her shoulders positioned so that the chest is not cramped; and to note that movement can be supported by muscular coordination and strength. This can involve the surprise of the return of sensation to a previously numbed or constricted part of the body or the extension of a gesture beyond the limited range it had been allowed. For example, a woman learns to feel the strength of her own legs as she plays out in fantasy a confrontation with her dictatorial husband. A young man discovers that he enjoys making broad sweeping gestures with his arms instead of trying to remain colorless and stiff—in contrast to his flamboyant but unreliable father. Third of the personal supports is the cognitive ability of the patient. Perls (1969) noted that one of the main techniques of the underdog is to play dumb, to forget or deny some knowledge that might facilitate or support the patient in time of emergency. Therefore, a patient may feel overwhelmed by the realization that she wants to speak angrily to her mother and scared that she might come on too strong. The memory of what her mother has endured—being orphaned at an early age, coming to a strange and unfamiliar country as a nine-year-old immigrant, losing a baby, tending to a dying relative—can provide proportion that places an angry confrontation with a daughter a little lower on the scale. Perls et al. (1951) observed that "It is the accepted way of posing the problem, and not the problem, that is taken for reality." (p. 394). To get a fresh restatement of the problem, or a new way at looking at some of its features, to make new connections or deductions can prove supportive and encouraging in moments of discovery.

In addition, there are two sources of support from the environment in which discovery is made. First, the therapeutic setting: the quiet and seclusion of the office or group meeting room, the confidentiality assured in the therapeutic contact, and the guarantee of time adequate to confront the arousal of discovery. These important elements can sustain the patient during a difficult time.

Second, there is the person of the therapist. In appearing to be a person of some scope and personal experience and in the sense of having seen other people through dramatic personal explorations, the therapist provides perspective and support, suggesting—not necessarily in words but often in spirit—that there will be a next moment, and then a next...

It is apparent that most of these elements have the power to restore momentum to the breathless instant of discovery, when it seems that time itself stands still. It may need to stand still, in order to experience and to plumb the significance that the moment of discovery holds. The restoration of momentum is a beginning of the movement to place that stand-out minute in time back into the ongoing chronicle of the patient's life.

Accomodation

The second stage of the integration sequence is the stage of *accommodation*. Therapists are unwilling to settle for exciting insights that occur only in therapy and have little to do with how the patient actually lives in the everyday world to which she returns after the session. The accommodation phase is that necessary step where the patient begins to behave in her actual world in accord with the discoveries made during therapy. This is the point at which the patient realizes some of the implications and consequences of the original discovery and makes further adjustments which could not have been predicted initially. The patient who discovers the depth of her own sexuality may begin to react differently to friends and acquaintances and evoke a different reaction from them. Their reaction—differing from the supportive or concerned response of the therapist—can call for the patient to improvise, faithful to the spirit of the earlier discovery, but moving beyond it into fuller discovery and exploration of its implications in her interactions outside therapy. People will respond uniquely and unpredictably, sensitive primarily to their own needs and not necessarily reacting as the patient may have predicted. In this stage the environment has expanded outside the therapist's office, it responds unexpectedly, and the patient is forced to improvise, for better or for worse.

It is at this stage where behavior may by awkward and poorly coordinated, and the patient feels clumsy. There are distractions, as contrasted with the single-minded focus of the therapy session. The world is not as obliging as one might like: People have headaches or indigestion, or they have an appointment, or they may just be uninterested. The patient may manage this complication ineptly and become discouraged. The therapeutic task is to continue with the mobilization of the patient's self-support systems. Environmental supports at this juncture are often less reliable and the patient's ingenuity and adaptability are challenged. The physical supports mentioned earlier, breathing, posture, and movement, sustain the patient bodily, but now they serve an additional purpose. They help tolerate the excitement and, furthermore, they temper the effect of too much sensation. In doing this, the cognitive system of the patient, which is crucial to adaptability, is more able to cope with the present situation, improvising and varying behavior instead of being frozen into inaction or habit.

The support system must allow the patient to move past exclusive focus on herself—an indulgence granted in the therapy sessions—and to pay closer attention to the effect that her words and actions have on others. This sensitivity to circumstance makes for more effective and rewarding interaction, for better quality contact. Furthermore, it signals a move out of excessive preoccupation either with oneself or with one's stale concerns and greater accessibility for engagement with others.

The ability to identify and locate environmental supports may be part of the preparation in therapy for the accommodation phase of the work. For example, a young woman suffered from debilitating anxiety attacks whenever she went to eat in restaurants. In therapy we worked with her management of anxiety attacks: restoring her spasmodic breathing, identifying some of the background concerns underlying her anxiety, articulating how she scared herself and what she feared would happen in the restaurant. Then, we began to deal with her fantasies of going into a restaurant, identifying what she would need to feel more comfortable there. Her main fear was that her anxiety would be so severe that she would vomit and everyone would see her. The plan we arrived at was, first, that she would eat several times in a drive-in, where she could stay in her own car. The next step was for her to go to a regular sit-down restaurant and select a table near the women's room so that she could get there in a hurry if she had to.

Assimilation

The third phase of the integration sequence is *assimilation*. What was at first a novel and innovative experience now seems more possible and representative; it is felt to be "like me" to do, think, or feel differently than before. At this stage, behavior is in the middle mode between spontaneity and deliberateness. The individual feels capable of dealing with the surprises that she might encounter—or even generate—and considers that the chances for a successful, or at least necessary, outcome are pretty good. The attitude combines an awareness of risk with a mixture of feelings ranging from optimism to determination. The patient's support system is sensed as dependable, and her behavior has a range of inventiveness which will stand her in good stead.

Often the behavior at this stage is situation-bound; that is, it is in response to a certain individual—as when a 40-year-old man reacted differently to his mother's disapproval, or when a social worker recognized her own needs enough to tell her supervisor that she was getting inadequate supervision. Or it may be a reaction to specific circumstances—speaking up in class or at a staff conference or at a family dinner. Behavior at this stage may sometimes feel like "taking a stand."

Integration

Integration, or when the new behavior or attitude fits seamlessly within the person's I-boundaries, is the final result of a unit of therapeutic work. This is the stage when the individual is able to respond with effortless and unselfconscious involvement to the situation-at-hand. Behavior has the quality of undeliberate response, where situation and person seem mutually interactive and where the result is a reciprocal exchange of influence, with a minimum amount of preconceived conditions or restrictions. By effortless, I do not mean that there is no energy or work involved; but it will be the interaction that commands attention. Behavior is directed by the organismic ordering of the individual's needs, in concert with what the environment offers.

CONCLUSION

Many years ago I taught psychology at an art school. One of the questions raised by students who learned that psychology is a science was, "If it's so scientific, why are there so many theories of personality?" Obviously I could not avoid the issue by merely pointing out that physicists have the same problem and they are workers in the hardest of the "hard" sciences. By way of introduction, then, one morning I asked my students to fantasize that there was a model for a life drawing class in the middle of our room and that in various parts of the room were Rembrandt, Modigliani, Gainsborough, Van Gogh, Picasso and Renoir, each painting from the model. Which one of the paintings would be the *true* one?

So it is with a theory of therapy. To claim that there is only one right way is presumptuous and, even more important, untrue. Each methodology evolves because its perspective illuminates some of the darker corners of contemporary existence and merges with the insights of theorists who have gone before. Gestalt therapy was born of the union between fertile minds and fertile milieus. What maintains the vitality of the theory is its growth in subtlety and application—through the enduring contributions of Perls and his colleagues, and through their students. It is a rich and elegant theory, providing orientation and range for therapeutic choice.

Part II:
Transformation of Principles

Therapy Without Resistance: Gestalt Therapy

Erving and Miriam Polster

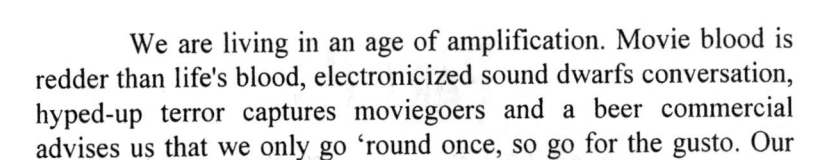

We are living in an age of amplification. Movie blood is redder than life's blood, electronicized sound dwarfs conversation, hyped-up terror captures moviegoers and a beer commercial advises us that we only go 'round once, so go for the gusto. Our culture is inundated with sensation-mongering.

Understandably so because these exaggerations make us attend to what is otherwise overlooked. They reverberate from a valid need to recover lost experiences of sensations and feelings and the accompanying respect for personal awareness.

The so-called third force in psychotherapy was spawned by these concerns. Its contribution to a new level of personal awareness in our culture is considerable and long overdue. Nevertheless, the consequences of the long period of stunted awareness which preceded the recent psychotherapeutic developments are evident in indiscriminate and poorly integrated behaviors which have made caricatures of some of these techniques. The grim beating of pillows, for one example, is an attempt to sensitize awareness of aggression and anger. What is frequently overlooked, however necessary these forced marches may sometimes be, is that there is *also* a more organic way into the sensate experience. Amplification of experience emerges organically when one pays attention to what is already happening.

Therapy Without Resistance

One of the great recognitions of Gestalt therapy is that attending to one's own personal experience from moment to moment mobilizes the individual into a growth of sensation and an urgency for personal expression. As this momentum gathers greater amplitude from each moment to the next, it impels the person to say or do what he must. This progression leads to closure; to the completion of a unit of experience. With closure comes a sense of clarity, as well an absorption in fresh developments without the preoccupation which unfinished situations call forth.

In working towards behavioral change, therefore, there are two "paradoxical" principles to follow (Beisser, 1970). The first is: *What is, is*. The second is: *One thing follows another*. Instead of trying to *make* things happen, the psychotherapist following these precepts must focus on what is actually and presently happening. The present moment offers an infinite range of possibilities which may interest the therapist: the patient's beguiling voice, dramatic story, contradictory statements, perspiration, glazed eyes, flaccid posture, unfounded optimism, and so on, ad infinitum. The therapist's own attitude, imagery, sensations, etc. are also fair game. From this range the therapist chooses a focus. When the therapist is absorbed with what is current, and brings the patient's attention to current experience, a resuscitative process is started which brings liveliness to very simple events.

A therapeutic fairy tale will illustrate. A man complains that he is unable to enjoy himself at picnics. He feels neurotic and dull. While he is talking his face is screwed up in a painful expression. The therapist suggests that the patient attend to his face. He is surprised, when he focuses on his face, to notice a tension there. As he stays with this sensation he begins to feel warmth developing in the tense area and he experiences a slight movement. It is an involuntary grimace, he says. As he concentrates on the grimace his tightness grows, revealing a pain. When the therapist suggests that he make a sound that would fit his particular sense of tension and movement, he screws his face up and grunts several times. When asked what that sound feels like, he says it feels like he has to take a shit but can't quite get it out. He feels weird about this fantasy but also feels some relief from the tension. Also, he likes making the sound but is embarrassed and blushes as he speaks. "Suppose," says the therapist, "that you just make the sound, temporarily setting aside any meaning it may have for you." He goes into the sound again and this time his hands begin to move slightly as though in rhythm with the sound. Asked to notice how his hands are joining in, he now says, in surprise, that they are giving a beat to the sound and he then begins to snap his fingers. Soon, laughing, he says this is incredible fun. He goes into lively song. Finally he is overcome by hilarity, falls to the floor saying this is more fun than shitting. Furthermore, he can do it publicly. He is aware of absorbed internal excitement and is also aware of being carefree; there is little concern about either shitting or any other mistake which free expression might lead him into.

This fairy tale took seriously the simple events that were happening. The process of moving from each event to the next had natural amplification powers and moved on to climax and closure. In the stalemate between the fear of shitting and having fun, new ingredients were recognized which changed the intensity of the struggle. Such ingredients, in this instance, tension on his face, grunting, snapping his fingers, song, etc. always change the chemistry of a situation so as to form a new configuration. *What is, is. One thing follows another.*

BEYOND RESISTANCE

Fairy tales are not reality, of course, and some of you may object that there is a complex set of forces, usually including resistance, which interferes with such easy resolution. This concept of resistance has, of course, had a useful history. Through it contradictory motivations which inhibit behavior and feeling have been recognized. People do interrupt behavior and feelings which *seem* to be in their best interest. People *should*, after all, enjoy themselves at picnics. They should succeed at work, cry when sad, play with their children, have orgasms when sexually engaged, etc. When it is obvious to us and to themselves that they should be doing these things but are not, we look for resistance. Ideally then, the resistance would be obliterated, leaving the individual free to be the person he or she could or should be.

The troublesome implication is that resistance is, first, alien to the individual's best interests and second, like a germ, its removal would permit healthy function. Psychological leeching of the unhealthy organism does not work, however, because what is called resistance is, after all, the individual's own behavior, not a foreign body. It is through re-incorporation of the alienated energy bound up in this behavior that the individual achieves more full functioning.

Reformulating the concept of resistance along these lines requires an altogether open mind about the priorities in people's feelings and behavior. Not assuming the person is behaving wrongly, "resisting," leads us to stay with each expression of the person, as it arises, moving always with the actual experience, innocently witnessing the unfolding of fresh drama.

There are several basic difficulties in encompassing such an attitude, and it is hardly likely that any therapist would wholly succeed. Some of the difficulties are:

1. It is only natural for people to look ahead in any process and to set goals for themselves. This is true, of course, for both therapist and patient. If not for the inspiration of personal goals there would be no therapy in the first place. People want to get better in specific ways. The task of the therapist is to be able to bracket off these goals so as to function in terms of present experience—even though at heart wanting the patient to give up alcoholism, improve relationships with people, find good work, say goodbye to dead parents, etc. The difficulty of coordinating goals with immediate process is not unique to psychotherapy. A home-run hitter in baseball will tell you he cannot focus on hitting

a home-run. He must attend to the ball and to his own stroke. Great novelists do not foreclose their own surprise at how their characters develop. Psychotherapists also must tune in and remain faithful to what matters in the unfolding situation.

2. In the age of the psychological detective, the uncovering of the hidden has been magnetically attractive. Most of us are fascinated by following clues until we find a hidden ingredient. The temptations of psychotherapeutic detection are supported by fact that we often *can* discover that which has already been there. Mother bakes a pie. Child hopes it is a pecan pie. It is covered, though. Child lifts the cover and sees a pecan pie. The excitement irradiates the child. It is a new delight. But the pie *was* already there. Only the discovery is new.

For these reasons it is difficult to transcend the magnetism of the uncovering phenomenon and to replace it with the creativity phenomenon. The creativity phenomenon is the development of that which has never existed before. It is more like what mother experiences when she bakes the pecan pie. Though she may have had a lifetime of experiences with pecan pie, this new one never existed before and her pleasure, if she is not already jaded, comes from the process of the creation and the freshness of experiencing an altogether new pie. So also in therapy do we discover that which is created anew. We discovered in the earlier illustration that the person unable to have fun at picnics did something which was initially reminiscent of shitting. We were not oriented toward uncovering the "original" and now anachronistic trauma about shitting. Instead, we were oriented to follow the sequence of experiences which culminated unpredictably in lively song. There are also, of course, uncovering aspects in the experience and those who prefer viewing it from that perspective are not "wrong." We just prefer to follow the freshly unfolding process itself rather than to view the process as uncovering something previously obscured. We would rather bake a pie than look for one.

3. The psychotherapist must exercise considerable connoisseurship in distinguishing between what is happening in

the present moment and what is distractingly preoccupying. The distinction is a subtle one; rules about what is a present experience will only clutter up one's good sense. The very act which appears to be a preoccupation, when focused on, may turn into present occupation. For example, the woman who looks around the room when talking seems preoccupied rather than presently engaged. When the therapist suggests that she notice how her eyes wander and that she say what she sees (rather than telling her she is resisting), what may be revealed is inordinate curiosity, which, when acknowledged and accepted, results in lively visual experience. So, although the original inclination of the therapist may be to consider looking around the room as irrelevant to the current process, a mere deflection, the fact may well be that looking around the room is basic and talking to the therapist would have been a deflection. The basic propellant to change is the acceptance, even accentuation, of existing experience, believing that such full acknowledgment will in itself propel the individual into an unpredictable progression of experience.

4. Though it is true that simple experience teaches, it is also true that people have an inherent reflex to assign meaning to the events in their lives. This meaning gives dimension, support, and context to events. Without the context which meaning provides, events are torn out of their natural settings, empty and discontinuous, as with the labile manic whose pressured liveliness accelerates into forced moments, each unrelated to the previous moment, springing in frantic isolation from any personal context. He walks on air, like the cartoon characters who, when they notice they have been walking off the edge of a cliff, suddenly fall.

According to the Gestalt theory of figure/ground relationship, there is an inherent integration of experience (figure) and meaning (ground). When this integrative function is impaired it may be necessary to formulate a verbal context for the immediate experience so that the harvest of the experience may find a place within the daily existence of the individual. To recognize the relevance of a current experience to other experiences in one's life gives coherence and continuity which are crucial to a sense of security and general well-being.

The proportions of experience and meaning vary from person to person. Some well-integrated individuals could not articulate the meaning of certain events in their lives event though the unity between figure and ground is, for them, quite sound; others, could articulate it well. Sometimes insistence on meaning upstages experience and interrupts the pure flow of involvement. On the other hand, sometimes the experience can be desultory and futile because there is no development of the sense of fit into personal context which would provide ownership and dependability. The therapist's artistry must take this into account when establishing the direction and the emphasis of work at any given moment.

COMPOSITION

When a therapy views expression as creative rather than resistive, how does the consequent internal struggle between two equally respected parts of the individual move toward closure? No need of the individual exists alone; its counterpart also exists. The combination is only rarely peacefully achieved.

The Gestalt concern with polarities addresses itself to this internal struggle. Each faction in this struggle wants to dominate, but each is also subordinate to the individual's struggle for internal unity. The course of these internal struggles is varied; where two parts of the person seem incompatible with each other there may be out-and-out ambivalence, or one side may be submerged in deference to the other. The subdued part may appear ineffectual or it may work underground, frequently in disrepute, sabotaging the dominant faction but making life uneasy at best, and panic-stricken at worst. Frequently the struggle is frozen in anachronistic concerns or in personal horror stories about the consequences of allowing full expression of one or the other of the competing forces. To bring the interaction up to date, the warring parts must confront each other, the struggle must be expressed and articulated. The neighborhood tough guy may, for example, also have a soft side which once plagued his existence. Showing his soft side may actually have got him into trouble, or he may have internalized the standards of his childhood scene and so views his periodic moments of softness as threats to his self-esteem. So, in the interest of survival, as he sees it, he covers over and subdues his soft responsiveness. He got the message of *toughness-uber-alles* early and forgot what he reflexively wiped out of existence.

The therapist must be alert to the surfacing of polarities because, although they are sometimes obvious, they are often discerned only through sensitive attention. A moist quality appears around the tough guy's eyes when he is talking brusquely about his mother being exploited by her employers or his father beating her up. There may be only a flicker across his eyes, a swelling in his lips, or a relaxation of his wrist. At first the disowned soft side would be easy to disregard; he has been doing it for so long. Even if the person is willing to engage the two parts of himself in dialogue, there would at first be a poor quality of interaction, including mutual disregard, scorn, low energy involvement and a sense of the futility of any interactions; what could they have to say to each other? The therapist, however, contributes his observations and brings to the patient's awareness the chronic discounting and stand-off. The patient is intrigued and some vitality enters into the dialogue. The two disputants address each other more vigorously, each insisting on recognition for what it contributes to the totality of the individual's experience. Gradually the acknowledgment comes, that each does something to define the person in full dimension; rather than being a one-dimensional stereotype of a tough guy, he can be a compassionate tough guy, a tender but outspoken professional, etc. He is free to invent for himself all the possible permutations of being tough *and* soft. When this happens, he is whole and more open than before to doing what had once seemed unlikely and troublesome.

CONTACT BOUNDARY

Bringing alienated parts of an individual back into contact with each other is a natural extension of the fundamental Gestalt principle that contact creates change. We are all bounded in our existence by the sense of what is ourselves and what is not ourselves. We are also bounded by the need to make discriminations between these two, always imperfect but indispensable. Perls said, "Wherever and whenever a boundary comes into existence, it is felt both as contact and as isolationism." (Perls, 1947).

As always, paradox befuddles the soul. Where the discriminations between self and other becomes most difficult to make, the individual runs the highest risk of either isolation from the world or such union as swallows him up, wasting his identity by living the will of another.

Since contact is to people as chemistry is to the relationship of physical elements in the universe, we conclude that "through contact one does not have to *try* to change: change simply occurs" (Polster and Polster, 1973). The philosophical equivalent of our chemical interaction is the Hegelian view that each thesis gives birth to its own antithesis and contact between these two entities results in a new creation, a synthesis. We see human contact, also, resulting in mergers between that which is ourselves and that which is not ourselves. We are, therefore, immensely affected by our environment and we must sustain a sense of ourselves while at the same time remaining open to these infinite influences. We are continually confronted with the artful choice between assimilation and rejection of what we encounter. As Perls, Hefferline, and Goodman said

> ...fundamentally, an organism lives in its environment by maintaining its differences and more importantly by assimilating the environment to its differences; and it is at the boundary that dangers are rejected, obstacles are overcome and the assimilable is selected and appropriated. Now (that) which is selected and assimilated is always novel; the organism persists by assimilating the novel, by change and growth. For instance, food, as Aristotle used to say, is what is 'unlike' that can become 'like'; and in the process of assimilation the organism is in turn changed. Primarily, contact is the awareness of, and behavior toward, the assimilable novelties; and the rejection of the unassimilable novelty. (Perls, Hefferline, and Goodman, 1951).

The rejection of that which is not assimilable saves us from becoming what we don't want to become, from relinquishing individual identity. There are limits, however, to a person's freedom to stave off what he or she is steeped in. Non-smokers would have to hold their breath to keep out the noxious fumes of smoke-filled rooms. Accordingly, it is important for the individual to select or create environments which will make healthy assimilation or rejection most likely without exacting too great a toll. The therapeutic environment, be it the one-to-one relationship of individual therapy, the therapy group, or the therapeutic community, must offer improved possibilities for making good-quality contact. This may be accomplished in therapy through five pivotal elements: (1) Creation of a new interactive climate, (2) Personhood of the therapist, (3) The expansion of I-boundaries, (4) Sharpening of contact functions, and (5) The development of experiments.

(1) The new interactive climate

People coming into a therapeutic situation quickly discover it is a very different world from the one they are accustomed to. First of all, it is a relatively self-contained unit of people with little seepage into the everyday world. This reduces, though of course it does not eliminate, the specter of catastrophic consequences. People are less likely to be shot, adjudicated, ostracized, flunked, ridiculed, or otherwise pilloried as a result of their actions or words. The general expectation is one of ultimate acceptance even during painful interludes when acceptance may be in doubt. Only rarely is a person working on a problem not seen from a respectful perspective by at least some of the group. People are not crowded by the complex, contradictory requirements of the world out there. The climate is usually one of live and let live; there is a subtle optimism that the puerile, the confusing, the disgusting, the frightening, etc., will soon turn the corner and become vibrant, touching, revealing of inner beauty, and restorative. Consequently, there is less need for people to interrupt themselves. When one believes that what is happening will turn out well, even though presently painful or problematical, acceptance becomes easier. Each individual may discover a new extent of psychological space within which to function. Crowding of one's psychological space supports prematurity or delay because these alien requirements impinge on the individual's range of possibilities.

The new community is, of course, not Eden. People do get angry with each other, misunderstand each other, trick each other, walk out on each other, and shower a whole range of kindred brimstone on their co-sufferers. Usually these mutual tortures are readily recognized and dealt with because of the basic exploratory climate, the extended time opportunities and the presence of a therapist who is commissioned to watch the store.

(2) Personhood of the therapist

In a therapy where contact is seen as a major organ of personality, the personhood of the therapist is given central importance in the creation of behavioral change. Most excellent therapists we have known have been exciting people. They are radiant and absorbed. They encompass wide areas of personal experience. They can be tough or tender. They can be serious or funny. They change fast according to the stimulations they receive. They are incisive in their perceptions, clear and simple in their articulations and courageous in assimilating new experience and in facing the dragons of the mind. If patients spend considerable intimate time with such a presence, some of it will frequently rub off on them. Patients absorb a new way of perceiving, articulating, considering. They learn to seek new perspectives. They recognize alternatives to whatever is happening. They engage in a new partnership of feeling. They experience someone who knows how to accept, frustrate, arouse. They meet surprise and adventure. Hopefully, they imbibe a respect for what it is like to be a human being.

In the face of such an awesome pattern of characteristics, the reader may well ask whether humility is also included. Fortunately it is not necessary that the therapist be such a marvel as we might all wish he or she were. What is more crucial than the specificity of desirable characteristics is the unavoidable fact that, social designations aside, the therapist is, after all, a human being. As one, he or she affects one. Once when we were referring a parent to a therapist for his fourteen-year-old son, we asked the father whether he would like his son to be influenced by a particular man. That is not a bad question for any person to ask about a therapist. It is plain that the therapist's personhood ranks high along with technique and knowledge as a determinant of therapeutic direction. A kind person will affect people through his or her kindness, a demanding person through his or her demandingness, a person interested in power through this orientation. Clearly many of the therapist's characteristics or interests evident elsewhere might not enter into the therapy session. What is important, however, is that the therapist not be required to hide these characteristics or interests (when they do organically appear) in order not to unduly influence the patient. On the contrary, the therapist's influence is indispensable and unavoidable, and if the exercise of it risks putting inappropriate demands on the patient this only reminds us that there is no guarantee of a good job. Permitting the influence to appear does not free the therapist of the transcendent requirement for exercising an artistry which unites his or her own personhood respectfully with the authentic personal needs of the patient.

(3) Expansion of the I-boundary

People's I-boundaries include the range of contact experiences which their identity will allow. They will make only those contacts which do not excessively threaten their sense that they are still themselves. It is therefore important that they learn to experience aspects of themselves which they had formerly obliterated so that as unpredictable stimulations arise they will not be unduly threatened by their reappearance. The prude endangered by forgotten sexuality, the macho man terrorized by his impotence, the chronically supportive person engulfed by disquieting rage, have all narrowed their I-boundaries and refused to accept certain alienated parts of themselves. The whining person, the saboteur, the leech, the ogre, may all be exiles from awareness calling for their right to be heard. Malaise ensues because the risk of reappearances of these characteristics causes unbearable disturbances for the individual's self-image. When unacceptable characteristics can be reassimilated and given a voice, individuals may discover themselves to be quite different in actuality from what they feared they might become if they listened to these alienated parts of themselves. Their sense of self expands, encompassing new possibilities in behavior and feeling, setting contemporary limits based on present experience, not past trauma. Fixity of behavior and feeling always limits the world in which people may live nourishingly. Since there are limits to their control over the world and its confrontations, the more flexible a person's acceptance of herself is, the more securely she can live in a changing world. When her own worst fears about herself are altered and they begin to assimilate the validity of these formerly alien characteristics, the possibilities for improved contact are increased. She can let the chips fall where they may, trusting her own ability to sustain herself in the face of the unpredictable or customary.

(4) Sharpening of the contact functions

We spoke earlier about the importance of making the distinctions between what is ourself and what is not ourself. Basic to this ability is the rhythm which exists between the individual's *sense* of his or her own organic identity and the *functions* through which he or she makes and maintains contact. The seven basic contact functions are: talking, moving, seeing, hearing, touching, tasting, and smelling (Polster and Polster, 1973). In focusing on these functions, the Gestalt therapist seeks to improve such qualities as clarity, timing, directness, and flexibility. All of these contact functions have been subjected to the erosive deteriorations of cultural prohibitions and interruptions. Growing up often seems like a long process of learning what not to see or touch or say or do. Each time a function is interrupted in its natural course, its impetus has been challenged. It is true that some others may be inspired by hardship, like Demosthenes. But, more likely, most deficiencies are not so dramatic and will go unrecognized. Many people have overlooked their own contact functions for so long that, although dismayed about their lives, they have little awareness of the simple, but far-reaching, deficit. Gestalt therapists are alerted to these interruptions and deficiencies; they must develop a safecracker's sensitivity to what is missing as well as to what is too much.

In working with a man who speaks incessant gobbledygook, the therapist may ask him to limit himself to simple declarative statements. Or the therapist may respond to the circumvented meaning behind circumlocutions. The therapist might ask a verbally stingy man to add a few words to his sentence once he feels he has completed it. Therapists must have as much variety in their inventiveness as there are linguistic positions. Following this tack, therapists will frequently meet with objections to making direct contact. Patients may fear they will offend people. They may believe that in order to be understood they have to give the full background to every statement. Or they may make curt statements, sourly requiring that if people want more, they must ask for it.

These objections must be faced. The circumlocutious man may find it objectionable to say what he means to say in fear of discovering he is far more critical than he wishes. When brought face to face with his own critical nature, he may feel pinched by anxiety. The therapeutic task is to turn this anxiety into excitement. How might the patient's critical facility be used right now, for example, in contact with the therapist? As the patient warms to his task he may discover a new clarity, a pungent sense of humor or an affection that endures through the expression of criticism. When the patient begins to respect the liveliness accompanying his critical faculty, he is on the road to magnifying his diminished zest. The original dread of himself as a tyrannical critic may evolve into the discovery of his genuine perceptual powers and the zing of not soft-pedaling them.

So also with the other contact functions. A man who was bombed out of looking because he couldn't stare at his mother's crotch may surprisedly discover the beauty of his therapist's eyes and no longer be willing to give up seeing. A woman having spent her formative years sitting stiffly with hands folded whenever company arrived may learn to fidget and feel the vibrant sensations which movement releases. People who have rarely been touched may be held or may explore the various textures in the therapy room or in their environment. Each time, the fresh recognition of the excitement and fruition inherent in the exercise of these contact functions supports, even inspires, the person to try them out further.

Repetition is crucial for assimilation. It is rare that one experience solves a problem once and for all, but one experience may light the way. Alas, it is also true that full recovery of functions rarely happens. More likely the individual sets new thresholds for the exercise of function and for better recovery from temporary abandonment of function. The circumlocutious man, for example, may return to his use of circumlocutions in situations which are especially difficult, but he comes back to clarity more easily. It takes more to throw him off the track and less to get him back on.

(5) Development of experiments

The functional psychology of John Dewey espoused the primacy of doing something in order to learn. It is better to take children to a farm and to a dairy than just to tell them about milk production. So, also, in Gestalt therapy we want to turn our "aboutist" habits into present action. Individuals are mobilized to face the relevant emergencies of life by playing out their unrequited feelings and actions in the relative safety which the therapist's expertise and guidance provide. In Gestalt therapy we call this a safe emergency. Although the safety factors are present in the nonpunitive and sensitively guided atmosphere of therapy, there is also a large emergency factor because individuals are enabled to enter into areas of their existence which were formerly out of bounds and which are still laden with fear. For example, a remark about her grandmother easily passed over in ordinary conversation receives new focus when the therapist asks a woman to play her grandmother, whom she remembered sitting like a sparrow with head tilted to one side. She tilts her head, assuming grandmother's posture, and regards the therapist with the same undemanding, completely loving expression which she remembers her grandmother had. Only now she feels what it is like to be such a loving person. She blushes with the animation brought on by the easy affection. Grandmother was like a star in the heavens beaming our from the deep reaches of the universe, but no longer an everyday part of existence. Now she returns to life within the patient's own skin. Reality begins to include unqualified loving. Mourning surfaces also for the lost birthright, misplaced when grandmother died: a lost right because now everyone—spouse, children, colleagues—needs her and when she doesn't give them what they need she feels unlovable. Then she can't love them either. The therapist says, "Be your grandmother and tell them about you." To her spouse, grandmother describes how, as a child, the patient wanted to know everything and was constantly coming to her with stories about new discoveries she had made. Spouse, in fantasied dialogue, responds by saying that's just what he loves too and what he has been missing. To her children, grandmother tells how the patient could always make up games and toys out of the most unlikely materials, a wooden crate, an old quilt. The children respond, turning to mother (the patient), observing the fact that she never just plays with them and would she please, please, and who cares about dinner. The patient, realizing what she has dismissed from her own adult function, is inspired to become again what she had once been, supporting herself even though the support of her grandmother is gone.

    This speculation is only one illustration of the consequences of recreating grandmother. The improvisational possibilities are endless. The action is open-ended, transcending accustomed modes for dealing with memories, fears, sadness, and moving the individual into untried and unpredictable directions. In the improvisational cycle which is played out in the experiment, the patient is moved to fresh ways of being. As we have said elsewhere

> ...the patient in therapy... may tremble, agonize, laugh, cry and experience much else within the narrow compass of the therapy environment. He...is traversing uncharted areas of experience which have a reality all their own and within which he had no guarantee of successful completion. Once again he confronts the forces that previously steered him into dangerous territory and the return trip (may) become as hazardous as he had reflexively feared. The therapist is his mentor and companion, helping to keep in balance the safety and emergency aspects of the experience, providing suggestion, orientation and support. By following and encouraging the natural development of the individual's incomplete themes through their own directions into completion, the therapist and patient become collaborators in the creation of a drama which is written as the drama unfolds. (Polster and Polster, 1973)

Two major forms which the Gestalt experiment might take are enactment and directed behavior.

In enactment the aim is to dramatize, to enact some important aspect of the individual's existence. This could be a dramatization of an unfinished situation from either the past, the present, or the future. It could be the dramatization of a characteristic of the patient, as, for example, playing out the monster in oneself which one is otherwise afraid to reveal. It could be the dramatization of a polarity in dialogue, as where the tough and tender parts of one individual talk to each other. It could be the dramatization of an exchange with a fantasied someone sitting in the "empty chair." It could be the dramatization of a visual fantasy or it could be the dramatization of the diverse parts of a person's dream.

In directed behavior, the individual is asked to try on a certain behavior. A man might be asked to try talking with his hands, to call a friend each day, to fidget in his chair while talking or listening, to say "dear" when he addresses the people in his group, to speak with the ethnic accent of the people who reared him, etc. This supports the actions-speak-louder-than-words credo. He takes his risks through the action, giving him the palpable effect from which his previous gaps in experience have distanced him. Also, in present action, he is free to improvise, to take a new tack instead of the familiarly doomed course of action he may have tried before.

The experiment is also a route by which the unfinished business of the patient may be brought into the present. This not only fosters more than a dry narration of past events, it holds opportunities for action and improvisation and for the resolution of persistent but anachronistic limits on the patient's experiences. The woman who keeps her distance from all men because her father kept her at arm's length becomes freer to express her longing for closeness to a man and to find ways in which this longing can be satisfied—not by sitting on daddy's lap, but by fantasying sitting on his lap and telling him what it means to her and expressing also what she would like to have received from him then. She could try moving, at first awkwardly, into an embrace or a supportive gesture that a man in her life is now willing and ready to offer, remaking her assumptions about the inevitable distance that must exist between herself and men.

These are some of the fundamentals of Gestalt therapy which lead to behavioral change. The functional objective is to heighten present experience; the faith is that the ultimate objective, change, will be accomplished when one optimally experiences the present. Always, the return to experience, to the acceptance and reengagement with what is, leads to a new orientation for behavioral change. Animating these principles is the move beyond the concept of resistance into the view of the individual as a population of ideas, wishes, aims, reactions, feeling, which vie for full expression. Giving voice to these multiple factors is like giving suffrage to a previously disenfranchised segment of the population. It allows these parts of the person to vote and to be attended to rather than relegating them to dissension and sabotage.

Gestalt therapy is a phenomenologically inductive system in which an individual's development unfolds from moment to moment and in which we are more concerned with opening the person to a continuing process of discovery than sending him or her back through time to concentrate on that which has existed before. This distinction is, to be sure, a subtle one. We believe that supporting a person's potentialities for creative improvisation with a contemporary focus rather than an historical one is a basic ability that he or she needs—now in therapy, ultimately, out of it.

ADDENDUM / QUERIES

QUESTION: Gestalt therapy, at least as Fritz Perls promulgated it, seemed a defiant cry against the historical excesses of psychoanalysis. It now seems, by counterreaction, and by example of the phenomenologist and existentialist, to overreach itself with its emphasis on the current experience. What do you see as a proper balance between the here-now experience and those historical and hereditary forces which make up the personality?

DRS. POLSTER: Past experience, pungently and vitally relieved, gives historical and contextual substance to the individual's present action. What has occurred earlier in his or her life informs, illuminates, and yields to the present as it is freshly re-engaged, not dutifully or technically recounted.

The requirement is to accommodate the individual's past experience within a figural development of what is happening right now. To be stuck as though one were *indeed* living in the past promotes staleness and obsession. So the resolution of unfinished business from the past has a central position in Gestalt therapy and the reenactment of such situations has important methodological leverage. The present is the only time slot in which awareness and expression are possible, sensually and motorically. To return to the unfinished situation with these possibilities achieves a new balance between respect for the patient's history and the fresh opportunities for resolution offered in the present.

Presence is ubiquitous; only its quality is uncertain. There are innumerable stories people tell which reveal past experience and which arouse the most poignant union between the teller and the listener. Many other stories may be distractions or bores. The Gestalt therapist, in spite of the theoretical proscriptions to the contrary, is always faced with discerning the many shades of difference in the quality of presence and moving toward the quality of greatest immediacy that can be evolved.

QUESTION: I can find nothing in your very fine chapter which alludes to the causes of uneasiness, discontent, or illness in your patients/clients. Can you say something more specifically as to whether you believe in psychic disease and what its causes might be?

DRS. POLSTER: The concept of psychic disease imposes a linguistic tyranny to which we object. Though its fundamental meaning refers to malfunction of some aspect of the person, its implication is to set the pathological apart from the common experience. Obviously there are people whose personal malfunction is at a threshold which may conveniently warrant such separation. Then we say they are ill and take certain desperate measures which disregard the actual choices of the people involved, through hospitalization, medication, etc.

To say that one person is diseased and another not is simply a practical diagnostic and methodological aid and should not be mistaken for the fundamentals of malfunction which apply to all people. Human trouble exists when a person is unable to assimilate that with which he or she is confronted. This original failure to integrate may happen because of overstimulation, as for example, when one is severely frightened, or when necessary release outlets such as crying, objecting, screaming, embracing are shut off. When this kind of overload happens, we may become lopsided, bloated, emaciated, preoccupied, disappointed, disillusioned, disgraced, frustrated, etc. In these instances, individuals need either to get rid of the effects of what they cannot assimilate or to reintegrate these experiences in order to feel whole again. To feel whole, internally united, is a generic human need and good function is intended to bring about this wholeness. With each malfunction, be it of language, movement, seeing, or whatever, individuals are to some degree handicapped in their struggle to feel whole.

QUESTION: The implication of Gestalt therapy without resistance is of a process and a set of people-healers who are more beneficent and presumably less cruel than those who call for a transference neurosis. But is not the resistance Freud talked about as a psychological process equivalent to the basic fear of losing one's boundaries, one's self, in any new intense and creative experience, and precisely a part of that growth experience? How can Gestalt therapy short-circuit or change this fact of growth-life by offering *no resistance*?

DRS. POLSTER: Greater beneficence or less cruelty has nothing to do with the position we are taking in respect to resistance. We are dealing with the prejudicial implications of the word. We are not proposing that one ignore the risks inherent to boundary stretching. There is plenty to be frightened about in the inevitable struggles within oneself as well as against what is outside oneself. The internal struggle is inextricably related to these boundaries, which we call I-boundaries, and which circumscribe the limits of supports or fears concerning any particular behavior or experience. On that score we have no quarrel with Freudians or others in their recognitions of the "intense and creative experience" as a vital part of growth. On the contrary, we intend to renew the necessary internal struggles.

What we are saying is that we do not view that patient's stuckness, evasiveness, blankness, stubbornness, dumbness, blindness, wiliness, etc., as resistances to what some identify as the *real* problems or directions. We view this growth process as including a struggle *between* or *among* parts rather than the unilateral view of the individual resisting what might be in his or her own better interest. The concept of resistance implies preset goals which are frequently stultifying to growth, particularly when these goals are inculcated either by society or by the therapist.

So the Gestalt therapist seeks to give full expression, either in fantasy or in action within therapy, to otherwise discredited behavior. We might tell a person to emphasize his dumbness, to let his jaw hang slackly, his shoulders slump and a vacant, non-fixed stare take over his vision. And lo, the bright, energetic, but driven young man discovers his capacity for relaxing; that being dumb is not the panic-laden state he had dreaded but instead brings with it an ease and an absence of fear that he had not known he could feel. Now, this means that he will be less likely to panic in the inevitable moments of not-knowing that overcome him. This looseness, which he found in being dumb, can make his intelligence an agile and dependable part of him and can open him to accepting his ignorance with grace.

One might say this is merely a change in wording and that we are just calling resistance something else. There is an element of truth in this, but it is also true that changes frequently revolve around just such changes in words. These changes are responses to previous abuses of words. The change of perspective implied in the rewording of resistance to struggle does indeed suggest change in our methodological emphasis as therapists. Many concepts that have influenced behavior are only small turnarounds in perspective. It is too much to expect that a new concept be something altogether new under the sun.

QUESTION: In my study of the lives of therapists I have found that they love life-detection and are still unconsciously detecting their own covert and unresolved lives through their clients/patients. Is it possible in Gestalt therapy to practice such a pure phenomenology and experiencing as to say that it is without the need to life-detect? Perls himself had this as a greater need than others, as I observed him.

DRS. POLSTER: We have already said in our paper that it is difficult to "transcend the magnetism of the uncovering phenomenon." There is little likelihood of purity in experiencing each moment and remaining altogether open to discovering only what has never been there before. We have described a methodologically useful difference between the uncovering phenomenon and the creativity phenomenon. To expect purity in the process of transformation would be absurd.

It is true that Fritz Perls remained always heavily influenced by his history as a psychoanalyst and that psychological detection probably fascinated him. It is also true that in spite of this characteristic in his work, even casual observation would reveal large differences between his step-by-step processing of experience as it was happening and the psychoanalytic interpretative mode. We must take both our similarities and differences where we can find them instead of discounting just because we are not altogether different.

QUESTION: Do you find other modalities valuable in Gestalt therapy? For example, do you do games analysis according to the transactionalists, painting and creative activity according to the Jungians, meditation according to Yoga, etc.? There is no indication in your chapter of what specific techniques are used in Gestalt therapy or whether all of them come in sooner or later as required by an intuitive therapy.

DRS. POLSTER: We find many technical modalities very important in our work. The methodological concept of the experiment is our entry into the entire range of exercises and games which have been invented over the past twenty-five years. Not only is this given repertoire valid for us to include in our work but each Gestalt therapist also uses his or her inventiveness to develop experiments individually for individual needs. In working with an artist involved in a troublesome painting, we may have the artist enact one segment of the painting talking to another—one color to another, one figure to another, etc. We have used music. We have used movement—dance, shadow boxing, stretching, playing rigid, fidgeting, etc. We have used metaphors, played parts in allegories, told life stories as they might be made into a comedy by Laurel and Hardy or as a film by Bergman or Fellini. We have played out fantasies. We have played out a day's experience as it might have been treated in a soap opera, etc.

Yoga exercises, meditation experiences, free association, mandala drawing, visual imagery, pantomime, group dream workthroughs, etc., are all possible ingredients in the repertoire of any gestalt therapist. All that is required is that the individual experiment with that which may further his or her own awareness and contact powers.

Escape from the Present

Erving Polster

Theories of therapy require continual freshening up for at least two reasons. One is that their concepts spawn connotations which either corrupt or desert the original meanings. The other is that the concepts compete with each other for centrality and the winners in popular esteem may crowd out equally vital ones. With these sources of error in mind, I want to examine one aspect of Gestalt therapy, its here-and-now emphasis. This emphasis has been corrupted from its original intent and it has won out in centrality, crowding out other more important concepts. After sketching the strengths and weaknesses of present orientation, I shall offer two correctives to this emphasis.

THE PRESENT AS A RALLYING POINT

For the psychotherapist, it seems only natural that the full dimensions of time and space be taken into account because things do obviously happen anytime or anyplace. It is therefore curious that the more narrow emphasis on here-and-now should have gained almost cult-like ascendancy over the past 35 years. Shortly after World War II, many people began to believe, with repercussions still going on, that the here-and-now was the center of psychological living. Although the reasons are not altogether evident, there are some obvious speculations. For one thing, the threat of a nuclear wipe-out offered a fearful justification for shunning the future. For another, new values concerning "relevance" were being adopted and high among them was the call for immediate gratification to replace the oppressively familiar delays for almost everything people did.

For psychotherapists, however, these common allures of the here-and-now were joined with some important technological advantages. What we found to be a therapeutic bonanza was the mind's extraordinary resiliency when it was freed to concentrate on only one thing. Focusing only on the present was a large step toward just such narrow attention. Kierkegaard (1948) long ago recommended that purity of heart was to will one thing, and his credo—originally intended to invoke total attention to God—was then put to a more mundane practical application. It became clear that if you cut out all distractions, either internal or external, the resulting concentration would release new personal awareness and maximize function. Anybody studying for an exam or trying to pitch a strike in baseball knows this; yet, it is hard anyway to achieve such pointed attention.

The here-and-now emphasis served as a bridge to thorough absorption by underscoring simplicity in a world gone haywire in complexity. This narrowing of attention—dissociation, in a sense—helped to close off many debilitating habits of mind that normally fenced people in and made therapy slow going. It was an exciting turn of the psychological kaleidoscope. In this new mode, any single point of keen concentration might trip off a chain of internal events. As simple a sensation as an itch, for example, when receiving such concentration, might at first get stronger. Then it might move to another area of the body, then another, then back to the original place. In continued concentration each awareness might ignite the next until the whole body would be warmed as though with a soft fire. The growth of sensation came like dominoes rising instead of falling, collecting waves of feeling which released pent-up energy, invigorating the person who originally only had an ignorable itch.

Such absorbing effects of simple sequences of sensation were comparably experienced in the more complex behaviors. Here-and-now dialogues with a visualized father were more dramatic than conversations *about* him, hitting pillows was more potent than telling *about* lost aggression opportunities, and expressing held back criticism right now to group members was better than discussing vague grievances. Uncounted exercises in immediacy were invented. These experiments led many people into previously unimagined highs in personal concentration. A new term, *peak experience,* became adopted as a nationally well known code word for total absorption and its scintillating consequences.

The impressive effects of concentration led to a widespread adherence to what was identified spuriously, I believe, as the power of the present. It was much easier to say *now* than *how;* and this emphasis on the present did indeed reduce the complexity of attention, fostering improved concentration. When the instruction to stay in the present caught on more readily than the more arduous mechanics of concentration, it was not long before there was a swelling of the numbers of people who endorsed the idea of living in the present. They had presumably come to realize how much they had lost by allowing their lives to be delayed and deflected. For them to put life on the back burner until some future time when they would graduate or get married or retire, understandably, was no longer acceptable. Nor was a brighter twenty-first century consoling to the underclass of the society. Many people came to believe that the present was all they had in life, the only reality.

Fritz Perls, among others, was unusually skilled in publicly demonstrating the power residing in simplified experience, and his followers were often amazed at the depths of the experiences he speedily induced. In his early theorizing, Perls (1947) emphasized the present as "an ever moving zero point of the opposites past and future" (p.95), still recognizing the past and future as live reference points for the present. Though he never actually changed his mind, his penchant for communicating quickly and without qualification, especially when addressing mass professional audiences, led to oversimplification. Thus given over to sloganizing, Perls (1970) was moved later to write: "I have one aim only: to impart a fraction of the meaning of the word *now*. To me, nothing exists except now. Now = experience = awareness = reality. The past is no more and the future is not yet" (p.14).

To make such distinct equations between now, on the one hand, and experience, awareness and reality, on the other, is excellent sloganizing but only loosely accurate. Since the present is simply a point on a time continuum, it is actually neither experience, nor awareness, nor reality. They are occurrences in time, not time itself, just as a jewel in a box is not the box. A person has the choice, on the one hand, to describe his sadness about his mother's death without caring about time; caring instead only about the sensations, thoughts, intentions, hopes that may enter his consciousness. On the other hand, he could also relate his sadness to time by saying that he is *still* sad about his mother's death two years ago or that he is sad because she is *soon* going to die. *All* details of experience exist within either time or space dimensions, and everybody is free to take account of these dimensions as he sees fit. Minds will not stay put and their freedom to roam over the years is self-evident.

Many of my fellow Gestalt therapists would cry foul at my sticking Perls with his own slogans. They would have a point. It is true that, in spite of its simplistic overtones, the here-and-now approach of Gestalt therapy was more comprehensive from the beginning. A major provision giving equal billing to the there-and-then was the premise that remembering, imagining and planning are validly taken as present functions. This qualifier, though it supports illusory connotations about the present, does look beyond the present and it restores dimension. However, it suffered the fate qualifiers often do; it took a back seat. Unfortunately, the past and the future, though taken into account by most serious students of Gestalt therapy, were widely disregarded by those who were superficially knowledgeable—practitioners and lay people alike. The consequences of this misunderstanding are one element in the total cultural configuration that has popularized the notion that "the future is now."

Too tight a focus—with a highly concentrated emphasis only on the "here and now"—will foreclose much that matters: continuity of commitment, implications of one's acts, preparation for those complexities that require preparation, dependability, responsiveness to the demands that people will assuredly be exposed to, and so on. When these inevitable requirements of living are chronically set aside for what should be only *temporary* technical purposes, alienation from large parts of the relevant society is one consequence; living life as a cliche is another.

PRESENT AS DISSOCIATION

One example of a person infected by the stereotypes about present experience will help show its *dissociative* effects. Abigail, a 25-year-old woman, was alienated from her parents who, for religious reasons, objected to her living with a man if they were not married. Though greatly distressed about her distance from them, Abigail stood firm on living with this man, whom she loved. She wanted urgently to reconcile with her parents, though not at the cost of her freedom of choice. In telling me her story, she spoke in the tone of a person younger than her 25 years, fighting her parents from a hopeless childlike position. She knew much more than they about contemporary living but she still spoke weakly. I asked her to talk out loud to her parents, imagining them sitting in my office. She said that they would ask her acidly whether she was going to get married. In response, she said she didn't want to talk about it. Normally, in actual contact with them, she would either melt while dripping tears or go into a catatonic-like paralysis. I encouraged her to be as generously verbal as she could, cashing in on her knowledge by saying what she knew to be true. Then, taking both sides, she played out the following dialogue between her and her parents:

Abigail: The reason we haven't gotten married is because we enjoy living together and I don't want to do something just because I'm supposed to. . .I have to feel like it's important inside.

Parents: (Caustically) Well, isn't the church a good enough reason for you?

Abigail: The church is very important to me. To me what is important is the spiritual part of it, to experience God. To me it's not just following the rules. According to our church, marriage is a sacrament. And I don't know why... I don't understand it at all. (Cries, looks confused again, resigned)

    A crucial point was reached. For a moment, Abigail did well at stating her position clearly. Then, characteristically, she got confused. She couldn't make the shift from firmly knowing something in her current environment to knowing it also with her parents. Her own truths, though she believed in them, were dissociated, therefore inapplicable, when talking to her mother and father. They were from an alien world. She told me, as she visualized them, that they were looking at her critically, neither understanding her nor even attempting to. What she felt—common for her—was that she was doing something wrong. In spite of her discomfort with her parents, she was still vaguely attached to her past, beleaguered like a punched-out fighter looking for his corner. She needed them not only for the relationship itself, but also because she felt isolated from her entire past. Her sense of disconnection was like an amputation, which cut her away from her supports, leaving her with a cosmic whine. To feel bereft about losing her parents was sad enough, but the malaise was multiplied when she invalidated her lifetime of experience, which, of course, was not owned by them.

At this point I told her she looked like she wanted to stop talking to them because she thought they wouldn't listen—but she may be stopping too soon. Whether they listen or not, she needed to get the clarity that words provide. When I asked whether she would be willing to go on with the conversation, she returned to it. Again, she played both parts, this time in a rather softer tone. Her parents told her how deeply hurt they were by her leaving the fold; they said they are worried about her wasting her life, that she has no future. In response Abigail replied,

> I don't think that's the way it is. I have a darn good future. To me what's important is what I have right now, not 20, 30, 50 years from now. And it should be. I don't know what's going on that long. What I have right now has nothing to do with the future. This is the way I have chosen to live my life now. It may change, I don't know *(starting to get a marked whine in her voice again and sounding contrived).* What I know is that I am happy with today. *(Unconvincing)*

She seemed enmeshed in the liturgy about present experience. I explained to her that she started out saying she had a darn good future, then abandoned this belief by discounting the future entirely. I explained that she probably does have expectations about the future, some subtle and some quite evident. I suggested that her parents thought she was wrong when she told them the future doesn't count, rather than, as she had started to say, that she merely had a different opinion about her future. She probably thought she was wrong, too, because the future does count. This was contradicted, however, by the people she associated with who were heavily present-oriented. Her confusion left her without a leg to stand on. At this point, I suggested she speak to her parents again, saying what was actually true for her.

Abigail: When you say I have no future, that has no merit, that if I'm not married it could end too easily and if I were married it couldn't and wouldn't. Nobody could just drop out of it... I don't think this is true . . I believe we have a very strong commitment to each other . . . Whatever problems come up between us, we think in terms of long term, not in terms of it's good for now only and we'll not be married because it's easier to pick up and leave.

By this time, her voice had lost all trace of whining. She was clear in her gaze whereas, ordinarily, she had a questioning look on her face. She now seemed unconcerned with whether her parents accepted what she was saying. She obviously believed what she said and when I asked her how it felt to say it, she simply replied, "Clear." She now looked like she was well-grounded and later remarked about her lifetime of accumulated understandings, "It's a process of changing what I was taught and taking everything else I've learned and putting it all together."

What was apparent in Abigail's mindset was the ascendant place of the present. This focus permitted her to have a relationship that her background would not allow. Since she could not manage the contradiction, she had to cut out her parents' influence, unnecessarily also detaching from other large regions of her life. She had mistakenly equated her parents' influence with her past life. But her past—anybody's past—is much larger than her parents' attitudes and may remain as hospitable background to her current life whether her parents accepted her or not. This whole interwoven mosaic of her past, present, and future became hopelessly confused, much as the state of a brainwashed person returning from internment to their usual culture. Putting it all together was not as hopeless a prospect as she assumed, once she recognized the truth in her own argument. Once she believed in her actual future instead of relying on dissociated jargon, her rights to her relationship to the man she loved were seen as a part of the simple continuity of her life.

To escape from the cramped scope of the here-and-now, I propose two remedies. One is to emphasize the transition point between now and next; the other is to accent the there-and-then by awakening the storytelling faculties inherent in all people.

TRANSITION AS THE CENTER OF FOCUS

First, the transitional experience: If we start by looking at the digital clock, we see an apt symbol of a fixed present. In the interests of simplicity, the digital expunges the context within which any specific time appears and it nullifies the visual experience of continuing transitional movement. For all but an infinitesimal fraction of a whole minute, time stands still, and, always, whatever time the clock shows is the only time anybody can see. That this invention is more than a mundane convenience, representing larger social concerns, is illustrated by observations of a New Jersey educator (Jacabowitz, 1985), who noticed that children don't learn fractions as well as they once did. She wondered why and decided that, among other things, the digital clock deprives children of the direct representation of whole, part, half-past, and quarter-to, always previously visible in clocks. Nor do the digitals give any sense of before and after.

Standing against this illusory sense of arrested time is our knowledge of the inevitability of time's passage. I propose that, built into this awareness of time's sequences, people have a surge to focus on the transition points between now and next. One simple representation of the excitement of this experience of transition is the thrill of traveling at high speeds, whether on a bicycle going downhill or in an auto going 90 miles an hour.

Speed thrusts people into nextness, highly accenting the transition point, as it changes palpably in each instant.

For the reader to get a personal experience of comparably simple transitions, I suggest this experiment. As you continue to read, alter your focus slightly by attending not only to the present word but also by simultaneously anticipating the next one. Nextness is the key angle. You are always in between and always moving. Notice whether it makes a difference in your reading experience when you consciously lean into nextness. You will probably have tapped into a reservoir of your energy, creating alertness, excitement and fluidity. Leaning forward might also cost you a measure of comprehension, particularly if you move ahead more quickly than you can readily coordinate. If you have already been accustomed to focusing on the transitional, it is probably easier; many readers already do this spontaneously, actively anticipating nextness.

There may be some eyebrows raised by this perspective. Isn't this a frantic way to live, always alert to whatever is next, never settling into whatever is already going on, rushing headlong into the future? Though people may, of course, stumble over themselves trying to get ahead into nextness or trying to predict what is next, what is proposed here is nothing so clamorous as that. Rather it is a reminder of the naturalness of movement into the future—normally effortless and ingenuous. A telephone rings and we head toward it. A sentence emerges from a strung-out series of individual words. A question is followed by an answer. Events flow naturally, one after the other, just like the more primitive sequences of inhaling and exhaling or landing after leaping. Unless called to our attention, generally we don't even notice the relationship of one moment to the next.

This trip through continuity is, of course, not always so easy as these reflexive and peaceful sequences might intimate. Instead, the management of sequences often is filled with complexity or danger, which slows us down or even stops us. Every event, whether simple, like a single word or a flickering in facial color, or complex, like a policy announcement by the government, will point *arrows* into the future. As one illustration of the varieties of direction possible even in simple circumstances, note the headwaiter in a restaurant who says, "Your table is ready now." Almost always if you hear these words you will readily follow the waiter to your table. The choice of arrows is clearly made and you ride it happily forward. Even in this simple exchange, however, there may be elements which create greater complexity. You might have wanted a table outdoors and the waiter is leading you indoors; you might have waited an hour and feel either relieved or annoyed; or you might suddenly remember a phone call you must make. Nevertheless, in spite of unique personal possibilities, the direction of arrows most likely will move you toward the table.

Where there is a larger array of competing arrows, some luminous, some dim, a greater sensitivity will be required. Suppose, for example, that a friend says to me, "I want to call Henry." Simple words, leading to a simple act. If, however, I foresee unhappy implications of her calling Henry, I might warn against it. Or, I might remain silent, believing I shouldn't interfere and hoping it will not work out as badly as I suspect it might. Or, my friend's tone of voice may relieve me as I think she is at last going to call Henry and I may smile happily. Or, knowing my friend as I do, I may realize she doesn't really want to call Henry herself; that she would prefer that *I* do it. I then may offer to make the call. Or, I may tell her to get on with it and do it. What I choose from among all the options is important because if I choose the wrong arrows from among diverse signs there will be interruptions in the grace of our movement. As my friend goes her way and I go mine, there may be a silent gnashing of gears. Sometimes this will provoke severe incompatibility. More commonly there will only be a vague sense of not getting anywhere. Unfortunately, just such missed connections will often decay relationships.

To further illustrate the surges imbedded in each expression, here is an example of a few short exchanges with a research biologist, who was a patient of mine. I was trying to influence him to talk more than he did about his activities—to the woman he lived with and to others. In response, he said, "It's a lot easier to talk about things I am excited about and that are going real well than if I was being really frustrated." From this sentence, there are a number of arrows which could give me an interesting ride into nextness. I wondered about his need for things to be *easy*. There was a whole story which could evolve about just that simple theme. I passed that one up. Then there was the word, *talk*. Did he prefer showing people things to telling them? Who listened when he talked and who pulled a veil over their faces? I didn't follow that arrow either. Then there was the word, *excited*. What excited him and what happened to him when he got excited? That didn't draw me either. Any of these might have been prime arrows for other people or for me at another time. This time, though, the arrow I rode was his difficulty telling about things which *frustrated* him. So I said to him, "Frustration is interesting too. Novels and movies are filled with frustrating events."

Then he told me about his work which was, according to him, "99 percent frustrating." I asked him what was so frustrating. After some generalizations, he went on to tell me about one of his experiments. In spite of knowing little about biology, I became engrossed in his description of working with two proteins which were similar but serve quite different metabolic roles. He gave details of his time-bound struggle to crack the problem and how, after about a week of work, he "finally got very lucky and found a way to solve it." He told the story of his frustrating research well and, while telling it, presented any number of new arrows pointing toward new nextnesses. His allusion to luck was the one I rode.

Imbedded in this idea of luck are two contradictory possibilities. One was that he was blessed with nature's bountifulness, a lovely feeling to have, but not one which he ever exhibited. The other side was belittling himself, ignoring that his own strong hand created the solution. So, I said, *"Lucky* sounds like you had nothing to do with it. I'd like to know more about your luck." As he went on, he soon came to recognize that he had made a skillful guess in experimenting with proportions of the proteins and how they would affect each other. In further acceptance he also recognized that good research allows luck its best chance to work. That made him a partner of luck, rather than a passive recipient. In summary, during these simple sequences, he told a story with important elements of drama. The characters were chemicals, not people, but he gave a lively account of how these characters related to each other and what happened to them in one or another set of circumstances. He allowed his frustration to be a part of his story, facing up to it and feeling the fun in it. He described the risk of making certain choices, and, as it happened, created a happy ending, though that would not be required. Furthermore, as a vehicle for personal message, the story gave him a good perspective on luck and a precedent for accepting his own good function.

STORYTELLING

The story which unfolded through riding the arrows from one in a series of units to another leads us to the second general remedy for the here-and-now emphasis, namely, storytelling, which is always composed of experiences of there-and-then. Each moment in a person's life is host to an infinite number of events, and as these events occur the raw material for stories is formed. However, the span of these events is wretchedly limited. Most are given no more notice than the effect of your car on the pavement. Some may be given unconscious notice, for example, continued resentment of forgotten insults. Even so, only a fraction remains in the mind's merciless exclusion of most of life's happenings. Those which live in memory and in story remain understandably dear; they are carriers of a personal sense of enduring reality, prime vehicles for linking together the selected survivors of personal experience. Without this linkage, only the most dim sense of reality would remain—isolated pulses, unmarked.

In Jean Paul Sartre's (1964, p.39) novel, *Nausea*, through his character, Roquentin, a gloomy view is presented of the contradictions that may sabotage an enduring reality. His gloom is caused by the paradoxical clashes that are common to "living" and to "telling" about it. Though the dilemma is not as hopeless as he sees it, it is one which must be taken into account. Roquentin says, "Nothing happens while you live. The scenery changes, people come in and out, that's all . . . Days are tacked onto days without rhyme or reason, an interminable, monotonous addition." For him, the solution to this nihilistic state is to tell about these happenings and he even thinks "for the most banal event to become an adventure, you must (and this is enough) begin to recount it." He goes on, though, to add his seemingly hopeless contradiction, "But you have to choose: Live or tell." The implication is that if you only "live" there is nothing really there; the fleeting experience is nonsense, hardly worth the attention it commands. On the other hand, if you tell about it, it can, through the telling, be a vibrant, adventurous experience. But, once you start doing that, the living is over.

Paradox is no stranger to human existence, though, and this one is neither more nor less vexing or challenging than any other. Rather, it is illuminating because through Sartre's confrontation of the paradox between raw living (untold) and confirmed living (that which his told) he gives unaccustomed centrality to storytelling, normally accorded only a peripheral place in any person's life. Though it is, of course, difficult to live something out and tell about it at the same time, this seeming mutual exclusivity is served well by the remarkable integrative skills of the person. Integrative dexterity is evident everywhere, ranging from the crucial coordination of the disparate functions of the brain hemispheres to the frivolous trick of patting the head while rubbing the belly. This deftness is equally available for coordinating living and telling, a feat which, in spite of Sartre's Roquentin, we all accomplish every day. It is, of course, evident that some people do it better than others. Some will be fooled into

ESCAPE FROM THE PRESENT

mistaking the tales for the events themselves, repeating them over and over as though that will restore the living referent itself.

All people vary in the proportions of attention they give to living and telling, as well as in how they time the telling or in the style of their interconnections between living and telling. For some people, telling a story enhances the living to which it refers; for others, it only distorts what actually happened. For some people, stories are marvelous elaborations on what is only a simple experience; for others, the most complex event will be worth only a grunt, the punctuation mark in a story to be fleshed out. Some people are wary about telling those things which they are afraid will make them look bad. On and on.

Much of what happens in life floats on the periphery of awareness. Jane may ask, for example, whether I thought Agnes was unfriendly to her; she had a hard time knowing. John seemed to talk more about his ex-wife than he recently had. Agatha vaguely sensed that there was more music in her life these days. These were all dim awarenesses, suggestive but undependable. In spelling them out by telling stories, details could be added giving broader perspective and greater clarity. Hints become realizations; bare facts, when recounted, expand like yeast; unvisioned feelings and their associations become revealed. When the poet is moved by seeing a tree, the tree is only the skeleton of what he wants to say. He fleshes out an outline with his personalized words. While telling about the tree he sees, he may say that it beckons him to climb it, or that he wants once again to pick its bark, or that its branches form an umbrella. He may become clear about fertility or gnarledness or grace. When people see trees casually, they are only trees. For those who tell about them, they may be much more, as they clarify what trees are like in their diverse characteristics and implications.

In psychotherapy, special attention is given to the elusiveness of experience. People want to change their lives but often can't put their fingers on just what it would take. One such person was Ingrid who, in her group, spoke about a general sense of shame, fear and self-criticism, untied to anything that would account for her feelings. She just thought she "should have it more together, more confident, more successful, more loving and more accepting." Her concepts didn't stand still long enough to hang a wish on them. When pressed further to spell out what she was ashamed of, it took her a while before she said that when she disagreed with people she got mad, gritting her teeth and becoming silently unyielding. That, she said, is what she was ashamed of—the dishonesty of her silence. Suddenly her shame seemed a little less elusive. She added that her mother always preached honesty at all costs, although when Ingrid practiced it her mother couldn't handle it. When lying was immoral and truth unpalatable, Ingrid, of course, found herself in a bind; she wound up silent over the years and forgot why.

In an attempt to flesh out the story, I suggested that rather than stay stuck with the contradictions about truth, which only paralyzed her, she try an experiment in lying, assuring her it need be only for the moment. She got excited, transforming a worried look into one that was loose, even a little wild. Tongue in cheek, she told about the really tough week she had, working so hard around the house that her fingers split open and her nails crumbled. She "cleaned at the office, watered plants, did lots and lots of work and lots and lots of reports, lots of letters." At this point she was still caught in the phoniness of the lie, but she was getting warmer. There were giggles about all she had done for the people in her house, when suddenly she realized she was saying something true; truths she normally would not tell. Then she licked her chops and went further to tell a true story about how she recently entertained Norwegian relatives. Here is how it went and clearly her experience by now is no longer elusive. She said proudly,

> I cooked for these people, I entertained them, I listened to their problems, their frustrations, I poured them drinks, emptied their fucking ashtrays. I spoke Norwegian for them so they would like me and be entertained by me, and

I gave them all hugs and kisses, and I cleaned the whole fucking house Norwegian style. I mean, I worked my fucking ass off. Then I set this beautiful table, with lace cloth and flowers and candles. I even asked my uncle to say a prayer before dinner, so they would feel at home and comfortable. Did this three nights in a row for three sets of people. I did an incredible job. . . There is a lot of excitement to that.

She could go on forever, but she stopped herself at this point in her prideful account. As it happened, in her family, men were allowed to go on and on about their experiences, some tall stories included, but the women were supposed to serve and tone themselves down. This realization clarified her shame about not being *counted.* By now though, she *felt* counted and her shame simply evaporated.

To extract stories from people's lives the therapist often has a mind-bending job, trying to lay bare the stories that actually count. On easy days these stories may be readily apparent and one may gather them like picking stones off the ground; at other times they are deeply imbedded in their host psyche. Only through sensitive, patient, and inventive efforts will the therapist recognize the signs of the story's existence and succeed in prying the right ones loose.

People often have difficulty telling these stories even when the outlines for them are already apparent. One woman spent her childhood getting beat up by her father but was reluctant to tell about it. For the listener the violence would have been absorbing but quite assimilable. For her, however, the extra stimulation of telling it might have drastic effects, like screaming or feeling as if her head might burst. She might also feel like a coward because she allowed the beatings, or like a wanton mischief-maker or a betrayer of her father (whom she also loved). Thus, the actual story may remain heavily veiled, but the story is always there, waiting for the right inspiration to bring it out into the open. As Loren Eisely (1975, p.3), the noted scientist-writer, says

> Everything in the mind is in rats' country. It doesn't die. They are merely carried, these disparate memories, back and forth in the desert of a billion neurons, set down, picked up, and dropped again by mental pack rats. Nothing perishes, it is merely lost till a surgeon's electrode starts the music . . . Nothing is lost, but it can never be again as it was. You will only find the bits and cry out because they were yourself.

The difficulties in finding the story line are further exemplified in the writings of Proust (1924), as well as a number of other twentieth century writers, including Kafka, Joyce and Faulkner. Proust is especially well-known for obscurity in story line. He paradoxically tells about his own early enthrallment with the novel. He loved it because of the dramatic clarity with which it condensed a lifetime of gradualism. He saw the novel speeding up life's process, replacing life's gradualism with a "mental picture." Through ingenious acceleration of events, the novelist crams his pages with "more dramatic and sensational events than occur, often, in a lifetime."

In his actual writing, however, Proust frustrates this expectation that the novelist will rescue the reader from gradualness. Instead of providing an easy story line, he disseminates detail so luxuriantly that the elements of story line are veiled and only gradually revealed. The story is, of course, there but recognizing it may seem like finding faces hidden in a drawing. As a result, a legendary number of Proust's readers have been awed by his perceptual masterfulness while never finishing his novels. Though the ingredients Proust lays open are far more scintillating than the ordinary sensations which people regularly experience, his gradualness nevertheless requires the reader to be continually attentive with unusual perceptual acuity to ferret out the advances in plot.

The therapist must also attend carefully to the emergence of story lines by highlighting the patient's "mental pictures" which otherwise would remain either shadowy or concealed. What usually stands out for the patient, emerging from his almost undifferentiated gradualness, is a generalized theme that serves as a distant pointer to events long ago locked away yet still anxiously throbbing for a return to awareness. This thematic structure, often no more than a title, is a guiding factor in each person's orientation toward himself but making no greater mark in a person's life than the title of a novel will in the novel itself. Whereas a title without a novel would be absurd, people will often find it difficult to look beyond the titles that have been given up to the experiences in their lives.

One woman saw herself as having had a terrible sexual relationship with her ex-husband, but at first she could tell me nothing about it. All she knew was that she had a Terrible Sexual Relationship. She surely knew more than the title and it, alone, was too tight a summary. I pointed this out to her, saying she probably knew more than she thought she knew. Only when she talked more did it become clear to her that she actually knew much more but, oddly, hadn't realized it mattered. As she went on, she remembered that every night her husband watched Playboy TV he was no longer interested in her. That, by itself, added substance to her feeling degraded and dismissed. Getting warmed up to the details, she then found it worth telling me that he had herpes and was contagious two weeks out of four. Moreover, he wouldn't tell her when he was contagious, so she had to be personally on the lookout for it. Fortunately, she never caught it. In addition to these severe interruptions in accessibility, the pernicious effect on his self-esteem was great and he compensated by treating her with great disdain. Her Terrible Sexual Relationship, more than a title, evolved into a fleshed-out tale of misery.

Perhaps this may seem a special case of shame, preventing this woman from telling her story, but when she told it, she didn't seem prohibitively ashamed. Once started, she easily went into considerable detail, with little probing necessary. For her to limit herself to the titles of her stories was simply a familiar style; she merely was unaccustomed to spelling out the events which gave her life substance. This form of narrowing life was more than one woman's neurosis; abstractions are a common shorthand system through which people come to assume too much about themselves and know too little. Too often, the titles to the stories of life are given so prominent a position as symbols or guides that they come to be accepted as substitutes for the real thing. For someone to say he is country folk, for example, will not be as uniquely identifying as the details of the Baptist revivalist meetings he lived with, the games he and his friends played, the whippings he got, or getting lost in the woods.

Patients who come for therapy are commonly oriented to their own special abstractions which title large sweeps of their lives—marital troubles, homosexuality, school failures or fear of elevators. These titles crowd their minds; only by unfolding the titles into the specific elaborations will the special qualities of each life be restored. Once actual happenings can be re-experienced for their own sake, the titles may change and their lives too. Marital Discord may become Boiling in the Kitchen or The Homosexual Life may become Better Than to be a Boxer. Yet, no matter how intriguing the new titles may be, sometimes even helpful through the new perspective they give, they can never substitute for the story. Though many people hope they can change their lives by changing their titles, on such a wish hangs a multitude of fruitless searches.

It is also evident that Gestalt therapy, concerned with movement through time and with the entire range of a person's experiences, would be well-served to reexamine its title as a here-and-now therapy. With its revelatory technology having established the value of amplified existence, it seems timely now for a new phase of Gestalt therapy. Although a fundamentally broad-ranging approach from its beginnings, intending to widen the realms and fullness of human engagement, the emphasis on technique dramatically upstaged what was always methodologically crucial: the centrality of simple, high quality contact and the versatility of a person's awareness. These instruments of simple humanity can generate fascination. In concert with supporting technology, they highlight the drama, therefore the reality, of each lived life. Such engagement includes much that is ordinary: support, curiosity, kindness, bold language, laughter, cynicism, assimilation of tragedy, rage, gentleness, and toughness. The principles of Gestalt therapy orient therapists to notice not only how people presently live, but also how they have lived, and will live, not only *here* but also *there;* not only *now* but also *then.*

Tight Therapeutic Sequences

Erving Polster

In 1953, when I was first attracted to Gestalt therapy, one of its major claims was that it shortened therapy. It contrasted sharply with the more leisurely paced therapy common in those days by accenting immediacy and action, and it provided specific procedures and perspectives that got down to business pointedly. The consequent sharp focus, considered radical when it was introduced, is now recognizable in many contemporary methodologies, especially in brief therapy.

To illustrate sharp focus, when a patient rambles unhappily, only touching on his sadness, the therapist must attend keenly to that sadness, amplifying it in any number of ways. He might guide the patient to describe the sadness more poignantly. Or he might guide the patient to tell his dead mother what he missed in their relationship. Or he might direct him to localize the feeling of sadness in his body. The procedural inventory from which to select is large and serves two purposes: (1) to *accentuate* what might otherwise remain a veiled reference to sadness and (2) to *connect* the sadness to a range of possible consequences—crying, anger, resolve, and remembering, rather than settling for chronic and unsatisfying allusion.

Therapeutic pointedness is a corrective for psychological *slippage*, a mechanical term I am adapting. In mechanics, slippage refers to the loss of motion or power through inadequate connection between gears. When gears mesh properly, the rotation of one gear impels the other; the resulting movement is fluid and powerful. When the gears are poorly engaged, power is lost and movement is sluggish and uncoordinated.

In human metaphor, people must also integrate connections among their experiences. When they are able to mesh each experience with succeeding experiences, this produces a confident directionalism. Therefore, the tightening of the experiential connections between one moment and the next is a primary task in psychotherapy. Loose connections often result in feelings of aimlessness or being stuck, omnipresent in neurosis. Session after session the patient may wander, alluding almost absentmindedly to his life's complaints, struggles, confusions, and so on. The therapist, when not oriented to the tightening of the relevant experiential connections, may collude by offering explanations without observable consequences, often feeding new material to the wanderer.

TIGHT SEQUENCES

In a recent book (Polster, 1987), I introduced the concept of tight sequencing. Tight sequences are those sets of experience where the perceived consequences of any event happen right away—or very soon. The most simple satisfaction of this requirement for consequentiality is achieved by focusing on the transition point between "now" and "next". Each moment serves as a springboard into its future and will announce that future in sometimes clear, sometimes cryptic, signals. The therapist reads each of these signals, edging forward like a detective, to discern the hints for what is going to be next.

But unlike the detective, who is concerned with recognizing what already has happened, the therapist also must help to create new experiences by leading the patient into the "naturally" next expression or feeling. This requires intricate discernment because each moment calls out for a number of possible moves, *arrows* in a sense, each pointing to a different nextness. Furthermore the patient may not want to go forward and will use diverse means, familiar to all therapists, to avoid the trip. He may care more about other matters, as does the paranoid person preoccupied with fixed expectations, or the anxious person careful to keep his muscles tight against new experience. We well know that any patient proceeding forward might discover dangerous characteristics, such as his viciousness if he were to say more about his mother, or his homosexuality if he were to express tender feelings, or his selfishness if he were to satisfy his own needs.

In the face of such fears, pointed and sensitive evocation is required to move the patient's statements gradually in the direction for which he only gives hints. Here is an example of a session where the sequentiality between one statement and another was dogged by slippage. The process of tightening the sequences may often bank on verbally strong interruptions of the evasive process or on experimental arrangements like the empty chair technique, visualizations, or accentuating sensations. But in this case, each step in the tightening process came through a gentle increase in the spiciness or directness of the language. Each remark, small though its force may have been, tightened the connections between one statement and the next until, at last, the ingredients came together to form a moving story.

The patient, Kevin, started the session by talking in his meandering style

> Well, um, let's see. Um, today I found myself, a lot, ah, a lot more enthusiastic about coming in today. Um. Yet, as soon as I sit down here and try to tell you that, um, it's it kinda goes. (Laugh) I don't know why but (laugh), damn, I mean it's always, I always get intimidated. I told you that. (Quiet voice) Anyway, um, one of the things I was thinking about was the way I'm here, um, in a way, (nervous, forced words) another way in um that I'm in here that's like being with my Dad, the way I'm like with my Dad. Um, it is ah kind of

saying or presenting myself in a way that's um a more innocent or more adolescent or something along those line to you then. I mean it's like I'm purposely trying to be....

I knew from previous sessions that this could go on and on, so I interrupted to get at the substantive kernel, obscured within. "How do you play innocent?" I asked. His answer tightened the connection somewhat, but his words were anemic. They only thinly disguised the fact that he pretended to need my advice or leadership more than he really does. I said, "(you're) sort of building me up," to emphasize both his generosity in protecting me and the possibility I might not need it. He replied, "Yeah, yeah, yeah," excited this time about the simple truth. The excitement made him somewhat bolder—enough to say he was thinking last night about something, now forgotten, which he had decided not to tell me because it was *too assertive*. That's some riddle, I thought. When I teased him about dismissing me by saying, "How quickly they forget," he guffawed. By now, his assertiveness had overcome his fear and I could confidently tell him his memories would come. He went on, still hazily, and apparently changing the subject, saying, self-congratulatorily, that on the way over he had thought that he was being a good friend to himself these days, though not yet to others. But he still didn't remember.

I guessed aloud that he didn't want to hurt me with his assertiveness. He demurred, unsatisfied with my guess. Based on his earlier confusion between me and his father and my interest in keeping the connections tight, I asked him whether his father could handle his assertiveness. The gears meshed perfectly. He remembered a clear example and he spoke, at last, with a marked reduction in slippage. With greatly increased clarity and drama, he told me

> Yeah. Sometimes when I do get assertive, oh yeah, times where I have been assertive, it's felt like I've defeated him. I can remember one time when we were,

myself, my Mom, and he were sailing. We went for a week on a sailboat up into the coastal islands. And there was one very windy day where we had the big jib up, do you know about sailboats very much?

(I said, "not much," and his voice became instantly more animated. He continued to describe the events with great excitement. His authority was not only greatly increased as he lucidly instructed me, but he did it with animation and color.)

The jib is the forward sail. And you can have different sizes of jibs. And the bigger the jib, the more wind it catches and the faster it makes the boat go. But the bigger the jib you have the more unstable the boat can be. Particularly because it pulls from the very front of the boat. So we had a huge jib on that day. We got up in the morning when the winds came up and it was really rough. But we were screaming along with this huge jib and I loved it. And the boat was kinda shaky. And my dad wanted to take the jib down. And I really wanted it up, I wanted to cruise. So, we got into a fight about it. And he finally just said, (imitates his Dad's angry voice and smiles, also, having found his own angry voice) 'Okay, take the jib down, do what you wanna do, I don't care, leave the jib up.' So we did for a while. At one point, it got caught in something and I had to crawl up front to undo it, and I cut my finger kinda badly when I did it. And that just made him feel worse. He just said, 'Oh God, now you cut your finger, this is awful.' And I just felt tremendously guilty after that point. Like I really usurped his authority.

Once the momentum got going, the of-course quality of his story caught on, just rolling from one incident to another. This lubricated him to continue elaborating about his father's fragility and the assumptions he now makes about the fragility of others, including me. He was then able to say what seemed unspeakable: that there were some things he didn't like about me. But I turned out to be neither as fragile nor as wrathful as he thought, which was good for both of us.

The creation of consequentiality—words that matter—is a major force for quickening and heightening therapeutic pace. That which in ordinary conversation may proceed airily, with little notice, in therapy takes on great amplitude and is thus transformed into a vibrant, life-determining, fulcrum-creating moment, with the energy to move wherever the individual's direction requires.

The better the therapist swings into the momentum, the more likely will his remarks bring on the "naturally" next behavior. Therapy, in its greatest moments, provides masterful examples of what can be called the *"sequential imperative"*—the sense of the irresistible sweep into nextness. Experience appears to be seamlessly and inevitably interconnected. Perhaps the word inevitable is excessive since we all know that experiences have a variety of possible consequences. It is more accurate to say we are seeking, with variable success, the sense of exquisite rightness, so right we would want nothing better. Yet, inevitable or not, the *sense of inevitability* offers relief from the plaguing questions that immobilize the mind. Am I going to alienate people, am I going to get promoted, am I going to get sick, fat, or put in jail? Of course, the sense of inevitability also has some harmful connotations and must be distinguished from driven, monomaniacal, and compulsive behavior, where rigidity governs the person's movement. Rather, it represents the simple, unmediated grace that comes with an organic progression, within which all the parts fit beautifully together.

Inducing confidence in this progression is a therapeutic mandate and it impels the patient from the static moment of the present into the engaging experience of nextness. Just as the Olympic diver's taut body is unerringly directed and knifes gracefully into the water with hardly a splash, the therapist's intention is to guide the patient to follow the natural directions of his words and actions, one after the other, with a minimum of circumlocution, qualification, allusion, illogicality, self-suppression—what I have called *slippage*.

This primitive predisposition to be swept into the stream of continuing nextness is the basis for a number of mind-influencing procedures that have in common the invocation of high fascination, a feeling of heightened emergency, and a sense of the inevitable succession of events. These procedures include the induction of hypnosis, as well as meditation, drugs, and brain washing (see Polster, 1987), each of which reduces the interval between stimulation and reaction, between what has happened and what happens next.

Among these high-focus methods, hypnosis is the system most clearly relevant to brief therapy (Erickson & Rossi, 1979). The sense of inevitability is set up through a series of highly narrowed cause-and-effect sequences—counting, giving easily resonant suggestions, and so forth. These are each small in impact or risk but in series they add up to the feeling "of course;" the individual may ride this "of course-ness" into the most surprising consequences (Erickson & Rossi, 1979). Meditation is comparable because the repetition of the mantra creates a sense of ultimately welcome choicelessness, a release from the individual's thought processes or other background influences that distract from narrowed attention. Once this narrowing occurs, the sequence of awarenesses seems altogether natural and conflicts recede into the background.

The phenomenon of no-choice (to be distinguished from resignation) when accompanied by fascination, reduces the awareness of, or anxiety about, danger. While this feeling of safety is advantageous for movement in therapy, one should be mindful not to induce a greater sense of safety than circumstances merit. Dangers do exist, after all: bosses fire assertive employees, sexual fantasies can create debilitating panic, and recognizing rejection can be severely depressing. It is risky to sweep patients into that for which they are poorly equipped.

Before going on to describe some particulars of tight sequences, I'd like to say a few words about loose sequences. Loose sequences are those moments in therapy which do not have observably compelling consequences, even though they may be very interesting and important. Though not always immediately located on the path of problem-solving sequences, these experiences are valuable because they offer unrestrained opportunity for the patient to find his own way while verbalizing and to explore diverse, sometimes chaotic, wisps of experience. Free association is one technique that offers very loose constraints on purpose or communicative style. Loose sequences also exist when the therapist "listens" but inserts little of his own thought into the stream of therapeutic interchange. In loose sequences, inevitability and concern with direction take a vacation and there is freedom for trial explorations and the tentative meandering that allows new thought to catch on. Even surrealistic connections may occur and exercise the mind's potentialities. Many specific therapeutic advantages accrue to these and other loosely sequential procedures, but right now I choose to disregard the roaming power of the mind in order to examine the power of narrow focus and tight sequences.

CONTACT—TRANSFERENCE

As I have proposed, the generic source of slippage is discontinuity between one moment and the next. The content that determines the tightness of sequentiality is influenced along three major psychological dimensions. One is the dimension of contact as contrasted with transference. The second dimension is action as contrasted with awareness. The third dimension is abstraction and as contrasted with detail.

First, the dimension of *contact and transference*. At one pole—contact—the patient is talking to the therapist as the individualistic person the therapist really is. At the other end of the pole—transference—the patient is talking to the therapist as though he were someone from his past—a father or mother in many cases. These polar markers were transparently evident in the case of Kevin, who blurred the differences between me and his father, thereby diminishing the tightness of sequential development.

To the extent that the patient operates at the transferential level, there is slippage in his expressive system. He is not accurately guided by his past, so his words are off the mark. The result is flabby existence, where momentum and directionality are reduced. With greater tightness—an improved connection between past and present—each experience contributes support and energy for the series of coming experiences.

The psychoanalyst and the Gestalt therapist have historically approached this problem from opposite ends of the pole. The analyst has tended to expect transference and has often found it, using it to understand the effect of the past on the present. His purpose was to move people from transferential errors into an improvement in current contacts, thereby freeing themselves from the long arms of their parents.

The Gestalt therapist, on the other hand, often expected that in immediate contact with the therapist the patient would learn directly how to live life as it really is. However, that expectation was thwarted by the inevitable unfinished business still influencing the patient. To take account of this unfinished business and to try to finish it through current action is a Gestalt fundamental. When accomplished, this not only enables the patient to rise beyond the past, but it also tightens the patient's connections by synchronizing the present with the past, increasing the coherence and unity of life. Though their procedures are significantly different, both psychoanalysis and Gestalt therapy hold one goal in common, namely that the individual's feelings and actions be up-to-date so they may be wholeheartedly included in the moment-to-moment stream of experience.

Davanloo (1980), a short-term, analytically minded therapist, has shrunk the distance between transference and contact. Though the transference understanding is an important facet of his work, he also holds his patient to the immediate consequences of treating him mistakenly. For example, in the case of a woman handicapped by her passivity with men, he repeatedly points out her evasion of contact. He asks, "Do you notice that you leave things hanging in the middle of nowhere?" When she says "yes," Davanloo says, "...if you say there is, and at the same time say there isn't, and continue to be vague and evasive, then we won't be able to understand the problem..." (p. 107). Furthermore, Davanloo stands tough in this patient's denials of his interpretations by specific arguments that are both simple and convincing. When his patient tells about having been booted into the back seat of a car, he guides her to the angry consequences implied.

Through Davanloo's continued focus on the quality of her communications, the conversational momentum grows and blossoms into crucial stories about her past, as though it were the most natural thing in the world. He says, "Though the tone is always gentle, the language is extremely confronting, giving the patient no chance to escape from the impact of what he is saying" (p. 106). *No chance to escape* is an apt way of describing his pointedness and the ensuing sense of sequential inevitability. While giving high emphasis to the transference phenomenon, Davanloo has, by accenting current experience, corrected a common source of slippage in the psychoanalytic system. The slippage between past and present would theoretically be reduced by understanding the past, but the faith was often misplaced because there were too many escape hatches for the person avoiding good, quality contact.

AWARENESS—ACTION

A second major influence on the tightness of sequence is the *integration of awareness and action*. Awareness and action are the results of the generic sensorimotor system. When they are united, the person reaches an apex of personal absorption. When people act without awareness, their behavior will often be mechanical, empty, purposeless, and unrewarding. On the other hand, to be aware without acting also has troublesome consequences: dreaminess, for example, or implosiveness when the energy becomes strongly compacted. Whether a person favors action or awareness, if the connections are only loosely established, they must be restored for the person to move forward with the power that united function provides.

Here is an example of a poor connection between awareness and action. A woman, admired and well-loved in her community, was disturbed because people did not approach her; she felt isolated because she had to make all the social moves. She was unaware that her face did not offer easy welcome and so people were careful not to approach her uninvited. As she talked about her sense of isolation, she became more and more distressed. Immersed in sadness, she put her hands to her characteristically contracted face without awareness. To heighten her awareness of her face, I asked her to just feel the relationship between her hands and her face.

This awareness itself might have been a therapeutic step, since a strengthened awareness often arouses action. But to facilitate that connection, I asked her to let her face move against her hands just the way it wanted to. Her face stiffened all the more during this movement. Then, swept into memories by the new connection, she began to talk about her drunken father, who would be "all over" her when she was a child. Now she felt both futility and rage, but when the movement of her hands and her face became more vigorous, the rage won out and her face fought what felt to her like a suffocating invasion by his drunken body. Finally, in revulsion, she released a desperate sound and cried. Soon after this, when she was ready again to face the group she was in, it was with an unfamiliar open look and an unreserved connection with the people. Plainly, the amplified *awareness* of her father's oppression and of her own facial sensation became more tightly connected with the *action* represented by her hand/face movements and the accompanying sounds. It was through this heightened connection that she was impelled forward, beyond dispirited complaint, into aggression and release.

ABSTRACTION AND DETAIL

A third major impact on the tightness of sequentiality is the *relationship between abstractions and the details they summarize or introduce*. Sometimes the relationship of abstraction to detail is either self-evident or not worth exploring. For example, a man says I love fruit, eat it three times a day, and that's why I am so healthy. One probably would have no concern with the kind of fruit he is talking about or about the manifestations of his healthiness. The danger in therapy, however, is that both therapist and patient may be geared to communicate on an abstract basis about important matters, often settling for the empty and distorted understandings that many generalizations offer. Abstractions are containers of life experiences, and they offer rich signals for what should be happening next.

For example, one patient, Robert, an architect, complained about procrastination, so common a complaint it would have been easy to take its meaning for granted. That would have been fine with Robert, who wanted to talk about procrastination with a shapeless assumption that we both knew just what he was talking about. But the word begs for elaboration. Instead of doing what he is supposed to be doing, he may daydream about alternative things to do, he may converse with his secretary, he may go to the bar for a drink, he may endlessly go over what he has written, he may forget what he wanted to do, and so on.

When I pressed Robert by asking him how he procrastinates, he first felt misunderstood and then humored me by mechanically telling me what he did. He stared into space, he turned business calls into social visits, he reexamined design plans blankly, all of which got him no place. But he was just warming up and soon the thought came that, while he was working, *his father was sitting on his shoulder*. In fleshing out this new and more fertile abstraction, he then cited chapter and verse about how his father debunked everything he did, drove him to accept his values, inveigled him to become an architect, and continued to live his life through Robert's work, kicking and screaming all the way about Robert's failure to do it right. Life with father and the anger that Robert had set aside opened new avenues away from procrastination as he transformed this stale abstraction into a fresh one, father-sitting-on-his-shoulder, a new wrapping for rich detail.

Without detail, the "understanding" provided by abstraction is like substituting a title for a story. It is surprising how often therapist and patient settle for titles. Patients are rejected by parents, they have moved nine times during their school years, they have been sexually molested. All these promising abstractions are often colored with only the most spare detail, enough to point to disturbance but not enough to profit from the rekindling effect of story line. The great writer Flannery O'Connor (1974) has some instructive words about the elaborative process

> It is a good deal easier for most people to state an abstract idea than to describe and then recreate some object they actually see. But the world of the fiction writer is full of matter, and this is what the beginning fiction writers are very loathe to create. They are concerned primarily with unfleshed ideas and emotions. They are apt to be reformers and to want to write because they are possessed not by a story but by the bare bones of some abstract notion. They are conscious of problems, not of people, of questions and issues, not of the texture of existence, of case histories and of everything that has a sociological smack, instead of the details of life that make actual the mystery of our position on earth. (p. 48)

In the four cases referred to in this chapter, the core realizations came when these patients began to tell the stories their abstractions called out. One was concerned with being innocent and adolescent; one was depressed that people did not invite her places; one suffered passivity with men; and one was bothered by procrastination. As long as they neglected the sequential nature of the events underlying their abstractions, they were missing an important link in the chain of experience, bypassing a source of personal fulfillment. Abstractions are the mind's housing for the stories that furnish it; one may be said to be living in an empty house in the absence of these stories. But the stories are abundantly available. When nextness counts, stories multiply and the suspense of the narrative keeps the mind alert to every new prospect. As the investment in each element of the sequence grows, the patient will almost invariably produce a story of some therapeutically pertinent part of his life. These stories spotlight his life and help him to recognize that he is the central player in its drama. With each realization of this centrality, he becomes more hospitable to the union of disparate events, restoring connections within a previously disjointed existence.

This was implied by the whole of Freud's works long ago. He evoked extraordinarily interesting stories from his patients, and most therapists have subsequently done the same. The value of telling these stories has been variously attributed, among other purposes, to catharsis, to clarifying the reasons for current behavior, and to the restoration of the mind's free associative power. These are all valuable aspects of recounting events and feelings. But the story also helps to confirm the individual's existence, the realization of which has fragile roots in the most ephemeral experiences. People pass through life with flimsy purpose, stereotyped meanings, empty rewards, and unregistered presence. The story serves to give content and organization to that part of a person's life; it addresses and restores the energizing effect which events should have on each other.

In conclusion, pointedness, tight sequentiality, and the resulting story line are powerful factors in all therapy. For brief therapy, there is hardly anything more. Though therapists intend to bring the events and feelings of a lifetime together by creating a sense of inevitable consequence, this succession of experiences may be hopelessly derailed within the infinitely intricate lives people live. In the face of these complexities, the artistry of the therapist rests on creating simplicity. While neither unaware nor disrespectful of complexity, he whittles it down in size to the point where the human mind can cope with it. In brief therapy, the therapist is especially directed to this simplification, where he knowingly sets aside some explorations for which the complexities of life might otherwise cry out.

Every Person's Life is Worth a Novel

Erving Polster

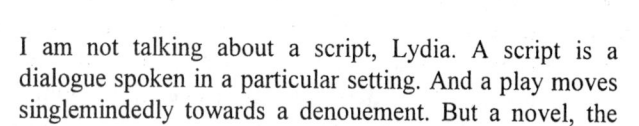

> I am not talking about a script, Lydia. A script is a dialogue spoken in a particular setting. And a play moves singlemindedly towards a denouement. But a novel, the sort of novel one could imagine one's life to be, at any rate, seems to meander, with a ragbag of concerns.
>
> -Lynne Sharon Schwartz *Disturbances in the Field*

People are often the last ones to recognize the drama in their own lives. They marvel at the adventures of others, but don't look inside to see that their own lives hold just as much possibility. Ralph was one of these people. If he had not been in my therapy group he would never have gotten my attention. He was a model of anonymity, indistinct as he sat there listening to other people's experiences. Silent all day long, though privately attentive to everything that was happening, he gave no hint that any of it held any relevance for him. Instead, his face glowed emptily, like a turned-on light bulb.

Ralph's lonely luminosity was not crazy, although the constancy of it might make one wonder. He looked rather like an eastern guru—meditatively absorbed, expecting nothing from anybody else. He didn't look frightened, but it was obvious he wasn't going to say anything. I thought that talking might fracture the wholeness he was trying to hold together, a wholeness hung in midair, like the "OM" in a meditative chant. But how long could this protective wholeness last?

Smoked out by the pressure that had been quietly building up in him all day and finally realizing that the day might end without his having said a word, Ralph forced himself to speak. Right away I could see that my speculations had been wrong. Ralph's silence had not been part of a mystical formula; the unchanging facial tone was only one element in his typical disavowal of importance. From this one-down position, there remained an urgent wish to salvage something, but it was almost too late. As he finally tried to speak, he was apparently so numbed by silence that it had become altogether too easy for him to know nothing and say nothing. I tried to help him out of his paralysis but in response he could only mouth psychologese. Using all the familiar words to explain his immobilization, he said he was frightened by "challenge," by "making contact," by "change," and by "authority." That's as far as he could go in spelling out what he wanted to say. On the face of it, he was a jargonized shell.

However, I still had reason to believe that Ralph, under the right circumstances, would come across. Now that he had spoken, I intended to get past his blank mode and flesh out suggestions of interesting story line. There was already a wispy hint of sweet radiance, although he offered little incentive for any indifferent person to explore further. As a miner of experiences, I could recognize the signs of any number of other interesting characteristics, but I had to watch out for the contradictions with which he threw people off. He had intriguing green eyes, but they looked painted on and were shadowed by his protruding brow. The lines in his face turned downward, bespeaking an actively troubled depth, yet his look of resignation would distract most people from climbing down into those depths. His lithe body lines, intimating fluidity, were contradicted by his fixed posture.

And in his empty expression one could envision a stonewalling toughness, like that of a caught spy. Already I had plenty to go on! Yet, even if these contradictions had not been so evident, I would have been certain that the stuff of drama was there in Ralph; it is there in everybody. All people start with a journey through the uterine canal to enter a foreign world. Surviving the crisis of birth, people continue to live in life-threatening dependency upon unselected strangers, who speak an unknown language. They are intimidated by unpredictable events which make them cry, kick, scream, and bite. At other times, they are ecstatic. They undergo dramatic changes as they pass through various life phases, such as sucking, crawling, self-awareness, sexual swelling, and vocational discoveries—each of which provides new opportunities and new threats. Always, at whatever stage, they are bewildered by contradictions between their needs and the needs of others, who may have strange and often unassailable customs. Whether realizing it at the time or not, each person is recurrently party to mystery, violence, suspense, sex, ambition, and the uncertainty of personal resolutions. And eventually, there is death for all! Like a mountain stream that carves out a river bed, these and many other experiences cut through people's lives, engraving character.

No one can escape being interesting. People can ignore the profusion of influences, however, and many do so with exceptional talent. Ralph was unusually adept, like the cartoon character Mr. Magoo, who blindly walks through the most devastating dangers as though nothing is happening. Although Magoo is virtually blind, we, who are watching, can see his narrow escapes. We laugh hilariously as he comes through time and again without a scratch. Magoo delights us with the tempting delusion that we can get away with blithely ignoring the world around us. Many other imaginary characters are not so lucky as Magoo. Verdi's Camille dies of tuberculosis after ignoring her health, and Tennessee Williams' Blanche DuBois lives in a dream world until she gets carted off to a madhouse.

Ralph's evasions were not as dramatic as Magoo's or Camille's or Blanche's. With those characters, the suspense about what might happen remains alive; we care right to the end. With Ralph that wasn't the case; the way he composed himself made it hard for others to care. So it is with many people. They may appear linguistically sterile, morally neuter, visually plain, or depleted in energy. However, these are all camouflage, intended to deflect from what is actually interesting. In my 40 years as a psychotherapist, I have seen great masters of camouflage. Some of them have been more skillful in hiding their exciting qualities than I in finding them. But I always know they are there, as the hunter always knows that the unseen snakes and birds and chameleons in the woods are there for the undeflected eye. Sooner or later, when I have alertly hung around, the faded person will usually come out of hiding. For moments, at least, he reveals something so arresting as to merit, like a character in a novel, even more widespread attention than the private reading of my special attention. In giving up the dulled image, such persons offer remarkably individualistic, suspenseful, and colorful memories, attitudes, expectations, and insights. Having revealed these hoarded gems, some will stay open and remain continuously interesting. Others will revert at the first sign of danger to the emptiness they have always banked on.

At first Ralph spoke only with a cliché-infected mind. He was all intention, nothing substantial. After playing for a while in his gobbledygook pen and finally realizing there would be no payoff, I got out. Instead of trying to satisfy his psychological ambitions, I lowered the stakes by looking only for those details which I knew he could give me and which nearly everyone would understand.

As a starter, I told him about a few events in my own life, hoping to establish credibility for the importance of one person's life to another. I told him I was born in Czechoslovakia and gave him some information about particular hardships my family and I experienced as foreigners in this country. Then, since turnabout is fair play, I could ask him where he was born without being dismissed as a simpleton. By this time he was willing, though stiff. At first he sounded like a card file: Born in Baltimore, Dad in the diplomatic corps, lived in Baltimore three years, another place two years, went to Catholic school for eight years, diagnosed cystic fibrosis. Cystic fibrosis! He was ready to slide right over this. When I stopped him, he elaborated matter-of-factly. "Spent my childhood, me and my two brothers, on a respirating machine three times a day." With these words his card-file style began to break down. Soon he started to cry, asking seriously, but with a shade of incredulity, "What seems so bad about it?" and adding, "You can stand it. It's no big deal!" "No-big-deal" turned out to be the theme of his life. Nevertheless, his tears had already warmed him, and he then went on to describe with the full attention to detail that a novelist would value - what his life had been like. Shots once a week, one in his ass and one in his arms. Sweat tests, wrapped under a 500-watt bulb for eight hours. Had to leave school every lunch hour to get on a respirator. Couldn't feel normal.

Then another stunner. The diagnosis of cystic fibrosis turned out to have been incorrect! "It's a terminal disease," Ralph said, "You die before you're 18!" The misdiagnosis became apparent only because he hadn't died. Then he cried more deeply, still insisting through his tears that it was no *big deal.*

With the prospect of death facing them head-on all those years, most people would think it was a big deal. Even Ralph would, had he read it in a novel. When I asked him about the imminence of dying, he said, "It wasn't talked about that much. I guess I never really believed it. Kids don't believe that kind of stuff. We were members of a group, though, and everybody died. One of the kids I remember well had a bike. He died. This one other kid, he was black, he used to go with me all the time for the sweat tests and the shots, so we spent some time together. He died too. He was about 16 when he died. It's bad—it hurts!"

By this time I was sitting close to Ralph and he just came into my arms and said, "It just fucking hurts—just hurts. When I think about my childhood I think about lots of things, but never that—ever!" Now he let go even further and cried in my arms as if he were cracking open. When at last he opened his eyes he was amazed to see how rapt people were, because he had long ago foreclosed on others being interested in him. With such a large stake in reducing his misery to "no big deal," Ralph had screened out the immense fact that while others were dying around him he continued to live. Worse than that, in screening out one thing he had also subtracted much more of his life. His crying now was like rain in a drought, releasing the agony contracted in his body, renewing his grief about the actual tragedy of those children who had died, and recognizing his own astonishing survival. Ralph, once realizing his singular existence, continued to value it. Two years later, after a number of important events, some joyous, some sad, he remarked warmly, "It's strange to be affected by my own life!"

EVERYDAY DRAMA

In drawing out the drama in Ralph's life, it was necessary to set aside prejudices about what was interesting. In therapy that is relatively easy, since the time is arranged especially for that purpose. Under ordinary circumstances, setting personal priorities aside in order to ferret out what is only obscurely interesting is less likely. People have such a large variety of purposes in mind that it is often much too distracting to probe for the hidden drama in the lives of others. To care about certain people and simply set others aside is a perfectly good bargain for most of us. If some people don't catch our interest, they just don't. We encounter this every day at parties, at work, in families, in politics, and even in walking the streets of a city. A life of unprejudiced attentiveness to everything is out of the question. Yet more modest expectations are within everybody's range; it is possible to appreciate the drama in one's own life and to lower the threshold for seeing it in others. To be open to these implicit dramas, even in small doses, can be pivotal in the enhancement of personal experience. As novelist Jerzy Kozinsky has said, in a *Psychology Today* interview with Gail Sheehy,

> Nothing bars me from perceiving my life as a series of emotionally charged incidents, all strung out by memory... An incident is simply a moment of a life's drama of which we are aware as it takes place. This awareness and the intensity of it decides, in my view, whether our life is nothing but a barely perceived existence, or meaningful living. To intensify life, one must not only recognize each moment as an incident full of drama, but, above all, oneself as its chief protagonist. (Kozinsky, 1977)

Here is one woman Kozinsky would recognize, a woman who had missed her chance to be the "chief protagonist" in her own life. In a therapy session with my wife, she complained that her father, in dying, had left her his shoes to fill. She described a death bed scene that ended with her father's head in her lap as he died. In the story, her father was the major character and she only a minor one. It was clear that she lived her life that way too.

The therapist asked her to tell her story again, this time making herself the main character. As she did this, this woman experienced herself as free of the legacy of walking in her father's shoes, free to be a person with a centrality of her own. The shift in her story was quite simple. She just described her own feelings as he died and found them to be as colorful and touching as anything she had previously said about *his* behavior. The accent on her centrality released her momentarily from the heavy weight of her dead father's shoes. Whether she was able to continue this freedom is unknown, but on this day at least her mind was opened to the possibilities of experiencing authorship of her own life.

People often squander their authorship. They don't grant the same importance to experiences in their own lives as they do to those of the characters in romantic novels or popular television soap operas. Instead, they set high standards for interesting experience, sifting life's waters with a large-holed fishing net, letting a lot go through untouched. They may think verbal fluency is necessary for others to be interested, or they may think they have to be affable, sexy, or famous. If they have ugly lip formation, quiet manner, ethnic dialect or naive political attitudes, they expect to be shunned. They will also turn their minds away from what they think they can't handle, avoiding what might infuriate them, entice them, confuse them, or frighten them. It is much easier to experience drama as consumers of novels, where events are often simplified, can be safely experienced, and have clear beginnings and endings. Only occasionally do readers use this drama as a stepping-stone, recognizing that the characters, with a few personalized changes, could be themselves, protagonists in their own lives rather than voyeurs of the fictional.

What often escapes notice are those simple events which give context and continuity to life. One person, for example, asked me what interesting things I was doing lately. Although I knew he wanted to know about bigger things, I told him how I had especially enjoyed walking across my house that morning to get a glass of water. The feel of my soft shoes against the wooden floor, the view outdoors as I passed my living room windows, the change of pace from my work, and the pleasures of just drinking water, one swallow after another—all of them mattered more at that moment than anything else I was up to. He smiled, bemused, thinking I just didn't feel like answering the question. Perhaps I should have told him how this experience of getting a glass of water joins with other experiences of daily life to provide the reality, the context, for more intense moments.

Alertness to everyday experience creates the background for special drama. If you can appreciate the timbre of a familiar voice, or sense the mystery of a helicopter swooping low over the house, or know the urgency of a sneeze in the middle of a sentence, or feel the anticipation in opening a certain letter, you will gain the linking experiences which give the wise, beautiful, adventuresome, far-reaching experiences the continuity within which they matter. A ride in an amusement park, a special gift, an evening with friends, an award in school, a defeat in a fight, a disappointment when stood up by a date—all help a person to claim the bits of existence which are the markers of a known life. There are a billion of these experiences, each of which, alone, is dismissible; in sequence they are the spark plugs for those climactic events to which people are more likely to pay homage. People who omit too many of these elemental experiences from their awareness may become frantically active, seeking other experience fruitful enough to make up for what has, usually unknowingly, been lost. Others do just the opposite, resigning themselves to a deadening accumulation of stale, zestless living. Hyperactivity, on the one hand, and deadening, on the other, are among the consequences of skipped-over experience.

TRANSFORMING THE ORDINARY INTO THE REMARKABLE

Transforming the ordinary into the remarkable is one of life's recurrent and compelling themes. The ordinary waits for an inspirational force to release it. Consider the Scarlet Pimpernel, the adventurous rescuer who masquerades as a foppish nobleman, the scullery maid who proves herself a princess by feeling a pea underneath many mattresses, the plain brown nightingale who sings more sweetly to the Chinese emperor than the bejeweled mechanical bird, saving his life, and Clark Kent, who turns into Superman. All are examples of the pervasive human wish to emerge from unexceptional guise as a unique and wonderful creature.

Contrasts need not be so marked for drama to be discernible. However, where the contrasts are smaller and where transformations from ordinary to remarkable are more easily attained, a fine sensitivity is required. An artist like Vermeer guides people to this sensitivity, looking not for the obviously special event, but instead for extraordinary grace in simple household moments. Bringing his eye to our own households, we may warmly mark the private familiarities of smoothing a bedcover, mending, fetching the newspaper, pouring a cup of coffee, taking warm clothes out of the dryer. Or, just outside, we may honor the sight of an elderly person crossing a busy street or a youngster mastering a bicycle. Such experiences give support and inspiration for the moment-to-moment focus, which offers a sense of continuity lacking in the more easily recognized highs and lows one may reach, for example, when falling in love or recovering from critical illness.

Novelists are foremost among artists delineating those experiences that many people omit from their personal awareness. In the opening lines of *Sister Carrie*, Theodore Dreiser tells of a moment of transition between a life at home and a life away—a moment of no return. He populates this moment with ordinary possessions, a surge of feeling, a taste of the past, and a hint of missed relationship. With his combination of simple awareness and fateful prospect he electrifies this moment. If not for Dreiser's skill in animating the simple experience, one could easily say Caroline Meeber just went off to Chicago for the first time. It is that and much more when he writes

> When Caroline Meeber boarded the afternoon train for Chicago, her total outfit consisted of a small trunk, a cheap imitation alligator-skin satchel, a small lunch in a paper box, a scrap of paper with her sister's address in VanBuren Street, and four dollars in money. It was in August 1889. She was 18 years of age, bright, timid and full of the illusions of ignorance and youth. Whatever touch of regret at parting characterized her thoughts, it was a farewell kiss, a touch in her throat when the cars clacked by the flour mill where her father worked by the day, a pathetic sigh as the familiar green environs of the

village passed in review, and the threads which bound her so lightly to girlhood and home were irretrievably broken. (Dreiser, 1900)

In this paragraph, everything that happens matters. Each detail contributes to the scene, our understanding, and the moment's suspense. Nothing is too small or too large to be included in the rush of words leading to the climactic sense of connections "irretrievably broken!" By then, the details have lit up the implications of a great adventure begun.

For the psychotherapist, similarly intending to light up the experiences of a lifetime, everything that happens in a session has similar potential. Unlike in the novel, where each ingredient is already finely selected, in therapy many of the words, sensations, movements, and expectations will be superfluous. Yet, using the same creative selection process as the novelist, the therapist accentuates key experiences and provides leverage for the emerging dramas.

One woman, Jean, told me about calling home and remarked, incidentally, that her father answered the phone and "turned her over" to her mother. This incidental detail, elaborated, proved to be a spotlight, illuminating influential elements of her life. In everyday conversation one would slide past such phrases. The miniscule curve of her lip while saying it would be disregarded. A misty hopefulness would be passed over. As the tiny incident was elaborated, however, it became apparent that this woman felt lifelong disapproval by her father, who characteristically sloughed her off. Although in her generosity she always excused his rudeness as innocent ineptitude, she nevertheless felt the isolating effects of being unwelcome in his world, the world of adulthood. Her belief that something was wrong with *her* was altogether incongruous when, on the one hand, she saw her college professor father as though, alas, he were the family idiot, therefore unchangeable, while, on the other, she swallowed his judgment of her.

Actually, Jean was a remarkably beautiful person, one with whom most fathers would have felt blessed. Extrapolating from her words and my own disbelief that anyone would dismiss her, I guessed he loved her too much, not too little, and didn't know how to handle it. Would his feelings open him up to being captured? Would he be distanced from his career? Would he feel too awkward? Would loving make him feel like a sissy? Neither she nor he will probably ever know the answers to these questions. What she could do, though, with a slight boost in her confidence, was to help him to expand his recognition of her. She did this by gently encouraging him to stay on the phone with her a moment longer.

Once Jean realized that by feeling unworthy of a better relationship with her father she may have prematurely foreclosed changing it, she became free to be the guide rather than the outcast. She could actively bring him along to accept her rather than making foolish excuses for him. Soon she was able to extend their conversations and to change the quality of them. He was no stone, after all, and she became altogether less dismissible. She began to have unprecedented conversations with him, and later, without prodding, he visited her from his distant home. Once her mind opened to him, she also reached beyond him to find a new welcome in the world of adulthood. Her impact at work grew, and she fell in love with a man who, for the first time in her 30-year life, gave her the reciprocal love she had coming to her. When she married this man her father unfortunately reverted to his old ways by failing to come to the wedding. But then, his absence was more regrettable than debilitating.

INFLATION OF EXPERIENCE

As a paradigm for the therapist, showing the way toward recognizing valuable human experience, the novel comes closer to the scope of a person's actual life than do poems, plays, music, or sculpture. The time span and the variety of places encompassed by the novel provide a broader spectrum than is available in other art forms. When Elaubert said that every person's life is worth novel, this was a testament to the large stock of happenings from which the novelist's work can be drawn.

From this stock novelists freely forage material; with shifts in emphasis, intensity and timing, their characters could be anybody. They put them through every form of dilemma, sometimes guiding and sometimes helplessly witnessing the way their characters carve out their lives. That they invite the inclusion of everything under the sun is well described by Henry James who, in paying homage to the writings of Honore de Balzac, says

> ... his subjects of illumination were the legends not merely of the saints, but of much more numerous uncanonized strugglers and sinners.... The figures he sees begin immediately to bristle with all their characteristics. Every mark and sign, outward and inward, that they possess; every virtue and every vice, every strength and every weakness, every passion and every habit, the sound of their voices, the expression of their eyes, the tricks of feature and limb, the buttons of their clothes, the food on their plates, the money in their pockets, the furniture in their houses, the secrets in their breasts, are all things that interest, that concern, that command him and that have, for the picture, significance, relation and value. (In Miller, 1972)

To apply an uncommonly lively receptivity to the "bristle" of living is a most fundamental task for the novelist and for the therapist. Yet there is a constant challenge to the person responding; sensitivity calls for a rightful choice from all that teeming presence. Milan Kundera, for example, in *The Unbearable Lightness of Being,* writes extensively of Tomas. He is a surgeon, but Kundera has chosen to give no description of his actual surgical work. On the other hand, Kundera makes sure that the relevance of Tomas' chance meeting with an old friend, not fully apparent at first, becomes apparent later. As large as the novelist's landscape is, it does contain a tight system of relevance; each detail matters An the total picture.

The same is true for therapy—perhaps even more so. Desultory conversation, for one thing, is regrettably rare. Much that a client might say while sitting around with friends never comes up. Partly because of time limitations, partly because of narrowed purpose, attention is given only to what seems immediately pertinent to getting better; what doesn't seem pertinent is commonly viewed as an evasive tactic and its acceptance as incompetent. Therefore, much that might be interesting, be it love of opera or a special hobby, may never arise. In attending to relevance, however necessary, both therapist and novelist face the danger of becoming so technically narrow that they present, paradoxically, only a caricature of any actual person.

This winnowing process is also inevitable, though less deliberate, in everyday life. We don't expect everything that happens to fit together. We do not even notice many of the people we pass on the street. What someone has said three days ago may be only a blur. These omissions are usually welcome, since they cut the huge glut of daily concerns down to a manageable few. Much of what happens is actually worth very little notice, a wisp of interest passing swiftly through consciousness. A stray impulse to quit a job, a flash of anger, even a suicidal thought—all minor in the lives of most people—may tilt a person's consciousness when given the inflated attention common to both therapy and fiction. An apt commentary on such inflationary hazards is given by Diane Johnson reviewing *Austin and Mabel* by Polly Longworth in the *New York Times* Book Review

> Mabel Todd has all the attributes of the villainness in a novel of the period - a self-centered, trouble-making adulteress with a disdain for housework and altogether too much willingness to display any of her seemingly numberless and genuine talents - musical, dramatic, literary, artistic... if she had been in a novel, Mabel would have to

expect disgrace and painful death. As it was, she had only to endure a little gossip and disapproval, and that from by no means everybody, for she had her partisans. (Johnson, 1985)

Neurosis will also often inflate the importance of events or characteristics. A spanking does not really mark a person as evil, a failed test does not mean a person is stupid, and a smile from a date is no assurance of intimacy. "Life goes on" is a simple homily for setting proportions right. Although this saying may sometimes be rueful commentary, it also offers a peaceful option to overreacting. The novelist may sometimes want to show that life does go on and let a character go against society and get away with it. But the condensed world of the novel often calls for a lesson to be taught, a symbol to be created, an entertainment to be fashioned, a tragedy to be encompassed. Since so much is to be omitted, the mere writing down of that meager remainder of all that could be written guarantees that it will be given special significance by the writer, at least, and if successful, by the reader.

The therapist joins the novelist in making a big deal out of small selections from all that is actually happening, taking each event not only for its own sake but also for its meaning in an enlarged perspective. While participating in this artful inflation, we need to remember that things don't work that neatly in everyday life. Chance meetings with old friends, trips to the hardware store, lost car keys, and forgotten appointments may or may not slip right through the ordinary person's consciousness. But in the hands of the expert novelist or psychotherapist any of these events might be the focal point of a spellbinding story or a successful therapy. Everything counts; in daily living there is no such likelihood.

Since the importance of any experience is so subjective, everybody is faced with inflationary potential. Suppose, to illustrate the challenge, that a 45-year-old man has just had his all-time most exhilarating sexual experience with a 19-year-old woman. He starts a brand-new life. Now he wears tight jeans instead of a suit and tie. He is captivated by the newest musical fad and is no longer interested in his old friends. He leaves his wife, intending to live an unfettered life, and he gives up his job to work more independently as a freelance consultant. Judging from this bare-bones description, we might say that this man is inflating a temporarily delicious escapade. It is the kind of inflation common to manic people who go haywire; for them proportion is difficult to measure. If this man is indeed making more of this experience than it merits, he is soon going to be out in the cold.

It would be necessary for the novelist, if this man were his character, or the psychotherapist, if he were his patient, to wonder how this precipitous change would fit into a life which must take past and future into account. That's where good drama parts company with mere inflation. Some hint would be expected presaging the change - dreams of surprise and adventure, a sense of lifelong personal confinement from which the man is surging to be released, a supportable belief that he can pull this change off, a willingness to bet his life to rescue himself from the mundane. These hints may or may not be immediately observable. since a person's preparatory mental rearrangements are often subterranean. Given the variety of people's motivations, distinguishing inflation from drama requires a sensitive knowledge of the circumstances surrounding an experience.

Lacking either the sensitivity or opportunity to get the necessary insight, people will often follow custom in making their judgments. According to most standards, this 45-year-old reborn is inflating his sexual experience. Most people would agree that you just don't change your life that precipitously, setting aside all that has previously seemed dependable. The custom might very well be right in this man's case. If it is, he is in trouble. It also may be wrong, if his motivations genuinely call for great changes. An uncertain future with many fingers beckons to this man. By way of consolation, if he has made a reckless mistake, he might be able to benefit from his bumpy experience. The lessons learned become part of the "at least syndrome" At *least* he may learn endurance in the face of pain; *at least* he may experience the spiritedness of "going for it"; *at least* he may know the continuity of a self undergoing radical change; *at least* he may see how comical a turned-around head may be. Alas, the gloomy truth is that it would be better to have gotten it right the first time.

An example of someone who got it right over and over again is the father of writer Maureen Howard. In her description of her father's extravagant exits, she shows the fine line between that which is out of proportion and that which is endearingly unique. Her father always enlarged his minor departures from the house into major ones. He recognized, in his staging of the common-place, that he was playing to an adoring audience. His farewells were always trumped up. At the same time, he implied a mystery about the world out there. He played on the suspense implicit in any farewell. He emphasized his importance to his children and theirs to him. He showed them his work as an actor, hinting at its shape. And he greatly pleased them. Here are Howard's words about her father

> An actor manque, my father had one routine that was magic and, though he never guessed it, was the very essence of the modern story-teller's art—worthy of Borges or Beckett. When he was going out someplace in particular, he'd stage his departure. Standing at the door in his coat and hat, he'd say: "I'm going away, but before I go I have something to say." And then with measured solemnity, with a hush of terror, with pride, pomposity, with tenderness- "I'm going away..." He put down his hat, unbuttoned his coat as if reconsidering but then, launched again with full resolve, hearty, upbeat, fearless, "I'm going away..."
>
> Nothing followed. Neither plot, nor meaning. It was all in the performance, what he invested in and yielded from a few silly words. I suppose it thrilled me absolutely, and

left me strangely unfulfilled. In this version of why I've come to be a writer, I imagine that I want to hold an audience as completely as he held us at the kitchen table and at the same time, though it is hardly possible and cancels his game, have something to say. (Howard, 1982)

The idiom of Howard's father, unforgettable to her, inflationary though it may have seemed, gained valid proportion because he always took his children into account, concocting his trickery as much for them as for himself. Not only were his amplified departures entertaining, but they also gave birth to an enthrallment in Howard which impelled her to continue, as a writer, what her father only hinted at as an actor.

Other themes more commonly satisfy the need for inflation. Sensational murder or divorce trials, love affairs of the famous, corruption in government, daring rescues, unbelievable wealth—all are amplifications ensuring popular attention. However, while corruption by powerful officials may be of concern to millions of people, it may provide no more drama for any one person than when he receives an extra $5 at the checkout counter. For the shopper, the moment of choice between honesty and dishonesty or between compassion for the clerk and the pleasure of getting away with some money is instant drama.

Personal experience has the power to surpass grander events. What *matters* to people is the essence of the divorce struggle of their friends, the grieving experience of relatives, the elation of a neighbor upon graduating from college after many frustrations. The arts, while risking inflation by lighting up the ordinary, open people's minds not only to the large effect but ultimately to their own perceptions, continuity, and context.

RHYTHM BETWEEN PAIN AND DRAMA

The death of a son, dramatic when it occurs in a novel, is nothing less than traumatic in actual life. In the face of the pain, little attention is left for those other realities which may ultimately provide shape, meaning, proportion, or inspiration to the suffering person. For those who are in pain, the pain is all that counts. There is a figurative swelling which forms around it, ensuring that this presently unassimilable experience will receive all the attention it has coming. The swelling, by guaranteeing attention, is a barrier between *the* experience and all other experiencing. Those who try to restore perspective will only be rushing fruitlessly toward an unlikely rapprochement. Resolution depends on an evolving series of experiences, all serving to release the individual from confinement to the painful event.

It is only after the pain is lessened that the drama inherent in the tragedy may be honored. That is to say, once the painful event, whether current or remembered, is restored to membership in the whole of the person, the conditions for drama are formed. The event comes to accentuate a valid, though scarred, existence. This confirmation of existence, forged out of a severely narrowed consciousness, is the nucleus of drama. From this nucleus, one may expand beyond the nullifying prospect of pain, eclipsing it by seeing once again the actual range of what matters.

In the novel *Disturbances in the Field*, by Lynne Sharon Schwartz, Lydia has four magnificent children, whose sprightly minds and child-color freshen everything they touch. They are already intimates of the reader when the two youngest are killed in a bus crash. Lydia is enveloped in mourning. The shock is also great for the reader, who, through absorption with this family, has become a party to their devastation. Still, they are Lydia's children, not the reader's. Having this measure of distance—far enough away to prevent inconsolable pain and not so distant as to preclude a concentrated sadness—helps the reader to experience a larger scope for Lydia's life than she herself can muster. The reader knows, for example, that Lydia has two other great children, is blessed with musical talent, and has a marvelous husband, as well as unusually loving friends. Although all of this counts tangentially to Lydia, it doesn't measure up to dissolving the pain. Inside her pain there is little room for perspective. There wouldn't be for the readers either if the children had been theirs. But from their position they can see the hope for resolution. Nevertheless, while rooting for her, they are not sure Lydia will ever make it. It is possible that her pain will blind her permanently or until it is too late. For the reader, the suspense builds and builds. Meanwhile, for Lydia hope, suspense, and resolution are nonsense. Only the pain counts until she is able to catch up to the reader's perspective.

The word "drama," according to Webster, derives from the Greek "deed" or "act." For the person in pain, necessary deeds help to recover perspective and dissolve the pain. These deeds have great variety and include such commonplace behavior as crying, shivering, talking, telling stories, lamenting, going back to work, drinking hot toddy, going for long walks, or enjoying those people who are still there to be enjoyed. The psychotherapist is well aware that the individual is a charge-discharge organism and that staying up-to-date with oneself requires release of the energy which is stored up. The bottlenecks created by seemingly irreversible events or immutable self-images must be opened up. Sometimes the breakthrough is sudden, like the lancing of a boil. Usually, though, the release is more gradual, each single episode contributing to the total restoration. It is said that time heals all wounds, which means that in the natural course of actions a person's function keeps on registering, over and over, that the person is still intact and still has the basics of the pre-wound identity. The pain of mourning, of shame, and of failure is washed out as one's normal fluids course through the channels of self-awareness.

Whether restoration is quick or gradual, all solutions have in common some form of action that will discard a stuck perspective in favor of new possibilities in feeling and deed. As Derek Jacobi, the actor, has said in an interview with Michiku Kakutani, acting is one opportunity to "ennoble all the sad, distressing things that happen to you in your life.... You can transform an emotion that was originally a hurtful one into something very soothing. For instance, my mother's death several years ago was hugely traumatic for me. And yet on stage... it is no longer hurtful inside. It's a kind of purging process." So, also, in therapy entry into the disturbing feelings of any person provides an opportunity to cast out those feelings instead of remaining with a stagnant self-image.

Narrative action served to flush the pain out of Daniel, a 30-year-old member of a therapy group. He was an affectionate, bright and engaging person, who was suffering over a frustrating love affair, one in which he felt awkward, inarticulate, selfish and disrespectful. In his misery he judged himself to be a creep and insisted he had always been a creep. Since pain obliterates contradiction, he could only give attention to things that would confirm his creepiness. Deciding to go along, I asked him to spell out his creepiness further. He then recalled how, in his adolescence, he had never known what to say to anyone. He gave us some unhappy anecdotes about those days, picking on himself mentally as he might have picked at adolescent pimples.

Among his stories was one about a high school dance, where he had naively humiliated a girl he had a crush on. The memory hit a special nerve and he began to cry. Crying was only further evidence of his creepiness. To the rest of us, listening from the outside, the story was a touching note in the wet, contorted comedy of adolescence, familiar to all of us. As Daniel continued to cry I pointed out that, although he judged his actions as creepy, he was actually just crying, spelled c-r-y-i-n-g. This wry reminder seemed to turn on a different switch and set him off on a new rush of adolescent stories that were in no way creepy. To his surprise, he remembered the time when he had shrewdly outwitted a bully who was out to get him for dating the bully's former girlfriend. Soon after telling this story Daniel began to laugh and went on with other recollections of his high school life—successes, both funny and warm.

Daniel *had* survived adolescence, a notably torturous time. But he had so enveloped himself in his persona as creep that for years he had blocked the narrative of his life. Every chance he got, he reverted to his self-image as a creep, with critical judgments so rigid there was no way out. He was installed as a creep. When his labels of himself were replaced by action—telling stories and crying—new experiences appeared, as they always will. With the arrival of suspense, perspective and relief—important elements of drama—Daniel was then able to join with others in the group in personal celebration of his victory over youthful awkwardness. Soon after this, although drama would not require it, Daniel ended his frustrating love affair, without self-recrimination, and began a new, rich and more graceful relationship.

Had Daniel read, say, *Catcher in the Rye,* he would have easily recognized and sympathized with the struggles of an adolescent trying to catch up with those new complexities which make it hard for him to know what he feels and to say what he means. By means of drama, Salinger helped to clarify what would otherwise be only faintly known. Were Daniel to read *Catcher in the Rye* he would come to know that Holden Caulfield was no creep, even though some people in his life might think so.

The therapist, like the novelist, has cultivated a capacity for what Henry James calls the "prodigious entertainment of the vision;" the zest to see what is there to be seen. What is obscured or disconnected is given a sense of direction and excitement, so that the patient feels he or she is going somewhere. Simple perceptions point the way. A stiffening upper lip, a look of muted horror, a contradiction between a tight jaw and a plea in the eyes will all serve as introductions to the dramatic life experiences. While looking and listening, one may also envision a bully, a swindler, a kid-sister, a stubborn brat, a lothario, a traffic cop, a dancer, a lost love, a dethroned prince. With such casting of a person's life, the full artistry of the therapist, like the novelist, may honor the unrealized self by releasing all the poignancy, sadness, frustration, anguish, sweetness, love, fury—everything that belongs to the confirmation of a person's experience.

THE THERAPEUTIC POWER OF ATTENTION

ERVING POLSTER

Over the years, we therapists have played and replayed certain theoretical themes. Every time we replay them they come out significantly different, with some of the hidden implications of the original themes becoming more apparent. From Freud's early hypnosis on, the concept of attention has been one of these themes, always an impelling guide in therapeutic procedure, but so common a function that it has been easy to slip over the recognition it deserves. I want to take a look at the concept of attention again and offer a special slant on it, one which emphasizes its quasi-hypnotic, quasi-meditative role in opening the patient's hospitality to new experience. After giving you some historical background, I will propose three procedural avenues for heightening and redirecting attention in the ordinary therapeutic engagement.

Before addressing the shifts of attention to be produced in our patients, it is worth looking first at theoretical changes which shift the attention of therapists.

As we all know, Freud started his psychoanalytic work by using hypnosis—*funneling* the patient's focus in the induction process in order to *redirect* attention from current suffering *back* to the early events the patient had disconnected from this suffering. What he didn't know was that this process—transforming therapeutic focus from the common style of doctor's interviews into psychoanalytic incisivenes—constituted the beginnings of a *focus revolution*. Freud was concerned with the content of the unconscious, which was a container of the patient's unattended experiences, and he sought to reconnect the patient's troubled attention to current experiences with her disconnected unconscious experience. He wanted to shift a chronic, fixed attention—obsessions and phobias, for example—believing the resulting reconnection with unconscious experiences would establish greater fluidity and broader dimension to the person's current attention options.

But, even though he did restore attention to the early events, hypnosis didn't satisfy him. He believed hypnosis bypassed the patient's resistance—something which was crucial, he thought, to genuine growth. Perhaps Freud put the blame in the wrong place, however. Not only did he bypass resistance but, more importantly, I believe, through his classic way of inducing hypnosis, he caused too drastic a shift in attention, too far removed from the patient's ordinary experience. The patient suffered what I would call a configurational failure since he could not make the connection between the recovered early experience and his currently real and complex life. That is, the *hypnotic* memories were as dissociated from the patient's *everyday* life as they ever were when hidden away in the unconscious. Though the new attention Freud had induced through hypnosis was narrowly focused on the patient's immediate inner experience—a momentous innovation—it lacked the versatility of attention required in addressing the diverse considerations in anyone's life.

Current hypnosis theory, especially as it comes from Ericksonian circles, contributes instead to the union between such narrow focus and the ordinary versatility of everyday life. The induction no longer requires such extreme disconnection as do the more classic forms; it may often be indistinguishable from ordinary interpersonal engagement, but Freud was not ready for this. Instead, he went on to free association, which, to my mind, served as a new vehicle for the induction of personal absorption, *less* disconnected from ordinary engagement than his classic form of hypnosis but nevertheless *quite* disconnected. Still, *through free association, Freud remained on the trail of a vital factor in therapy—simplified attention.* He simplified attention by releasing his patients from *interference,* from previous values and standards of expression. The patient was still disconnected from everyday life but not so much as under Freud's hypnotism. Through free association he offered the patient expressive innocence, unchaining her for a freedom which swept her into profound concentration and deeply inward attention. It is difficult for most people to recognize the sense of emergency and heightened attention which is created by the quasi-dissociative disconnection from familiar morals, grammar and habit. This escalated level of attention was novel in its day and prophetically antecedent to current high focus systems such as Gestalt therapy, hypnosis, meditation, bio-feedback, visualization techniques, etc.

A corollary reinforcement for enhanced attention was Freud's transference formulation, a step even closer to ordinary engagement than free association. Since transference was regarded as a microcosmic phenomenon, expressions to the analyst achieved powerful registration, creating new intimacy—both symbolic and experiential—and giving huge technical primacy to the therapeutic relationship.

So entranced was Freud, however, with the material which emerged from free association and transference that, ironically, he did not notice the *trance-like* phenomenon he had created in his patients; he failed to see the new rhythm he had composed between finely pointed attention and the more versatile attention of everyday life. Then, as the search for understanding dominated the free association and transference processes, the power to induce deeply concentrated attention deteriorated. Instead, too often, therapy became a mind wandering exercise.

A key counterforce came from Frederick Perls, under whose inspiration Gestalt therapy came on the scene. In his 1947 book, *Ego, Hunger and Aggression,* Perls recognized the mind wandering accompaniment to free association and emphasized the importance of *concentration* as counterforce to avoidance. Concentration is a form of tuning in sharply to whatever one is attending and Perls' recognition of its role in therapy took its place alongside hypnosis, free association and transference in escalating the attention factor. He found concentration to be a lubricant to new experience, as its pointedness reduced the inhibitory intrusions of the ordinary context of a person's life, much as hypnosis and meditation do. Here is an example of the simple effects of concentration. In this case, the person had been asked to concentrate on his internal experience and this is part of what he observed

> I was feeling around my insides when I finally got around to the region of my rectum, and there I noticed what seemed to me a silly tension, because when I examined myself I found that I did not feel like defecating, but there I sat with the sphincters just about as tense as if I did.

This person had simply not noticed what had been there all along, unattended. The attention shift was disarmingly simple, one small but palpable representation of an otherwise mystical and elusive unconscious. Because of the greater obscurity of most unconscious/conscious interconnections, it is easy to forget that transforming unconscious phenomena into consciousness is actually the achievement of shifting attention. The smiling person, for example, who discovers a vein of anger inside, has just chronically ignored the anger until able or willing to give it the focal attention that would make it a tangible experience. A wife in couple's therapy, complaining to her husband, when expecting a rejection of the complaint, may not hear him say she's right. A particular patient of mine, who is a lovable, bright, energetic eccentric gives unremitting attention to himself as a bumbling freak. Nothing I say or lead him into has so far re-mobilized his attention, which remains stuck on the self-image which was embedded in his mind long ago.

Since such examples of the key role of attention are familiar to all therapists, we continuingly search for new ways to direct the attention of our patients. But we are not alone and perhaps can broaden our options if we cull what we need from our fellow explorers. People of religion, politics, advertising, martial arts and many others are all looking to harness the powers of attention.

From among these, our closest cousins in influencing behavior and feeling are the world's religions, which implicitly have made escalated attention a core factor in their process. They create pointed focus through prayer, meditation, music and finely honed belief systems and rituals. Chanting, bodily rocking, and spiritual singing have guided their people into full blown absorption. They have welcomed extravagant phenomena into their process, ranging from belief in miracles and immortality to the induction of devotional, even ecstatic, experience, through practices such as divine healing, laying on of hands, speaking in tongues and fostering visions. Cult groups also sharpen attention by narrowing the complexities of life through minute rules and strictly guided living. From our own psychological background, in comparable life focus groups such as EST and others, we also see an extravagant sharpening of attention. They have turned their communities on through advanced mind control procedures, creating great inspiration and often producing so-called altered states. The time may be rapidly approaching when psychotherapists will find their own way to such communal escalations of attention, perhaps building on the promise of new therapeutic designs for inspirational gatherings of life focus groups.

But for now the florid, exotic and fantasmagoric devices for achieving this high focus, proportioned for the masses of people, are largely unacceptable in therapeutic practice. What we offer instead is a condensed attention to experience as it emerges and to the accompanying implications which have a clarifying and mobilizing effect. Perhaps this is scaled down, as it should be, but

The Therapeutic Power of Attention

I remember the spell cast upon me in my first experience of therapy when this man, the psychoanalyst, actually listened absorbedly to me for session after session. The sign of his full-blooded attention was that what he said was exactly tuned in to what I was saying. To us therapists, it seems only logical that he would listen attentively but for me as a naive patient, it was an enthrallingly connecting experience, and for the time I was in his office, nothing else mattered as much. Through this heightened absorption, I became free to say many things I would never otherwise have dreamed to say.

But, on the whole, though often unwittingly utilizing techniques for enhanced attention, we therapists have been very wary of the sharp induction process, as represented in a number of mind altering vehicles, of which religion and hypnosis would be two representatives. This is understandable, because such constriction of the boundaries of attention often narrow the person, sometimes for better, often for worse, and may, in the wrong hands, make it difficult for the person to access his or her individuality and ordinary societal interests. But, it is nevertheless plain to me that we are already players in this game, and irrespective of the doctrinal dangers, we may still sensitively apply the mind-opening powers of enhanced attention in ways which are compatible with our more individualized therapeutic purposes.

How then, specifically, may attention be enhanced and directed in ordinary therapy? Can there be a coordination between the casual attention of face-to-face relationships and highly focused attention, providing the benefits of escalated attention while minimizing the risks or requirements which are usually reserved for the monks among us? How can we close the gap between a searing attention—fracturing fixed positions or melting them—and a diffuse attention, neutralized by vapid responsiveness and stereotyped positions? When the therapeutic mission is too abstractly and loosely conceived it provides poor ground for the full-blooded attention we see in the trance experience, or the religious experience, or the brain washing experience, or the meditation experience. Is there a middle ground where we may incorporate the lessons from the high focus systems and produce it in the ordinary therapeutic situation? With these questions in mind, I would like to address three factors which enhance attention within the parameters of ordinary therapeutic interaction. They are: 1) tight therapeutic sequences, 2) the unfolding storyline and 3) the summoning of self.

1) *Tight therapeutic sequences* are those experiences—they may be statements or actions or feelings—where the implied consequences are immediate. The creation of tight sequences calls for the restoration of a sequential imperative, which moves experience fluidly from one moment to its naturally next moment. I propose that, if resonantly advanced, this movement builds a momentum which propels people to greater freedom for continuingly doing whatever comes to be naturally next. The result is a heightened absorption—not unlike trance—that helps one to rise above the distractions created by a lifetime of competing experience.

The key is for the therapist to tune in resonantly to this natural momentum. Any statement will point forward, containing a number of intimations—what I call *arrows*—each of which may point toward what is ahead. A patient, for example, while talking about her family playing music together may also offer snide observations about them. Whether to follow the arrow provided by the snide observations or the family playing music is a choice to be made and this choice will steer the course of therapy. So will the next choice, and so on...and so on...and so on. As these nextnesses, sensitively tapped, are successively navigated by the patient, she is drawn by the momentum of this fluid continuity into a feeling which says, "of course" to succeeding experiences. It is as though someone were successively to say the numbers 9, 8, 7, 6, then pause. You immediately think 5. This impulse to continuity builds up an innocent absorption, generating an "of course" frame of mind. Through this restoration of continuity, we therapists guide the patient to *spontaneous receptivity*, much as she was open to it in her childhood. This time around, we hope for a happier consequence than that which followed the originally damaging introjections which bring her to therapy.

Here is one example of such tightening of sequences, as it was manifested in a demonstration session with a person at a psychotherapy conference. A young, energetic African-American graduate student in psychology, let's call her Denise, started the session with a lively but abstract account of her frustration about her development as a professional. Before I could follow the arrow represented in her concern with her professional development, she hurried forward into telling me that she felt guilty about benefiting from the exploitation of people around the world. It was soon plain that she would go on talking at length in a heated but abstract style, expecting nothing consequential to evolve from her valuable feelings; a stuckness familiar to all therapists.

In trying to honor and restore the neglected consequentiality of her remarks, different therapists would vary on the arrow to be chosen. One might guide her to flesh out her guilt, another to explore her professional development, yet another to follow her enthusiasm, still another to tap her courage. Probably no choice would wash right away because she is stuck on a broken record. For me, what stood out, though, was her grand energy, joined contradictorily with helplessness. In her helter-skelter eagerness she had little sense of the discrepancy between her zest and her helplessness and the resulting stuckness. So, my choice for tightening the sequences was to observe wryly that she had taken on a huge job and to compare it to the work of an aerial acrobat, suggesting perhaps we could first do a few of those flips here on the ground.

This would help to provide consequentiality by offering a do-able and relevant option. We will see later how this implication played out. Now, however, she looked surprised, perhaps because I took her ambitions seriously enough to tailor them for success. A moment of connection but still she went on almost as though I hadn't said anything, impelled forward by her great cause—but still overshadowed by her feelings of helplessness. So, then, with helplessness as my new directional inference, my arrow, to move this theme forward I mundanely asked what aspect of her helplessness we could focus on. She told me how helpless she felt about Mozambique and the fact that the South African army was killing and torturing people.

But she still gave me only a misty sense of the problem she wanted to solve. She seemed more caged in the rageful impotence of it all and wanting to make speeches than in showing any concern with the actual satisfaction of her needs. Her empathy for the people of Mozambique, obvious to me, was overshadowed by her rage and I thought her empathy might serve as a deepening element and might make her rage less mechanical. Therefore, I told her how important I thought her empathy to be and this softened her somewhat. She responsively expressed a measure of empathy in a slightly different direction by saying that she was bothered about the inappropriateness of her anger against people who were inattentive to the world's problems. This made her more clearly aware that she actually would like to be impactful with these people and it took her out of soliloquy, raising her chances for satisfaction. By this time she was getting the feel of continuity from one statement to the next and, looking for consequentiality, she said, "let's say if I was here at this particular conference, angry at the profession for not including issues of diversity... I want to make you and everybody else incorporate those issues so that I can learn and know that we as a profession are doing something."

The audience applauded resoundingly. But she was about to go on as though nothing had happened, to make a new impotence-raising speech, eloquent but stuck, like running on a treadmill. When I interrupted by asking her whether she heard the applause, she said, begrudgingly, as though I was interfering with the more important content of the budding speech, "Yeah, I heard a couple of people." Then she began to wonder about *their* neglect of diversity. Following the arrow pointing toward a connection with the applauders, I asked her to imagine them as a group of people and ask them that question. She followed this easily, empty chair style, and she not only asked them why they had not addressed the issue of diversity but also told them she felt isolated and alone.

For the first time she is, paradoxically, not a lone agent because she is implicitly asking for people to join with her. Can she allow them to? That prospect is veering her into the possible, as we are getting more and more of a sense of continuity and she is beginning to tighten her own sequences and encompass a new absorption with actual people. I asked her to play the applauding audience responding to her. Playing them, she said, "I was thinking a lot of the same things, (as she was) but I really didn't have the courage to go up and ask that. That wasn't a priority." Denise then, in her own voice, said, "How can you *not* feel that's a priority..." Good sequencing—but then she goes on to break the fresh absorption by reverting to her habit: starting to make a speech about demographics, etc. So I interrupt her, explaining that she is going to lose the flow of conversation in favor of speech-making. Could she allow them to answer her question about how they could *not* have that as a priority? She, still joined with me, says "Ahh, I see. Okay, I see." A moment of realization of how her speech-making would interrupt her process. She acknowledges that she really wants to make a speech and when I say speeches are fine in their place, she lights up and we laugh together, she feeling both caught and warmed. I tell her that I love the way she lights up, fantastic, like a Christmas tree, acknowledging our *joint* continuity.

Then, after several further steps of establishing the smooth flow of her experience from one moment to the next, she came to ask a concrete and addressable question. Why does the conference not deal with sociological issues such as women's rights and the presence of people of color? This moved her next into discussing the prospects for getting the names of those in the audience who believe the conference should expand in the future toward "diversity". We end the session when she happily says that she's going to be passing around a pad for people to sign, an action she now felt altogether at home with. She had changed in discreet steps from an "idealogue," recycling her futility, into a person pointed toward immediate satisfactions and a promise of continuity.

In what sense does this session compare to such attention enhancers as mantra meditation and classical hypnosis? It is, after all, a quite familiar therapy interaction, recognizable to every therapist, moving step by step, tracking, with a clear purpose to move from problem to solution. In contrast to mantra meditation and classical hypnosis, there is also a familiar complexity of ideas and perceptions: Mozambique, helplessness, ambitiousness, diversity, inter-communication, divergence from the therapist's sense of good direction. Yet, in this ordinary interaction, quite distinguishable from classic hypnotic or meditative inductions, there is embedded, almost unnoticeably, a sense of natural nextness, and this helps transform Denise from diffuse abstraction into a strong focus on the flow of actual experience. Though this induction would not be so enabling that a person could lift a car off the ground or have a transcendent experience of unity with the universe, we nevertheless see that through the induction of tightened sequences, there was a heightening of directed attention, which frees her to transcend her habits and do what originally would have seemed either impossible or prohibitively forced.

2) The second vehicle for attention enhancement is the patient's *storyline*. By storyline I mean two interrelated things. One is the *particular* stories and their role in organizing and animating the events in a person's life. The other is the *stream* of stories which mark the path of a person's life, building into experienceable themes. Both aspects of storyline are key elements

in the renewal and escalation of attention to events which have been defused.

Stories have always been attention enhancers. One need only observe the enthrallment of children when a story is about to be told. Stories exercise a major hold on the psyche of all people because they flesh out, color and organize the events of life. They spotlight experience and serve as markers of the person's existence. They stimulate the view into the future with their "and then...and then...and then..." suspense. They animate events and the players within the story. They open people to new empathy with their lives.

Denise, for example, had dimmed her storyline by speaking abstractly and repetitiously about the problems of women and blacks in our society, bypassing *events*—which are the crux of storyline. In this short session, she came to deal with actual and imagined people, with the live tension of real purpose and its struggles, and the climax created by the actual clash of forces within her world and within herself. The realization of relationship between herself and her audience of potential collaborators helped to animate her ideas and to join her with other people. The players, activities and conflicts are the elements of storyline which must be restored to help amplify attention.

The therapy office is a hot-house for the remembrance of storyline. A familiar example is a patient who is an 18 year old college student. She told me, in passing, that she was going to traffic school after her session. Always fishing for stories, even though she was about to go on to other matters, I asked her what had happened. She had gotten a traffic ticket when driving a group of friends in the middle of the night to a fast food restaurant. What grabbed our attention in this otherwise tangential story was that she, previously plagued by drinking, was the only one in the car not drunk. She would have slid right over this achievement without giving it the registration that comes with spotlighted attention. Moreover, inspired by this renewal of attention, she then went further to remember an earlier traumatic experience, the telling of which helped to pointedly register the person she actually is rather than only the pale evasion she usually fosters. It must be recognized that neither the telling nor the creation of stories gives assurance of their attention enhancing effect, because patients are often inured to their stories. They have either told them over and over without personal effect, or they leave out key details that would help to spin their minds around, squandering their fertility as the stories become limp fragments of a lifetime. The events need the energization that the therapist's technique contributes to transforming the story from an obsessive commentary on a stuck or painful existence into a palpable experience of a life lived.

The therapist's contribution to this restorative role includes, among other qualities, a combination of concentration, fascination and curiosity. This triad of attention enhancers calls for a pointed focus on the events which form the story, a sensitivity for story value—much as a novelist or an editor might have—and a recognizable wish to know what happened in the lives of patients. The therapist thus serves as an alerting force for redeeming squandered storyline and allows no escape except when the stories are too difficult to bear.

3) The third source of enhanced attention is the concept of the self and the particular application of it which I have proposed in my recent book, *A Population of Selves*, the gist of which I will briefly outline here. Rather than limit a view of selves to misty classes of a unitary self—such as real self, true self, false self, actual self or other pre-designated classes of self (grandiose self, nuclear self, narcissistic self...)—I have accented how selves are individually tailored and how they animate the range of each person's life experiences. What I accentuate is that the self is a *personification* of characteristics and experiences, which are organized into person-like entities. Each self has a name and a role to play within the total function of the person. Thus a person who characteristically comments on everything that happens

among his family and friends may be said to house a *commentator self*. To point out that he seems very often to comment on other people's behavior may be a perfectly valid observation for the therapist to make, often sufficient unto itself. But to add life selectively to this observation, the therapist may refer, instead, to his commentator self. When rightly selected this attribution of self to a cluster of experiences will often give it a brighter reality and one with which the patient may more strongly empathize.

Is this transformation from experiences or characteristics to self no more than linguistic cosmetics, dressing up an interpretation so as to force added attention where the person might otherwise slide by? What makes it more than cosmetic is its congruence with two human reflexes: configuration and anthropomorphism.

First is the configurational reflex, which makes a pattern of related experiences—a Gestalt fundamental. Without this integrative force, usually exercised without awareness, nothing in life would make sense. The naming of self serves to highlight and simplify this complex configurational process, which is a summation of personal experiences and is always taxed by the prodigious range of such experiences. This generic and often overburdened function is perhaps the reason that people are so compelled to find out who they are and to try to achieve dependable personal identity. How can they put everything they do and feel together so that this infinity of experience may be composed into a good fit? They go to great lengths to discover and then to defend the selves they are, carving out the strangest affiliations and fighting the most destructive fights to accomplish this. This is especially so during a time in history where flux and the complexity of experience has risen making a summary of one's nature all the more urgent. Failures in the immensely challenging exercise of the configurational reflex result in the isolation of experiences at all levels, creating the dissociation of certain personal characteristics which cannot be fit into the totality of what people already experience as themselves. A child believing he is generous, for example, may not know how to fit his stinginess into the picture, and he may dissociate either his generosity or stinginess. This struggle to identify the nature of one's self is so important to the person's configurational integrity that self-designation will usually draw highly focused attention.

A case example is that of a patient whose immigrant father spurred her relentlessly to be a person of accomplishment. Instead of expressing his deep feelings of love, he blamed her for every imperfection he could find, as though focusing on her imperfections would inspire her to perfection. She seethed and hissed but went with his game by succeeding in everything she did. But she became rigidly vigilant about any blame and would go into rages with her lover when there was any implication of his pressuring her or not accepting her. She also had many other selves, beautiful ones—accomplished, generous, verbally invigorating, beloved—but they were sharply threatened when she was faced with flaws and she disconnected from them while her vigilant and angry selves took over. This internal struggle creates a drama of near survival proportion. If she can be helped to face the contradictions among selves freshly, her attention level will help her to forestall the threatened dissolution of self and take on the challenge of internal conflict and coordination.

Secondly, in addition to satisfying the configurational reflex, the naming of selves also satisfies the anthropomorphic reflex, transforming characteristics into person-like entities. We do this all the time, as naturally as breathing. Among our well known precedents, love, war, and beauty became manifested in the humanoid gods of Cupid, Mars, and Venus. Closer to home, an office machine not doing what we want it to do may be seen as "stubborn". Similar animation is created by composing selves out of recognized configurations of a person's experience. This anthropomorphic designation often creates a greater understanding and empathy within the person for her own clusters of experiences and characteristics. We accentuate the commentator quality of a person (or her vigilance or generosity or gullibility) by translating these directly describable *characteristics* into the more tangibly accentuated language of *internal characters*. The conflicts, changes and purposes of these internal characters give a heightened level of realization to what non-personified characteristics might only have registered less brightly.

The criteria for the satisfactory inference of selves are similar to the requirements of good fiction. The images must be faithful to the raw materials one is animating. That is, the attribution of selves must indeed represent the patient. As with all human translations the congruence is vital. One may either enhance a person's sense of self by accurately naming the selves or violate the sense of self with wrongful understanding and summation. When well done, the realization of these selves will saturate the patient with personal identity, creating an absorption which is reminiscent of a reader's relationship to fictional characters, with whom she identifies. This empathy is a strong warming factor, loosening the old images and increasing the acceptability of a changing sense of self.

In conclusion, the three therapeutic vehicles I have described—tight therapeutic sequences, unfolding storyline, and summoning of self—serve to illustrate the ever-present options which exist in ordinary therapy for the arousal and re-direction of attention. They are instruments for focusing the individual so pointedly on his immediate experience that he becomes released, more or less, from the background constraints which are chronically inhibitory. We are all familiar with the disappearance of problems during times of absorption, as when meeting an exciting friend or watching a key athletic event. This prospect often not only amuses but, unfortunately, also distracts us from what is not ignorable.

But to create the level of focus I am talking about is a more dependable and inspirational force, because it moves to open the patient to experience rather than to avoid it. While working in the familiar therapeutic style, we incorporate the powers of attention more readily observable in the hypno-meditative experience and use them to sharpen focus on experiences which neurosis creates. Though the focus is not heightened as pointedly as in the classic versions of hypnosis and meditation, it is nevertheless sufficiently impactful to create comparable absorption in the ordinary world of diverse stimulations.

THE SELF IN ACTION: A GESTALT OUTLOOK

ERVING POLSTER

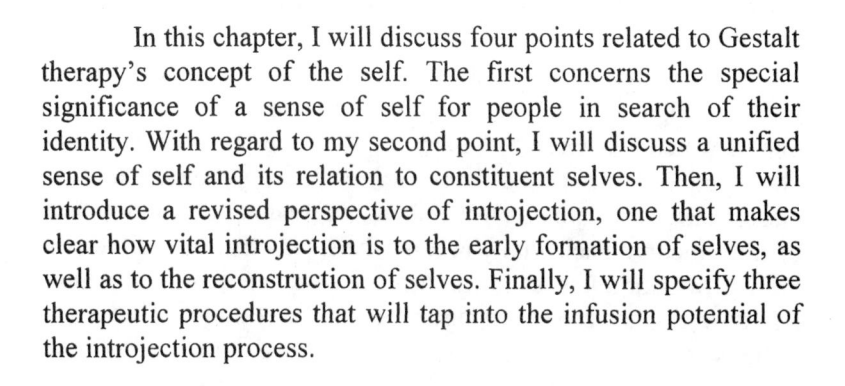

In this chapter, I will discuss four points related to Gestalt therapy's concept of the self. The first concerns the special significance of a sense of self for people in search of their identity. With regard to my second point, I will discuss a unified sense of self and its relation to constituent selves. Then, I will introduce a revised perspective of introjection, one that makes clear how vital introjection is to the early formation of selves, as well as to the reconstruction of selves. Finally, I will specify three therapeutic procedures that will tap into the infusion potential of the introjection process.

BACKGROUND

A concept of the self was one of Gestalt therapy's most important early contributions. However, the concept became a casualty—wounded, but not dead—in a post-World War II theoretical struggle. Many readers of this chapter were not yet born then, so it may be hard to realize the extremes to which therapists had gone in classifying people, often disregarding the person's individual experiences. In those days, we were replete with possibilities for understanding people, especially those of us who were psychoanalytically oriented. We often would assume this understanding prematurely, giving only superficial attention to what people actually wanted, what they actually felt, and what they actually did, using these concerns merely as intellectual stepping-stones.

I look back with nostalgia at those exhilarating days in the late 1940's when I was a graduate student. As young zealots, we exaggerated what we learned, for example by identifying someone as an oral personality, often obscuring—not even caring about—the person's unique individuality. To our credit, we were incredibly agile in divining each other's psyches from the barest information, and only the most stubborn among us would scoff at these designations. As a coffee-break calisthenic, it was a great exercise for our galloping minds, but a parlor game does not a person make.

A corrective to this system of stagnant classification had to come and it was most forcefully evident in existentialist circles, one of which was Gestalt therapy. In 1951, Perls, Hefferline, and Goodman, in their seminal book *Gestalt Therapy*, reacted against classifications and put the self into action, making it a centerpiece of their theory. Their view, in a nutshell, was that the self was a system of continuing contacts, a process rather than a structure, and they emphasized its engagements and its fluidity. They said, "The self is not...a fixed institution; it exists wherever and whenever there is...interaction. To paraphrase Aristotle, when the thumb is pinched, the self exists in the painful thumb" (Perls, Hefferline and Goodman, 1951, p.373). This was a key perspective because of the emphasis on flux rather than on an enduring class of characteristics; even though they said the *self* exists in the painful thumb, they made clear that the infinity of all of our experiences was of greater interest than the abstract self.

In a later work written with my wife, Miriam (Polster & Polster, 1973), we were more hospitable to classifications of the self and presented the concept of the I-boundary. Without going into details here, we named classes of self that were pivotal in regulating contact. But our interest in examining the activities and awarenesses of the person predominated, and we focused the rest of our book on those processes. The self once again receded into the background.

Misgivings about abstractions and a yearning for a greater appreciation of actual experience went beyond psychology. One of the voices warning against the petrification that occurs in classifying experience was that of the novelist Joyce Cary, who said that if you tell a child the name of a bird, the child loses the bird (Cary, 1961). That fear was and remains, real. Yet it also seems timely now to recognize that, although the danger of losing Cary's bird is substantial, there is an equal but opposite truth—if you know the name of the bird, its history, and its habits, you may know the bird better. Given these opposite truths, losing the bird and enhancing the bird, it is evident that the principles that win out in any method—that come to be a method's melody, so to speak—always are accompanied by counterpoints. These counterpoints could enrich the melody, like the harmonic undercurrents that deepen primary musical themes. In music, however, the different voices resonate spontaneously in the listener's ear, but in therapeutic theories, the mind easily narrows in on the main theme, shifting away from contrapuntal intricacy.

I do not think this has to happen. Let us revisit the self as harmonic counterpoint to our focus on raw experience. After 40 years of growth in experiential know-how, we see again—perhaps more than ever—a yearning to know who we are, to know the self that evolves from an infinity of ephemeral experiences, unnamed wisps, each by itself having no form and going nowhere. Perhaps now, less defensive about being classified, we can respond to this craving for a personal synopsis by searching out raw experience and, at the same time, as musicians do with their counterpoints, using the concept of self to add depth and identity to these experiences.

WHAT IS THE SELF?

The concept of the self calls for the person to transform the pronoun "I" from a grammatical stand-in—without further meaning—into a recognition of essential qualities with which the person may be identified. Real self, narcissistic self, nuclear self, and false self all refer to essential qualities of the person. But the self is more than essential qualities. It is also a representative of the person. This inner being is formed through those patterning powers of the mind that unite elemental experiences into wholes. Long ago, Gestalt learning theorists pointed out the innate capacity for gestalt formation, a magnificent capacity that enables us to see unified faces rather than disconnected eyes, ears, nose, and lips. Beyond this simple perceptual feat, it is only a short step to believing that the same patterning process also organizes personal characteristics into coherent clusters, from which we form our sense of self.

Where such formations of self are concerned, patterns are much more freely created than in simple perceptions. At a high level of generalization, we may see that the self integrates the events of a lifetime, of which an epitaph is one example. The 19th-century novelist Machado de Assis wrote, "Among civilized people (epitaphs) are an expression of a secret...egoism that leads men...to rescue from death at least a shred of the soul that has passed on..." (de Assis, 1990, p.202).

This rescue of a shred of our souls does not wait for death, however. Many of us spend our lives reaching for measures of our true proportions in a potentially shapeless existence. The search for a single guiding image of our enduring nature is a temptation at least as old as the Greek adage, "Know thyself."

Let me give you an example of a blessed unity of self. One chronically angry patient of mine realized one day, as though hit between the eyes, how hard his life had been. In great self empathy, instead of getting angry, he cried convulsively. After he emerged, released from his anger and tension, he said, "This is the real me, peaceful and soft." He loved this self, the self that was free to cry when overwhelmed and to enjoy the breath of fresh air inside. But was it real? No, it was no more real than his angry rigidity had been.

The appearance of my patient's "real me"—peaceful and soft—gave him a unified sense of self that we all seek; he was all of a piece, à la Kierkegaard, who wrote a book titled, *Purity of Heart is to Will One Thing* (Kierkegaard, 1948). The marvelous wholeness my patient felt in this self was devoutly sought as he was happy to identify with it and to pray that it would become more easily accessible. However, this was only one elusive aspect of his self. At other times, there would be other states of mind—religious, scholarly, sexual—that also could cause him to experience himself as whole, and even "real."

Whatever this unified self may be, no matter how pivotal in restoring personal cohesion, the one self that represents his "all" also is accompanied by constituent selves. These constituent selves may coordinate well with each other and with the unified self, or they may compete or be alienated. They may live in war or peace. They may be cunning or resigned. They may each go through periods of being favored or neglected. And they face stimulation, accepting it or fending it off.

In the consequent fluctuations, selves may be formed with great versatility. Let us examine a man who has the following four characteristics: he is careful in his choice of words, noticeably obstructionistic about things he is told to do, passive in conversation, insufficiently interested in his work. Given this cluster of characteristics, we may name the cluster a "procrastinating self." Or this formulation may change according to the chemistry created by combining these characteristics with others. For example, if this procrastinating person were to show nonchalance, we might name this self his "who cares self." If he seems quite confident, we may call it his "biding-my-time-self." If he is clumsy, we may call it his "nerd self." How we resonate with our patients in identifying relevant selves from a multitude of possible configurations will be influential in treatment. Moreover, this sense of selves changes as new experiences call for change.

Before we move to therapeutic applications, there is one other consideration to take into account in formulating the concept of self. Ordinarily, we see people as having *characteristics*, not selves. At what point do the discrete characteristics—carefulness, obstructionism, passivity, and disinterest—coalesce into a procrastinating *self*? To use another example, when a person pretends to trip over your feet, tells funny stories, turns serious conversation upside down, one may laugh with that person or ridicule the person or stiffen against him or her as a matter of simple reactivity. At a certain point, however, these events and the person's evolving characteristics may be so enduringly interwoven and so clearly recognizable as a class of experiences that they may warrant designation as a self; in this case, let us say, a clownish self. This clustering, named or unnamed, will incline the person to clown, sometimes irrespective of current needs. In a sense, therefore, the self has a life of its own, a configuration extending its guidance, often without awareness.

The therapist often will recognize these influential clusters of experience before the patient does. He or she may then make an integrative leap, identifying these clusters as the entity we call the self. By naming the self, then by evoking the self's story with its struggles, climax, and, it is hoped, resolution, the therapist breathes life into these clusters of characteristics.

In other words (and this point is crucial) *the formation of self is a small work of fiction.* Characters are created and put into action in the context of the patient's life circumstances. Let me give you an example of how this creation of characters and their thematic development works. I have a patient whose anti-establishment self was so firmly embedded that it was damaging his life. We identified this self through his stories of many geographical moves, a largely absent but authoritarian father, the many exclusions that kept him from feeling part of the new communities into which he moved, and the frustrated, defeated attitudes he expressed toward his current employers.

Paradoxically, in spite of this anti-establishment self, my patient is an executive with a large corporation. With his humane attitude, he tried to merge corporation and community needs, but his purposes were at odds with what the corporation saw as its bottom-line requirements. Because of this incompatibility, as well as his life history, he would speak of himself as an outsider, more like a token of corporate humanity than a serious contributor.

However, not surprisingly he also had an ambitious self, bordering on the grandiose and requiring him to succeed regardless of the clash of values. But the ambitious self as a servant to the anti-establishment self kept him tilting at windmills, dreaming the impossible. When he began to see his ambitious self more broadly, not as a servant of the anti-establishment self, but as a part of his own overall good sense, he found doable tasks to serve his humanitarian purposes. One of the things he did was to create a successful film on the use of company nurseries. He also set up a system to help needy workers. Subsequently, he developed respectful relations among his peers, and then his ideas were welcomed into the corporate decision-making process. Furthermore, cracking through his seriousness, he let himself enjoy his success, a pleasure previously strictly forbidden by the imperious anti-establishment self.

These new experiences called for revision of his anti-establishment self, and one day I told him that I now saw him as a corporation man. He seemed insulted for a moment, but then laughed at the truth of my observation. Nevertheless, corporation man or not, he is clearly his own man—bright, diligent, kind, and cooperative. And all of these characteristics became real to him. He had previously subsumed these characteristics within his anti-establishment self and now they were released to be reapplied in his corporation self, a composite self-accepting membership in the workplace he had chosen.

In spite of what I have said, to talk about selves seems a strange way to talk about a person, as though these selves were the person's tenants or employees or internal sprites. Why not just say that my patient was a person who hated the establishment, but also was ambitious, and that he had overestimated how much he would have to sacrifice his values in order to do his job? Isn't that enough? Often it is. But, what is added by addressing selves is that they become agents of the person: brightly organized, spotlights on otherwise ephemeral existences, banners, so to speak, around which the person rallies his or her psychological energies. Just as a novel creates human images that echo in the minds of its readers, an image of selves also comes alive, giving membership and coherence to otherwise disconnected parts of the person. The therapist uses the device of the self to give life to the patient's experiences, registering them so vividly that the abandoned aspects may be more fully re-experienced, and the fragmented person made whole.

HOW DOES THE SELF FORM?

This brings us to another crucial point. Especially important in the formation of the self is the role of introjection, a much maligned function. Perls said that introjection "means preserving the structure of things taken in, whilst the organism requires their destruction... Any introjection must go through the mill of the molars if it is not to become... a foreign body—a disturbing isolated factor in our existence" (Perls, 1947, p. 129). This point of view, that metaphorical chewing is crucial, often has been taken to mean that the introjecting person is a passive vessel who ingests what the environment serves. If parents do not listen, for example, when a young girl talks, she assumes she is not worth listening to; if people laugh derisively at her, she believes she is a shameful person; if people play with her happily, she infers that she has a right to whatever she wants.

According to this limited and limiting interpretation, introjection, through its indiscriminate inclusiveness and its enduring effects, is seen as a major source of mistaken beliefs about one's self, which it often is. But that is only half of the story. To incorporate the other half, I would like to redefine introjection as *spontaneous receptivity, unimpeded by the deliberative faculties of the mind.* Introjection, in this sense, is to receptivity what Freudian free association is to verbal expression. That is not to say that deliberateness has no place; it is a partner. From this position, we may better appreciate two of introjection's major attributes, which were overlooked by Perls and which contribute enormously to the powers of therapy.

The first attribute of introjection is that it is a wondrous source of learning, extending hospitality to the abundance of the world's offerings. Though introjection is receptivity, it can be an appetitive receptivity. We see the effects of its vibrancy all the way forward from the infant who spontaneously picks up English as a spoken language to a concert-goer enthralled by the music. This same fascination is available in psychotherapy, where the patient may be introjectively infused with the messages implicit in psychotherapeutic exchange.

The second attribute of introjection is that it does not stand alone. In and of itself, introjection has no implications for psychological well-being, no more so than blood circulation does for blood pressure levels. *The key to well-being is not whether we introject, but how well the introjected experiences are integrated into the person.* This integration is facilitated by three operations that together compose the process of introjection: contact, configuration, and tailoring. Each operation will be examined in turn.

The Contact Function

Though the Gestalt principles of contact are extensive, perhaps it is enough to say that contact is the instrument of connection between the individual and the world. Only through contact does the individual meet the world and discover anything to introject. One *hears* one's mother's cooing or scolding voice. One *sees* a smile or a scowl. One is *touched* gently or harshly. When *drinking* milk, the infant *feels* the touch of the mother and *tastes* the milk and *senses* its fluidity and texture. Such contacts, multiplied in power and complexity, are the raw material for introjection.

Whereas it is often believed that a person in good contact is not introjecting, contact and introjection are actually interwoven. So close in touch is the contacting person, as a matter of fact, that he or she emerges momentarily with the other person while paradoxically maintaining and individual identity. This closeness enables the contacting person to tune in sensitively, providing a head start on integrating the introjection. In this sense, food contact is a lubricant for the introjective process. Take, for example, a person who has always felt isolated and lives life according to the expectations of this isolated self. If, in good contact with a therapist or others, the person were to feel understood and valued, this new contact might cause a relaxation of his or her isolated self, while newly introjecting a sense of belonging.

Configuration

The individual seeks a rightful place within the self for new experience and to give relevance and coherence to as much experience as possible. This configurational reflex is a crucial determinant of the future of the introjection, particularly as to whether or not it turns out to be "healthy."

At first the child, with only scant experience, has little that is already established to which he or she must connect any new experience; the child's skill in determining what fits is minimal. Certain early difficulties, such as terrible milk and brutal treatment, would be manifestly alien to the already formed biological needs. But most of what enters comes in on the ground floor of the organism, and the child's freedom to introject is great because it is easy to fit his or her experience into the relatively few requirements. Much of what happens just fits, and it is only natural to feel that life is just as it uncomplicatedly is.

The fewer the contradictions between what already exists in the child and what he or she is newly receiving, the easier the configurational process becomes. But as this world of connections achieves greater definition—as in learning a particular language, developing individual body posture, living by certain moral rules, or recognizing dangers—the requirements for acceptable fit become more challenging. For example, it makes less difference who is tending the baby at 2 months of age than at 7 months, as the connections with the mother have been strongly formed by then and the baby will find it difficult to accept a substitute.

Other examples of differing experiences that would be hard to integrate would be experiences of hunger and the contradictory delay of food, aggressive impulses and the contradictory behavioral suppression, or sensuality and the contradictory requirement for distance. Or a generous little boy may have to reconcile his own actual generosity with his father's scolding him for being stingy. Or a girl trained to crave success may be thrown by being told she is stupid. Clearly, it is no small matter to navigate through a sea of contradictions we all face, especially because the formation of our selves is always on the line.

Tailoring

This is a process similar to the Perlsian concept of the mill of the grinding molars, which calls for the destructuring of gestalt patterns. As the child grows and as failures in connection accumulate, causing psychological pain, the individual must first assess the prospects for successfully interconnecting new stimulations with those already in place, rejecting those that would not fit. Then he or she also remodels experiences that would not fit in their present state, but would if they were altered. The remodeling comes through a number of activities, such as criticizing, objecting, revising, educating, digesting, suggesting, commanding, and all the range of things people do to try to make the world of ideas, things, and other people harmonious with themselves. These tailoring functions are all devoted to maximizing the success of the configurational reflex in interconnecting all that is taken in.

Nevertheless, in spite of our skills in contact, configuration, and tailoring, we are all more or less in trouble because, in trying to get a coherent sense of self, we often will have to isolate those parts of our experiences that do not fit. In the service of coherence, alienation among seemingly incompatible characteristics or selves leaves the person with a narrow or fragmented self-image. Such alienation—dissociation, when it is extreme—is a major source of self-distortion because certain parts of the person begin to count more than the whole person. Thus it is not the introjection itself that causes trouble, as is commonly believed, but alienated introjections—and their dissociative influence.

THERAPEUTIC PROCEDURES

Because of the pivotal disconnections represented in these alienations, therapy becomes an exercise in reconnection. Three primary means for creating connections are (1) the extraordinary engagement between therapist and patient, (2) the restoration of engagement among alienated selves, and (3) the uncovering of a unifying story line that interconnects a sequence of events. Each will be addressed in order.

Extraordinary Engagement Between Therapist and Patient

The extraordinariness to which I refer is common psychotherapeutic fare. For most people, just walking into a therapist's office makes them feel as though they are putting their very selfhood on the line. It takes no special tricks of charisma on the part of the therapist to turn this event into a great psychological adventure. It is enough for the therapist in this extraordinary context to exercise ordinary kindness, simplicity, clear-mindedness, good language, recognition of implication, and an enduring fascination with life of the patient. I would especially emphasize an enduring fascination. With an optimal exercise of these qualities by the therapist, the patient's connection with the therapist develops considerable magnitude. The relationship is then in a position to compete for influence with the patient's lifelong adherence to anachronistic selves.

One of the special instruments of this paradoxical interplay between the extraordinary and the therapeutically simple is the concept of sequential fit. Here is what I mean: Each moment of experience gives off its hints for what would seem like a naturally occurring subsequent statement, feeling, or act. Without the therapist's help, the patient cannot move into these moments because he or she is preoccupied or is otherwise geared to disconnect whatever he or she is doing from its immediately following probability. The patient blocks—by repetitions, deletions, changing the subject, abstractions that do not get fleshed out, confusion, circumstantiality, and so on.

If the therapist helps the person out of this choppy existence and into the ensuing experiences, one following the other, the patient soon will enter into the stream of what seems like *inevitably* "next" moments, accompanied by profound absorption and open-mindedness. When the therapist sensitively develops this sequential fluidity, the patient's embeddedness in the process reduces internal deliberations. The patient thus slips into a mental groove where he or she becomes hospitable to thoughts and feelings that previously would have been unacceptable.

This confidence in the power of sequentially faithful experiences has long been evident in the way that Gestalt therapists focus on the awareness continuum. We believe attention to people's own continuing experience stimulates a directionalism that will help lead them to where they need to go. Carl Rogers developed a comparable momentum through his continuing clarifications of his patients' statements, always offering improved language that would better move them forward into the naturally occurring next statement. Milton Erickson's stories, as well, would incline the rapt listener toward moves that he or she would unconsciously pursue.

Upon developing a sense of the rightness of conversational direction, the patient is released from some of the control of the tailoring phase of the introjection process. With a lowered need for tailoring, the chances are greater that one will say whatever one wants to say and will accept new ideas, much as in the early days of guileless receptivity. Here is an example: A patient made a snide reference to his mother's effervescent way of speaking, although it was evident that he, with his heavy vocal tones, could benefit from her style. In discussing her effervescence, as one thing led to the next, I asked him to imitate her voice. At this point it seemed the natural thing to do, and when he did, the lighthearted self inside him appeared.

The appearance of his lighthearted self led him to further spontaneity and soon he told me what he would not have told me before. At the age of 5, he had had sexual feelings for his mother. It would have been difficult for him to admit these feelings before he imitated her voice, but he welcomed them after doing so. He then went on to tell me that he had been able to smell her and feel himself against her clothes and he adored her. But he was called a "mama's boy" which he accepted as though it were God's own truth. Since the stigma scared him, he stiffened against the mama's boy image, never at ease in closeness to his mother, believing his sexual feelings might betray a "mama's boy self." When I jokingly added that he had really been "mama's little fucker," he reddened and laughed lyrically.

Through these simple sequences, my patient had swung into a mood in which each next statement or feeling was spontaneously valid, untailored. These pieces just fit together and he absorbed the validity of his sexual self, undeliberately softening the old mama's-boy introjection.

So far I have been discussing the actual relationship between therapist and patient: telling, responding, suggesting, laughing, experimenting, all that is actually going on. Adding, however, to the power of the actual engagement is the symbolic component represented in the transference phenomenon. Historically, transference has been a prime tool of reconnection, but it has had double-edged implications. Transference has been used to take the therapist *out* of the relationship with the patient by assigning implications that deflected from the actual contact, thereby, unfortunately, diminishing connectedness. I think we are all familiar with therapists' denying the direct validity of what patients say about them.

There is another implication, however, that is more empowering. The transference recognition makes the therapist a *party* to the entire life history of the patient, *intertwined* as the interpretations insinuate the therapist into the most intimate fabric of the individual's history. Through the transference, the therapist is no longer just another person, but has elements of everybody who matters in the patient's life. Such consequences are extremely absorbing. This absorption and the accompanying trust often lead to lessened deliberation by the patient, who becomes more open to both the benefits and the dangers of new introjections.

This powerful leverage is often squandered by the therapist's limitations: our pretended knowledge, our undiscerning goals, our ambitions and shame regarding failure and success, our homage to stereotypical procedure, and our insensitivities to the actual process of the patient. It can also be used abusively or exploitatively by therapists who are willing to play God. None of us is safe from such professional hazards and we can only note them here. Yet, in concert with all the necessary cautionary factors, the therapist may make use of the introjective opportunities provided by his or her special centrality to catch up with the advantage already gained by the early infusion of alienating influences. The therapist as a newly unforgettable, merging force is an antidote to the embeddedness of those outdated impressions that are unaffected by *ordinary* new experience. The new experience, therefore, must be so absorbing that the patient will be influenced as though young again.

The Restoration of Engagement Among Alienated Selves of the Person

The therapist promotes reconnection by restoring dialogue among constituent selves. Befitting the experiential spirit, Gestalt therapy long ago developed a two-part concept of the self in action. First came the concept of neurotic splitting, which also found a place later in object-relations theory. Perls, Hefferline, and Goodman said, "In a neurotic splitting, one part is kept unconscious, or it is...alienated from concern, or both parts are carefully isolated from each other..."(Perls, Hefferline and Goodman, 1951, p.240). Second came the technique of personifying the split parts and creating a dialogue among these parts.

As I have previously written, "With all these characters living inside the person, the therapist working with any individual is actually doing group therapy" (Polster, 1987, p.115). Let me illustrate this kind of "group" therapy. One patient, a contractor, felt he had made a terrible mistake in taking a certain difficult and unusually lengthy job. He was angry with several people who had advised him to take the job and especially with the other party to the contract, who had lied to him. But he still blamed himself heavily even though he should have been relieved to be almost finished with the project.

I asked him to play out a conversation between his conflicted selves, which he saw as his naive self, referring to the time when he made the decision, and his bitter self, referring to the way he was currently behaving. The two sides spoke carefully to each other, the bitter self with cool anger and the naive self with cool apology. After a few more exchanges, the bitter self got more angry and the naive self became afraid.

At my suggestion, the naive self started to tell the bitter self how afraid he was getting. As he was talking, he remembered a long time ago when he had become furious at a boy in his neighborhood who had plagued him with insults, until he could no longer take them. The naive self said that he had "lost it" one day and finally beat the other kid up so badly that he believed he would have murdered him if the fight had not been stopped. He had blacked out and now "knew" he would have continued mindlessly to bang the boy's head on the cement. He went on to tell of other memories of his many rages and temper tantrums. The naive self, afraid of this murderous self, overlooked the spunkiness that was distorted into the specter of a mad murderer. The bitter self also got into the act, telling me he was afraid his bitterness might be escalated by the dissociated murderer. If not careful, he might throw his chair at my computer, break my statues, turn over my desk, tear my room apart.

Not surprisingly, my patient was greatly relieved just to be able to say these things. More important, though, he was able to reconnect his alienated selves. First, the naive and bitter selves were reconnected in their dialogue. Next, they unearthed another member of the "group," the even more seriously alienated self, the mad murderer, whom my patient was also able to accommodate. Then, his discovering the spunky self under the shadow of his murderous self added one more member to the group, a key participant whose voice merited attention. With all these characters operating safely together, my patient was able to talk to me without the earlier self-recrimination.

Unifying Story Line

A unifying story line is a vehicle for connection. Stories are the gathering of experiences; through their thematic development, they transform otherwise unconnected events into a meaningful unity. When a patient told me, first, that his mother had died when he was 7 years old, and, second, that from then on his father periodically would mope, and, third, that he would repeat the words, "It can't work," he was connecting these experiences. Then, when he also said that he had made up his mind right then, at age 7, never to feel like a failure, he put down a marker acknowledging the continuity through is life. Normally, stories are so readily heard as a whole unit that their role in connecting discrete experiences is overlooked.

Stories all contain elements of the teller's self, reflected in the characters and their behavior. My earlier patient's murderous self was revealed in his blacked-out battering of the neighborhood boy. When he told the story, he made vivid a vicious fight that had lived in his mind only as a pale abstraction, an immaterial dread of the wanton—felt not even as fear, but as resignation. A patient who tells such stories offers a peephole into his or her self, a hint about the breadth of the patient's life. When this hint is recognized and elaborated throughout the story line, we have gone beyond stagnant "titles" that, by themselves, keep self designations fixed in position. These designations come to life as they receive clarification from the action, continuity, and thematic developments that evolve.

CONCLUSION

I have tried to show the self as a harmonic interplay between classification and action. The formation of the self and its constituent selves is highly influenced by introjection, a process that creates strong embeddedness. To counteract this embeddedness, it is important to take into account the process of introjection, redefined to embrace its renewal powers. I have described three procedures for creating such renewal, each developing high absorption and each tapping into nondeliberative, introjective learning energy. The first was the immersion in the therapeutic relationship through an inclusive transference and through sequential fit; second was the restoration of connections among alienated selves; and third was the evocation of a story line that reveals the drama in the patient's life and reconnects many experiences. A patient who is enabled to harmonize these contributors to a sense of self will enrich the identity by which he or she measures existence.

Translating Theory into Practice: Martin Heidegger and Gestalt Therapy

Erving Polster

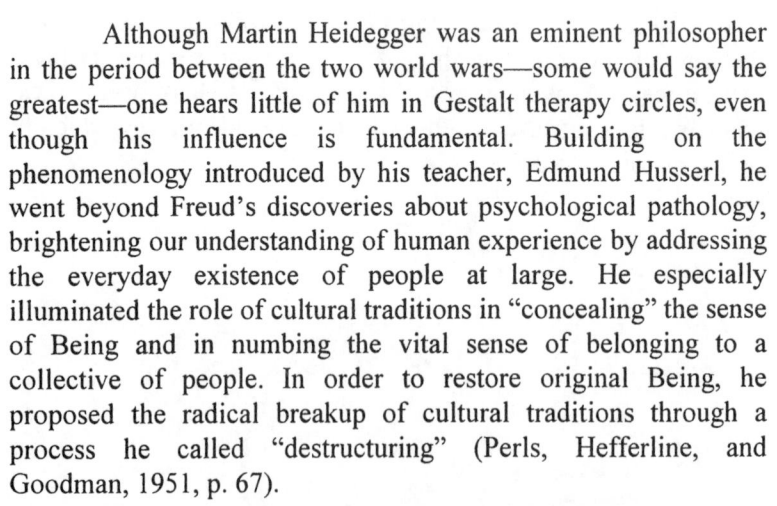

Although Martin Heidegger was an eminent philosopher in the period between the two world wars—some would say the greatest—one hears little of him in Gestalt therapy circles, even though his influence is fundamental. Building on the phenomenology introduced by his teacher, Edmund Husserl, he went beyond Freud's discoveries about psychological pathology, brightening our understanding of human experience by addressing the everyday existence of people at large. He especially illuminated the role of cultural traditions in "concealing" the sense of Being and in numbing the vital sense of belonging to a collective of people. In order to restore original Being, he proposed the radical breakup of cultural traditions through a process he called "destructuring" (Perls, Hefferline, and Goodman, 1951, p. 67).

Then, at the peak of his philosophical authority, he made the colossal blunder of accepting the Nazi party as an instrument for satisfying one of his philosophical imperatives; to unite concept and act. He became a partner with Nazism in trying politically to recover what he saw as Germany's loss of Being, which had been beaten down in the aftermath of World War I. In trying to apply his philosophical positions to social action, one might say he saw himself, as well as the Nazi party, as psychotherapists for the German society which, through their guidance, would be reunited with the destiny that remained hidden underneath obscuring cultural forces.

In addition to the drama of the fallen idol, Heidegger may also be interesting to Gestalt therapists for two other reasons. First, his philosophical positions concerning *Being, time, destiny* and the *manner* of people's expression were a harbinger for Perl's parallel development of his concepts of *awareness, awareness continuum* and the accentuation of *"how and now"*. Second, Heidegger's aborted union of his philosophical concepts with political action underscored the vulnerability also faced by Gestalt therapy in trying to transpose its theoretical complexity into an easily applied therapy. Both Heidegger and Perls did what the other theorists have also done; they oversimplified their message, largely through sidestepping the diversity of concepts, as well as the seeming contradictions, within their theories.

Neither Perls nor Heidegger was prepared by previous experience for the unprecedented social circumstances each came to face. They both got into situations calling for quick communication of complex concepts to large numbers of people. Heidegger, stepping out of his role as an abstract thinker, could do little more than provide a philosophical fig leaf for a vicious dictatorship. Perls, on the other hand, did not have to step out of role since he always worked as a psychotherapist. His theoretical and procedural contributions moved recognizably along pathways already implied in his previous work, revised by him to flesh out a new theory. Nevertheless, Perls also got caught up in new communication requirements. He, too, chose to unite concept and act, and he recognized the free-standing workshop format as an excellent vehicle for experiential teaching. Concept and act were easily united but time for getting ideas across was short compared with academic environments, and experiences became intense and narrowly personalized.

In both settings—Heidegger's political arena and Perls's workshop—attention to the interrelationship among diverse concepts was diminished, replaced by favored concepts, often received as slogans.

The heritage of oversimplification remains with Gestalt therapy even today. Perhaps that is the fate of any therapy theory; psychoanalysis doesn't really require free association, Rogerian therapy doesn't really call for repetition of what the patient has already said, cognitive therapists care very much about feelings, and Gestalt therapy is much more than the empty chair. Yet the idea that Gestalt therapy *is* this or that particular concept still influences some of its practitioners. The restoration of self-support, for one example, has been seen as a defining purpose for many Gestalt therapists. However, the theory itself gives equal billing to the persistent need for environmental support. Some writers have described field theory as an indispensable foundation, but Gestalt therapy theory, characterizing interconnectedness as basic to existence, is also consonant with holism or systems theory. Some writers think of the loss of ego functions as definitive in personal dysfunction, while Gestalt therapy also focuses on intrapersonal splits and their synthesis. There are many examples of such diversity and of therapists who choose one or another principle as the *sine qua non* of Gestalt therapy.

In addressing the question of the wholeness of Gestalt therapy and its accomodation of diversity, I would like to examine three themes: first, the lessons to be learned from Heidegger's failure to keep faith with his philosophical positions; second, Perls's version of Heideggerian themes, which had permeated the German intellectual landscape; and third, the proposal of two concepts, *point/counterpoint* and *dimensionalism*, which could help retain the integrity of Gestalt therapy theory while honoring a large range of compatible concepts and diverse personal styles and repertoires of individual Gestalt theorists and practitioners.

HEIDEGGER'S POLITICAL TRANSFORMATIONS

Heidegger's views on Being, destiny, depersonalization and holism signaled new realizations of the human surge for interconnectedness among any universe of experiences. Writing contemporaneously with the Gestalt learning theorists, he went beyond their beliefs in *perception* as a holistic phenomenon by also postulating the unity of past, present, and future and the primal quality of the human collective. This expansion of holism beyond the concept of perceptual Gestalt formation paralleled a later adaptation by Perls, who stretched the relevance of Gestalt formation to the complex process of psychotherapy.

Heidegger's ambition to change a nation was more formidable than Perls's ambition to change a therapy, but Perls also extended his work beyond his familiar constituency— psychotherapy patients. In the 1950s he became a key player in the new national excitement about psychotherapy, carrying its relevance beyond symptomatology and into the problems of ordinary growth. This contributed to the expansion of popular interest in psychotherapy itself and also to the creation of a new range of permissible experience, both prominent themes in the culture of the day. People of diverse populations who had not previously been drawn to psychotherapy began to flock to growth groups of many kinds and to psychotherapy itself. Both Perls and Heidegger were already represented by theoretical tomes, epoch-making for their professional constituencies, but these works were too complex for the glancing attention of their new publics (Perls, et al., 1951 Heidegger, 1962).

Heidegger had the greater challenge, of course, having gone so far from his philosophical roots. For a man aiming for the populist goal of awakening the German people to their spiritual mission, Heidegger's philosophical principles were unfittingly elusive. Furthermore, his writing style was composed of a mixture of convoluted philosophical discourse and misty poetic allusion, baffling even to philosophers. Isaiah Berlin, renowned explorer in the history of ideas said that he could not understand Heidegger's language or views, and referred to the "dark Heideggerian forest" (Berlin, 1996, pp. 50, 64).

Here is one example of Heidegger's dense philosophical/poetic style, from which he later created clarity by political oversimplification

> Insofar as Being constitutes what is asked about, and insofar as Being means the Being of beings, beings themselves turn out to be what is *interrogated* in the question of Being....Everything we talk about, everything we have in view, everything towards which we comport ourselves in any way, is being; what we are is being, and so is how we are. Being lies in the fact that something is...in presence-at-hand; in subsistence; in validity; in Dasein; in the 'there is'. (p.27)

Even the sophisticated reader will not walk away whistling this melody, but *will* get a sense of the importance and mystery of self-experience.

The political activist is nowhere evident in this philosophical/poetic portrait. Instead, the philosopher tells us about the certitude and ubiquity of Being, and the poet uses idiom and allusion to invite the reader to his own understanding of what it is to have a life revealed as Being. They both have a spiritual ring, more a catalyst for new insights than a direction to behavior and purpose. Certainly, neither uses the commanding words of a political activist.

Nevertheless, in spite of his spiritual tones, Heidegger was no softy; in fact he was apocalyptic, calling for the radical break-up of tradition and technology. As Lowith (1993) has observed, Heidegger's affiliation with Hitler was altogether faithful to his philosophical "will to rupture, revolution and awakening", which Lowith ascribes to Heidegger's post-World War I "awareness of ruination and decline" (p. 183). Isaiah Berlin

(1996), in similar interpretation, likened Heidegger to Bertrand Russell in breaking down traditional metaphysics (p.64). To my mind, Heidegger also shared much with surrealistic artists of his day in wishing to restructure—even fracture—the way we look at the world, seeking a fresh start by scrambling what Gestalt therapists would call fixed gestalt formations, the traditions we take for granted. Fatherhood, search for success, civil behavior, sexual boundaries, and other manifestations of social tradition would all be affected by this call for a new scrutiny of the ordinary sense of reality. But he saw society's constraints to be so fixed that only extreme acts of courage could loosen the bonds of tradition for a return to authentic Being.

In 1933, after some original unwillingness, Heidegger answered the call by agreeing to accept the rectorship of the University of Freiberg. In this role, he made huge leaps into demagogic simplicity. During the first year of his philosophical-political coalescence, he transposed high-level existential abstractions into cheerleading for Hitlerian politics. In the following speech, compare the sense of mandate with his philosophically exploratory language. After declaring independence from idle thought-without-power, he exhorted the student body by saying

> For a volkische Wissenschaft, courage either to grow or be destroyed in confrontation with Being, which is the first form of courage....For courage lures one forward; courage frees itself from what has been up to now; courage risks the unaccustomed and the incalculable....
>
> From now on, each and every thing demands decision, and every deed demands responsibility...The choice that the German people must now make is, *simply as an event in itself,* quite independently of the outcome, the strongest expression of the new German reality embodied in the National Socialist State. Our will to national self-responsibility desires that each people find and preserve the greatness and truth of its destiny. This

will is the highest guarantee of peace among nations, for it binds itself to the basic law of manly respect and unconditional honor. The fuhrer has awakened this will in the entire people and has welded it into *one* single resolve. No one can remain away from the polls on the day when this will is manifested. Heil Hitler! (Wolin, 1993, pp. 51, 52)

Here we see him close his speech with an authoritarian insistence to do-it-or-else. While still retaining the raw outline of philosophical concepts, he quickly transforms them into inspirational messages. Many of these concepts, themselves, are familiar to existentialists in general and to Gestalt therapists in particular: the courage to grow; every deed demanding responsibility; choice; simply an event in itself, quite independent of the outcome; the oneness of resolve; and participation.

What is disturbingly apparent in these exhortations is that Heidegger is no longer speaking about *what* the student body should do but only *how* to do it. However, this differs from his philosophical definition of Being, cited above (p. 6) where he generously encompasses the *what* of experience, including "everything we talk about [and] everything we have in view". This broad range of the events that are enveloped within his sense of Being disappears as he ticks off the necessary resolves. To have taken account of the awful events with which a call to courage would come to be associated would, of course, have diluted his politics and his inspirational powers. But, for some people, courage later included murder, vilification, book burning, and a mindless conformity to leadership. Heidegger's excess in emphasizing the *how* of experience over its content continued, however, even beyond the war, as is evident in the following observation he made, as late as 1949. He said

Agriculture today is a motorized food industry, in essence the same as the manufacture of corpses in gas chambers and extermination camps, the same as the blockade and starvation of countries, the same as the manufacture of atomic bombs. (Wolin, 1993, pp. 290, 291).

Clearly, Heidegger's philosophy was bent on damning technology. While he rightfully saw motorized agriculture and the manufacture of corpses and atomic bombs as having a common technological character, each with its own poisons, it is an empty understanding of the evils and benefits of technology if he disregards the differences. Such disregard of relationship between the "how" and the "what" of behavior oversimplifies Heidegger's observation about technology, and it fosters sharp communication. The price he pays for such one-sidedness is the diminishment of holism, an otherwise insistent theme in his philosophy.

Here are some further examples of Heidegger's political subversion of his theory.

First: when he recommended to his student body that any experiences is *"simply an event in itself,* quite independently of the outcome," he contradicted his philosophical concept of destiny. This concept had its roots in the merging of past, present and future into a unified whole, dislodging the familiar separation between event and outcome. What would have been more faithful to his own concept would have been to say that the current event, rather than independent of outcome, already carries the seed of the future, a key dynamism in the developing outcome. For the philosopher in Heidegger, each person is called to a faith that outcomes will indeed be true to one's authentic living. But, politically, for Heidegger to make the event *independent* of the outcome could foster unquestioning loyalty rather than faith in one's own process and could, further, be easily interpreted as an excuse for vicious behavior.

This is no small matter for Gestalt therapists either, who also gave primacy to the *event itself* and were often *misunderstood* to disregard experiences of the past and future.

However, Gestalt therapy holds that every event exists *in the ground* within which it happens. Both outcomes and precedents are indispensably included!

Second: Though he was willing to accept Hitler's obliteration of opposition when he was wearing his political hat Heidegger (1993), in his philosophical mode, said

> In essential striving...the opponents raise each other into the self-assertion of their natures. Self-assertion of nature, however, is never a rigid insistence upon some contingent state, but surrender to the concealed originality of the source of one's own being. In the struggle, each opponent carries the other beyond itself (p. 174).

This relational credo portrays dialogical participants who influence each other. If he had followed this credo more carefully, honoring the corrective impact of struggle with the "other" and wary of the single isolated principle, he might more readily have recognized his philosophical incompatibility with the Nazi regime. But he became so consumed only with the prospects of a restored spirit for the German people *themselves* and as *he* characterized them—to say nothing of the activist opportunity to confirm his philosophical postulations about Being and destiny—that he failed to counter the Nazi absolutism and opposition to dialogue. He dreamed instead of the new world of holistic Being he would have helped create.

Third: Heidegger was philosophically dedicated to the *collective* communal experience. Politically, however, it became expedient to exclude challenges to the collective's wholeness through the exclusion of those decreed to be outsiders. What is important to recognize about holism—and what he recognized philosophically—is that wholeness is continuingly forming and reforming; by its very nature it always faces the risk of fragmentation. As Heidegger (1962) himself said in his philosophical mode

> Being-in-the-world is a structure which is primordially and constantly *whole*...To be sure, the constitution of the structural whole and its everyday kind of Being, is phenomenally so *manifold* that it can easily obstruct

our looking at the whole as such in a way which is *unified.* [p.225].

This statement is a reminder that the fluidity of wholeness is maintained only through continuing responsiveness to its paradoxically "manifold" nature and requires continuing integration. The need for wholeness is so primordial, so compelling, that it is often achieved *prematurely* through the exclusion of contradiction and diversity, whether this be the exclusion of certain people or certain principles. This exclusionary process does not come easily because it is opposed by the alienated forces that continue to seek union. The resulting fluidity of this configurational process leaves much room for error and instability; unwisely formed exclusions will create losses that may prove to be haunting handicaps. A biblical example of the rigid need for wholeness is the admonition to those who "looketh" with lust: "If thy right eye offend thee, pluck it out," (Matthew 5:28-30) a heavy price to pay for exclusionary wholeness.

In keeping with Heidegger's urgency to enhance the German collective, he enunciated responsibilities for achieving wholeness. The first condition was the requirement that for each person to "bind" to the ethnic and national community through *labor service,* including sharing the "toil" of the Volk in labor camps. The second condition was to embrace *military service.* The third condition which he called *knowledge service,* called for knowledge to be geared to the spiritual mission of the *Volk.*

Professional knowledge, for example, would no longer be in the service of training for a freestanding profession. Rather, the professions were to "realize and administer the Volk's highest and most essential knowledge, that of its entire existence" (Heidegger 1993, p. 35), a large claim for knowledge and a stunning assignment of servitude.

This servitude reverses the freedom to discover and to accumulate knowledge, irrespective of its fit with already established purposes. So, for the unification of the *Volk,* Heidegger insisted that labor service, military service, and knowledge service were all to be consciously geared to the holistic needs of the *Volk*. Though he recognized the rightful place of struggle between teacher and student, this became mere lip service in an atmosphere of dictatorial holism. The concept of synthesis became paradoxically imprisoned by frozen purpose. Without the inclusion of contradiction and differentiation, synthesis becomes not only unnecessary, but meaningless.

After a year in the rectorship of the University of Freiberg, Heidegger realized what he had gotten himself into, and he resigned the post. What he did after his resignation has been a subject of controversy. Some people never forgave him for his collaboration. Some accused him of collaborating even after his resignation as rector. Some believed he did the best he could under dangerous circumstances. Some continued to honor his great philosophical contributions, and others remembered his charm and brilliance as a teacher. Whatever judgments may be made about him on those scores, the Heidegger phenomenon raises alarm bells for psychotherapists who, every day, face the risks of reductionism, oversimplification, and mechanization of the theories that guide them.

LINKS BETWEEN HEIDEGGER AND GESTALT THERAPY

Surprisingly, since Gestalt therapy has long recognized itself as an existentialist therapy, Heidegger himself is rarely cited. There have been other more direct influences on Gestalt therapy, including the Gestalt learning theorists and a number of psychoanalytic dissidents, such as Rank, Reich, Ferenczi, Moreno, Jung, Adler, and Horney. Still, it was Heidegger whose broad philosophical landscape set a tone that was a key link in the chain of influences. As Steiner (1989) says

> Sartre's philosophical writings are, in essence, commentaries on *Sein und Zeit*. The entire repertoire of

"engagement", "commitment", "taking upon oneself", "freedom of being", "authenticity", "the inalienability of one's death", in Sartre, Camus, and their innumerable epigones is Heideggerian in root and branch (p. 151).

Heidegger's ideas concerning Being and Time were forerunners for Perls' emphasis on the here-and-now. Heidegger declared that Being "always is as and what it already was. Whether explicitly or not, it *is* its past." Although Being was traditionally seen as a timeless essence of the living experience, Heidegger united Being with Time. He showed that the Being of any moment had a developmental urgency, that the seeds of any moment's evolving experience were inherent to and already represented in an indivisible future. In portraying this union, Heidegger was referring, as Steiner says, not to "living in time" but, rather, "living time" (Steiner, 1989, p. 78). Thus the past could not be seen to *cause* the future, as the prevailing view had been; they were permanently interwoven, a union which could only be blurred by the distractions of traditional attitudes of separation and isolation.

This indivisibility between past, present, and future was best represented in Heidegger's view of destiny, a guiding force in connecting events historically (Steiner, 1989, pp. 110-112). The "towardness" (Steiner, 1989, p.113) of destiny was an insistent momentum into the future, fed by past experience, both the individual's and, more importantly, the community's. Therefore destiny, while magnetizing the community to its own accumulated history, calls also upon each individual to yield to this communal "towardness" in order for his Being to be fully realized.

These concepts are difficult to understand. But the misty insights offered by the poetic allusion to the unity of Being and Time have been a force pointing us toward the goal of communal connectedness and feeling a bond among the infinite succession of events in a person's life, in spite of alienations and fragmentations. Heidegger's concepts, therefore, found a responsive chord in the psyche of a depersonalized culture, where the connectedness that Heidegger postulated served conceptually to take the individual out of his or her isolation and into a network of experiences as people. Heidegger's view of the unity of Being and Time and the personal themes they play out as destiny accentuated a growing realization of the primacy of a person's embeddedness in both the flow of time and the supernal community.

Perls abridged this intricate view of the indivisibility of past, present, and future by saying that the present is all that exists. Just as simple as that. He added a crucial stipulation, often ignored, by saying that the past and future were represented in the present through the functions of remembering and anticipation (Perls, et al., 1951, pp. 290-292). This stipulation brings him close to Heidegger's unified view of time. But the inclusion of remembering and anticipation as present function, almost as footnote, does not represent the full measure of Heidegger's profound inclusion of time as a key ingredient in a unified sense of Being. Rather, Perls' focus on the present itself was so strong that he weakened interest in those events that were not happening in the manifest here-and-now.

Therapeutically, Perls' accentuation of the here-and-now enhanced the powers of both therapists and patients to focus sharply on the issues they were addressing. The therapeutic empowerment was revelatory to many therapists and to their patients, but valuable though it was, it left Gestalt therapy vulnerable to a lessened attention to the relationship between "here and now" and "there and then", thus reducing the sense of a whole life lived (Polster, 1987).

Still, synthesis was very much on Perls' mind. He recognized the fractured holism inherent to disconnected experiences, which led him to one of his key understandings of dysfunctional living and to a key therapeutic procedure. He became sensitized to psychological splitting. To restore the patient to a sense of wholeness, he sought to improve the quality of contact between the alienated splits within the person. He dramatized these splits by calling them topdog and underdog, and he evoked the suppressed dialogue between them. This internal pluralism was a clearly understandable dramatization of what Heidegger might have described as Being's "manifold" characteristics.

Heidegger's philosophy filled the German intellect when Perls was forming his points of view, and he must have been influenced by it. But he was a psychoanalyst already burdened by intellectualism and wanted to accent simple experience. So, he incorporated a familiar word from everyday language, *awareness*, as a key focus of his theory. Where Heidegger's Being might have addressed the concept "I am", Perls was more concerned with "I am aware", bypassing as search for the more philosophical meanings of the nature of Being.

When the therapist asks the patient what he is aware of, the question points to particular experiences. The patient will respond concretely by saying I am hungry or I am sad or I am shivering or, even paradoxically, I am confused by your question. Therefore to ask about awareness, rather than Being, was a great increase in linguistic accessibility, making it a more therapeutically practical question. Though the concept of awareness moves closer than the concept of Being to ordinary therapeutic utility, it remains in the family of Being by calling for the revelation of qualities of existence, of is-ness, as Heidegger might put it, calling attention to sensations, emotions, acts, and values, all aspects of Being, normally "concealed" by intellectualism, tradition, technology or the funneling priorities of everyday life.

Building on awareness, Perls introduced the *awareness continuum*, which was a variation on Heidegger's concept of destiny (Perls, 1969, p. 51). With the concept of the awareness continuum, Perls helped turn psychotherapy away from its concern with *insight* and toward the patient's *movement* through time, each awareness revealed in a step-by-step process. He believed that if the patient would yield to the sweep of the awareness continuum, this would restore fluidity, dissolving the interferences created by unfinished business from the past. Then, once the business of the past was finished, the future would be open sailing, facing new problems released from fixed habits of mind—in Heidegger's language, having destructured tradition and technology for a return to authentic Being.

Perls' self-regulatory naturalism was one of the most impressive aspects of his original teaching. His *awareness continuum* shared with Heidegger's *destiny* a sense of the generic unity of the past, present, and future, a faith that the succession of awareness, accurately recognized, would in their interconnectedness surge forward, steering the patient to his organically right goals. Perls' awareness continuum differed from Heidegger's destiny through his accentuation of the freedom beyond the impasse to face up to a wide open directionalism. Destiny—in common usage and in Heidegger's own sense of historical urgency—is more prophetically embedded in the developmental process. It is only a slight exaggeration to call destiny a directionalism that sweeps one along by the force of an irresistible existential magnetism. With this view of destiny and its implication for a submission to a built-in holism, there is less room than offered by the awareness continuum to take account of the inevitable fragmentations, alienations, and disruptions of continuity and wholeness that plague every person.

Perls, though he expanded beyond the philosophical reliance on destiny and freed the person from historical determinism, nevertheless exercised his own brand of singlemindedness and oversimplification. The seminal text, *Gestalt Therapy*, is a complex articulation of the interwoven roles of awareness, contact, concentration, excitement, action, figure/ground interrelationships, and the centrality of communal effect on any personal experience (Perls, et al., 1951, p. 464) Perls et al. say, for example

The problem of contacting the lost ego-function is no different from any other problem of creative orientation and manipulation, for the unawareness, or the unsatisfactory kind of awareness, is felt simply as another obstacle in the organism/environment field. It is necessary to need, approach, destroy, in order to identify, contact, and assimilate. (p. 464)

The plurality of concerns reflected in "need, approach, destroy, identify, contact and assimilate" was too much for quick and inspirational communication. Instead, Perls proceeded, much as did Heidegger, to sloganize Gestalt therapy's theoretical position by saying, for example, that "everything is awareness" (Perls, 1969, p. 51). This blurring of the range of relational options influenced many Gestalt therapists to emphasize internal experience and to interrupt natural conversational process by exploring self-awareness. However, in theoretical faithfulness, the equal forces of *contact* and *action* must always be coordinated with the restoration of awareness. Perls' recognition of the therapeutic impact of heightened and expanded awareness caught on and helped to transform an overemphasis on insight into recognition of the therapeutic leverage created by strongly focused direct experience. But the increased attention to awareness would be empty if not joined with the creation of relationships, imagination, skill development, and many other functions with which self-awareness is reciprocal. Indeed, if anything were to be "everything" in Gestalt therapy, it would be the reciprocity among all the person's functions (Polster, 1995, pp. 7-10).

DIVERSITY WITHIN A UNIFIED THEORY

The reconciliation of diverse, sometimes seemingly contradictory, concepts is a requirement for maintaining the unity of a theory. The difficulty in accomplishing this reconciliation partially accounts for the skewing of theories. Therapists prioritize. So do the originators of theory. It is perhaps inevitable that Heidegger and Perls would sidestep some of their own diversity and contradiction. To do otherwise—to take contradictions always into account—is an action-delaying luxury that theoreticians can more easily afford than the political activist or engaged psychotherapist. Nevertheless, the practicality of personal priorities should not *define* a theory.

I propose two unifying principles that will both honor the breadth of Gestalt therapy, as well as its pointedness, and enable each therapist to exercise her own style and repertoire. The unifying concepts are point/counterpoint and dimensionalism.

The point/counterpoint relationship refers to the simultaneous relevance of two or more therapeutic concepts, with one ascendant, while others just as valid may serve as lesser guides. There are many examples of these point/counterpoint relationships in Gestalt therapy, too many to cover in this article. The one I will illustrate here is the point/counterpoint relationship between *process* and *content*, a relationship that both Heidegger and Perls neglected. Process and content are always simultaneously active though the therapist may at any particular time give greater emphasis to one or the other.

There are two meanings of process. One is the recognition that *flow* of therapeutic events is the major therapeutic vehicle, more important than attention to any particular single event or any single meaning. The process represented in this sequence of experience is reflected in the concept of the awareness continuum. In attending to this flow of experience, the therapist is enabled to help restore movement, but the *content* is also inevitably registered as the storyline unfolds.

Process also refers to the *how* of experience rather than the *what*, a distinction made central by both Heidegger and Perls. Heidegger said

> What is given and is explicable in the way we encounter the phenomenon is called 'phenomenal'. In this sense we speak of phenomenal structures.

Everything that belongs to the *manner of indication and explication* [italics mine]...is called 'phenomenological' (Krell, 1993, pp. 83, 84).

Perls stated his case even more strongly, paralleling Heidegger's emphasis on the "manner of indication and explication." Sweeping past a large range of his own theory, Perls (1969) said

> These are the two legs upon which Gestalt Therapy walks: *now* and *how*....*Now* covers all that exists....*How* covers everything that is structure, behavior, all that is actually going on—the ongoing process. All the rest is irrelevant—computing, apprehending, and so on (p.44).

However, "how" is *about* "what". There is no "how" without a "what". A person who speaks grimly is, after all, speaking about something. While the *content* of the grim person's speech may be temporarily set into the background in favor of the *grimness* of speech, the content nevertheless remains alive as a counterpoint theme. Perhaps this seems obvious and hardly worth mentioning, but there is considerable variation among Gestalt therapists in how much attention is to be given to the grimness of speech and how much to what the person is grim about. Keeping both process *and* content in mind may dilute the therapeutic focus on either content *or* process.

Wilhelm Reich recognized this difficulty when he separated psychoanalysis from character analysis (Reich, 1949). He believed that the psychoanalytic interpretation of content was futile if characterological fixities were bypassed, and he wanted to defer psychoanalysis until they were dissolved. He found that the psychoanalytic process was slowed when the patient was sitting stiffly or jumped to conclusions or breathed shallowly or used circumlocutious language. He called the attention to these structural interferences, the "how" of people's expressiveness, *character analysis*. Once the character barriers were dissolved, he believed, the patient would be open to psychoanalysis.

But to set content aside, temporarily as he intended, is unnecessary, and it is a high price to pay when it obscures the events of a lifetime. Coordinating these concepts requires fluid attention and sensitive timing, but it adds depth and relevance to the patient's experience. When a patient recognizes, for example, how he jumps to conclusions about his occupational prospects, he may be able to reclaim the story of his discouragements, fleshing out his life with eventfulness and discovering new thematic possibilities.

The point/counterpoint relationship is a variant of the figure/ground dynamic so basic to Gestalt therapy. Much as the reverberations between figure and ground are a source of stimulation, the simultaneity of point and counterpoint will also be a potential source of both the vibrancy and complexity of the experience. We need look no further than the musical use of counterpoint to understand the assimilation of simultaneity, where different melodies are sometimes richly harmonious, sometimes excitingly dissonant. The same is true for everyday experiences. The perception of a sunset while talking to a friend, reading a book while remembering that you had better turn off the oven, the lingering effect of a disappointment while starting to exercise—all are examples of simultaneity where one would be hard pressed to say what is salient and what is background. Nor must we be definitive about the relative saliency of any experience.

The experience of simultaneity challenges the organizing skill and will of a person. But the need for this configurational achievement is inescapable because diversity is all around us and options for our attention will not fall easily into figure/ground differentiations. The reverberations of simultaneity and the resulting pattern of attention may make for a rich existence, representing the complexity of a heterogeneous world of experiences. Or it may plague us with uncertainty and distracting conflict, the stuff from which psychotherapy is formed. But the dynamic which simultaneity effects in our awareness must not be avoided because of its inherent complexity.

Dimensionalism is the second of the unifying principles. Dimensionalism of time and space provide a source for locating one's self. On the dimension of time, I locate myself in the year 1998 or in the twentieth century or the date, hour, second, or millisecond. In space, I locate myself in my room or in my city, or I may give you the geographical coordinates.

So also we may locate ourselves along theoretical dimensions. The content/process dimension is one of these. At one end of this dimension, the therapist focuses totally on process and not at all on content, while at the other end the reverse would be true. Therapists could differ in their emphases on content or process while remaining altogether faithful to Gestalt therapy theory. All that is required by this theory is that *each therapist is called upon to take both process and content into account in his own stylistic proportion and timing.*

Among Gestalt therapy teachers there are wide differences in the emphasis given to content and process. In my own student experiences, I was impressed with this range and drawn to the freedom of style and repertoire. Two of my teachers, Paul Goodman and Paul Weisz, had opposite positions on the content/process dimension.

Goodman was highly oriented to content, repeatedly searching for the storyline of the patient's life, much like the novelist he actually was. His curiosity and the accompanying probing were geared to getting the story out, with its varieties of struggle and with its implications for the unique nature of each person's life. *How* the person expressed herself received little attention—only when it seemed clearly to interfere with the unfolding of storyline.

Paul Weisz worked at the other end of the content/process dimension, staying faithfully with the "how" of each moment of experience in exquisitely fine detail. Did the patient raise an eyebrow, make subtly self-critical comments, hold his breath, or speak in resigned tones? The gracefulness of small observations were like the pinpoints of Seurat's Pointillism. Through a meticulous arrangement of dots, Seurat's attention to form and color preceded the *content*. Nevertheless, in Seurat's painting of *La Grande Jatte*, for example, we see people, water, boats, and trees, and we come away with the sense of lives lived. There are parents walking with their children, people rowing boats, trees in full splendor, silent companionship, and so on. Paul Weisz's work, similarly process-driven through attention to tiny awarenesses, would nevertheless evoke the events out of which his patients' lives were composed. Though his major attention was to the process details, the reciprocal content was always emergent.

Some of the theoretical dimensions that characterize Gestalt therapy are contact/awareness, past/present, contact/empathy, figure/ground, impasse/continuity, support/confrontation and others. Greenberg and Paivio are thinking along similar lines when they refer to the need to integrate "being" and "doing" (Greenberg and Paivio, 1997. pp. 271-274). What I propose here is that there is a range of theoretical *dimensions* that define Gestalt therapy. These dimensions already exist within the theory, and the articulation of them would give perspectives for therapeutic choices among compatible, though sometimes dissonant, procedural options.

In conclusion, by incorporating the twin themes of point/counterpoint integration and dimensionalism, we may articulate basic themes of Gestalt therapy while maintaining freedom in applying these principles. Though simplicity increases theoretical leverage for clear action, to be sure, the advantages can easily be diminished by an insistence on compliance with narrow principles. For any particular therapist, such narrowing of focus may be advantageous because it allows for personal selectivity among procedures. It allows the development of each therapist's personal style and repertoire, and it allows the therapist to tailor his or her procedure to patients' needs. The problem comes only when this stylization is misunderstood to be the theory itself, confining others to the same choices.

Theorists and practitioners alike must therefore be vigilant about the temptation to narrow the theory when they need only to develop their own stylistic and procedural priorities. To do so and remain faithful to the theory's broad parameters calls for artful understanding of the relationship of sharp focus to a pluralistic world of options.

COMMONALITY AND DIVERSITY IN GESTALT THERAPY

ERVING POLSTER

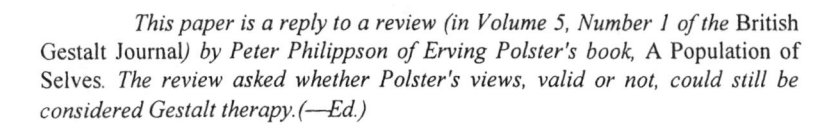

This paper is a reply to a review (in Volume 5, Number 1 of the British Gestalt Journal*) by Peter Philippson of Erving Polster's book,* A Population of Selves. *The review asked whether Polster's views, valid or not, could still be considered Gestalt therapy.(—Ed.)*

In Philippson's review of my book, *A Population of Selves*, (Philippson, 1996) he says "the function of this book is an explicit redefinition of a large proportion of the central terms in Gestalt therapy." He objects to many of these "redefinitions" and concludes that my views have now taken me outside the Gestalt therapy frame of reference. He adds a warning to the reader, saying, "the very fluency and humanity of this book will hide the fact that all the major foundations of Gestalt therapy are being removed." Philippson uses Perls, Hefferline and Goodman's book (hereafter referred to as PHG) as a measuring stick against theoretical heresy.

That is a more stark view of the supposed incompatibilities than I see. Philippson and some others before him have expressed a point of view which adheres more closely to the word-for-word language of PHG than I or many others do. The differences themselves are not surprising to me since any comprehensive theory must have room for diversity among its own people. *Incompatibility*, however, is another matter. I am going to try to show that the differences between my views and those of PHG are natural evolutions, responsive to the fundamentals but expanding beyond the original positions, often reviving neglected implications.

To examine Philippson's view of the differences between what he calls Polster-Gestalt and PHG-Gestalt, let's begin by presenting his diagram of these differences, below. Then I would like to comment on each, revealing a greater compatibility than he portrays. To seek out the commonalities in our positions is especially important because it gives a context to our differences. From this context of mutual interest, differences which are prematurely seen as incompatible may be re-experienced and, hopefully, integrated. That's what we try to do in therapy; why not do it in the angle from which we focus on our principles? If we were to succeed in encompassing these differences, I think it would provide fruitful diversity and greater depth.

POLSTER-GESTALT	PHG-GESTALT
Systems theory base	Field theory base
Emphasis on role playing layer	Emphasis on impasse
Task of therapist includes introducing new, more humane introjects.	Task of therapist is to encourage the awareness of introjects, and their assimilation or rejection
The client is encouraged to fit in with his/her community.	The client is made aware of the potential choices of identification with society's values, or of maintaining separateness.
Self is an 'internal' identification	'Self' is a polar, relational process, arising simultaneously with 'other'.
Awareness is primarily self-awareness	Awareness is primarily about contact with the environment.

1. *Philippson maintains that I follow "systems" theory rather than "field" theory.*

While I understand that PHG says Gestalt therapy is based on field theory, we must also remember that Gestalt therapy is a brilliant synthesis of a number of strong influences, including 1) psychoanalytic dissidents, such as Rank, Reich, Ferenczi, Jung, Adler, Moreno, and Horney; 2) Gestalt learning theory; 3) existentialism; 4) Jan Smut's holism and 5) eastern thought. From these forces, to choose field theory, itself, or one aspect of field theory, as the touchstone of Gestalt therapy, rather than only one of many guidelines, narrows it from the prodigious integrative accomplishment which it represents.

Looking at its identification with field theory, we can see two different dimensions of field theory which PHG takes into account. One is easy to reconcile with my positions; the other is embedded in paradox, always a tough challenge to fathom.

The first dimension of field theory addressed in PHG is the field as a representation of an interrelatedness among all phenomena, including the feelings and actions of people. I think it is evident that my book is altogether resonant with this dimension of field theory. I make it clear that, for me, the struggle to integrate the incredible range of phenomena we all live with is the reference point for all psychotherapy. A key ingredient of this position is the concept of a configurational reflex—a more active version of the concept of Gestalt formation—which "takes disparate details of personal experience and forms them into a unified pattern." (Polster, 1995 p.7)

From this perspective to heal is to make whole, as Webster's dictionary reminds us. What I have tried to get across is that in order to help patients to reconstitute as much of the wholeness of a lifetime as is available, therapists help people to incorporate disconnected or diluted events of a lifetime. When past and present, for one example, are reconnected with each other, this is a unifying experience. To see this reconnection as a unification process is a key alternative to looking at it as one event causing another. The squandering of personal experience created by disconnecting is a major fragmenting influence in our lives. The appreciation of the whole of a patient's life is partly reflected in the stories which patients tell, which I describe as "the signposts of a lifetime" and the communicators of "connectedness among people". (p. 108)

The second dimension of field theory, where I believe Philippson parts company with me, regards his conclusions about how I view the person's internal processes and the nature of boundaries. He compares *Gestalt Therapy Integrated* (Polster and Polster, 1973) with PHG to show the difference between our supposedly "systems" orientation and PHG's "field" orientation. Here is a comparison he makes between what we say about boundaries and what PHG says. We say, (Polster and Polster, 1974 p. 108) "Contact is a dynamic relationship occurring *only at the boundaries* of two compellingly attractive but clearly differentiated figures of interest." (italics mine) Philippson asserts, "PHG says it is *in our interaction* that aspects of the environment, and of our feeling response to it, become differentiated and bounded."

These two statements seem compatible to me. They both encompass interrelationship, boundaries and differentiation. I am guessing that a source of the confusion about these two perspectives is that we are dealing with a knotty paradox. The paradox is this: in Gestalt therapy, we say that psychologically relevant phenomena exist only at the contact boundary. When I see a friend walking toward me, I experience him because of the light from him which meets my retina, where it registers a visual image of him. The two of us are therefore joined as one since he exists psychologically only at the point at which we meet. At that level, there is no him and no me; only the sensory union at the point of our meeting.

From this oneness, our differentiation process paradoxically registers the fact that the image reflected at my contact boundary is more than an image; it is actually a person or thing which is *separate* from me. This differentiation registers boundedness, what PHG, itself refers to as "unified structures" (p. 227). Therefore I have no trouble recognizing that the friend walking toward me is different from another person who is not walking toward me, or who may even be walking side by side with my friend. I can relate *to* my friend, who is also part of me as sensory effect, by waving or waiting or whatever other way I want to handle what is actually both a *separate* him and a sensory merger of him and me. It is all so natural that the paradox is rarely of interest. Through the differentiation I create a clear understanding that my friend is indeed there, not an illusion. I behave and feel according to the way this internal organization evolves and whatever it leads me to. At bottom, the dual effect reminds us that we must deal with the paradox of separateness and union (which is, incidentally, a fundamental guideline of Otto Rank, one of Gestalt therapy's most important influences).

Does this view make me "systems" or "field" oriented? Though I have long been a Gestalt therapist, I confess I have never been a student of either systems or field theory, nor have I ever written about either of them, except once to quote briefly from Von Bertalanffy. At my level of understanding, the brand of holism, which guides me and which I have always associated with Gestalt therapy, would probably lap over into both.

Another reason for the confusion is that PHG itself is contradictory about boundaries. At one point they state that boundedness is "simply an illusion due to the fact that the motion through space and internal detail call attention to themselves against the relative stability and simplicity of the background" (Perls, Hefferline and Goodman, p. 228). PHG *gives very little attention*, however, to the concept of boundedness as illusion and only a page later (p. 229) makes several observations with which I feel my views to be in harmony

> Let us understand contacting, awareness and motor response, in the broadest sense, to include appetite and

rejection, approaching and avoiding, sensing, feeling, manipulating, estimating, communicating, fighting etc.—every kind of living relation that occurs at the *contact* boundary in the interaction of the organism and environment.

A little later (p. 230), they say

Fundamentally an organism lives in its environment by maintaining its *difference* and, more importantly, by assimilating the environment to its *difference*. (italics mine)

Still later (p. 462), they say

The functioning of the ego, we have seen, can be described as a setting of boundaries of the self's interest, power, etc.; identifying with and alienating are the two sides of the boundary; and in any live contacting the boundary is definite but always shifting.

My views also find resonance with the work of a different influence in the history of Gestalt therapy: the psychological field theorist Kurt Lewin. Lewin came closest among the early psychological field theorists in speaking to the complex requirements of psychotherapy. Let's take a bird's eye view of what he has to say about these issues. According to Hall and Lindzey, Lewin proposed two properties of the person

1) separation from the rest of the world by means of a continuous boundary and 2) inclusion in a larger area. The first property is that of *differentiation*, the second of the *part-whole* relationship. In short, the person is represented as being *separated from yet included within a larger totality*. (Hall and Lindzey, p. 210)

"Separated from yet included" is consonant with the way I have addressed personal boundaries and intra-psychic concerns. The surge to wholeness, which I believe is reflexive, matters so greatly in therapy because it is commonly thwarted by the fragmenting forces we all live with and which therapists focus on every day. Our biological and psychological configurational reflexes must be continually tuned in—mostly without awareness—to a large range of our experiences, many of which are not easily synthesized.

We should also take account of the boundary confusions recognized by a special circle of field theorists—Pribram, Bohm, Capra, Wilbur, Ferguson—who have been pioneers in portraying an omnipresent wholeness in the universe. Wilbur (1982, p. 168) says of quantum physicist David Bohm's work that he has postulated a universe in which physical entities, which ordinarily are seen as separate and distinct, are actually linked together—unified in such a way that distinctness would be only illusory. However, Wilbur also points out that Bohm "explicitly *excludes* any higher realms such as mind and consciousness." In the face of the oversimplification which many advocates of wholeness profess, here is what Bohm (1982, p. 199) says in addressing the greater complexity which this unifying, undifferentiated sense of living offered in his theory

> The mystic says that the good can be experienced: that it is wholeness, harmony. The trouble is that this unity doesn't communicate to ordinary experience, and that's why it is so important to understand what ordinary experience does have in common with this mystical experience of wholeness.

In human experience there are special complexities created by the union of a fluid awareness with a sense of enduring identity. In facing these complexities, theorists have tried to coordinate the seemingly contradictory views of both the mystical experience of cosmic harmony and the field principles of physics with the ordinary differentiations people make—often alienations—among ordinary experiences. These differentiations, in the form of conflicting purposes within any individual, make for a lot of personal trouble and we spend lifetimes trying to get it all together. Though people set up ideals of wholeness, there is a special distortion created in transposing to the ordinary experience that which is learned only under the most exceptional circumstances. Whatever ideals of wholeness may be realized in the meditations of our most "evolved" avatars, they come only in the most sacred moments, with the most devoted practices and with rare sacrifices. Thus, where they experience the universality of wholeness, the counterpoint—individuation—and its consequent fragmentation lurk in the background and always challenge the experience of wholeness.

Wilbur, in addressing the necessity for distinctions between wholeness and individuation cautions against the common oversimplifications of the concept of wholeness, saying

> The problem with the popular holographic theories, as well as the general 'new physics and Eastern mysticism' stuff, is that they... latch on to such phrases as 'All things are one' or 'Separate entities don't exist' or 'Isolated things are mere shadows' (Wilbur, 1982, p.256)

Wilbur then proceeds to spell out the theoretical dilemma which some leading spokespeople for the physics/mysticism union find themselves in

> Most of the people who either introduced the physics/mysticism thing or at least used it for effect have increasingly refined and sophisticated their views. David Bohm has clearly moved toward a more articulated and hierarchical view... Fritjof Capra never said that physics and mysticism were the same, although he did try to draw so many parallels that the public thinks he did...They have latched onto physics equals mysticism with such a passion that Capra's new and more sophisticated—and necessarily complicated—ideas will never reverse the tide.

Plainly serious thinkers in field theory have themselves come to understand that the field contains complex phenomena and that premature understandings blur these complexities.

We come now closer to home in responding to Philippson's questions about my Gestalt therapy allegiance. Let us consider what two Gestalt therapists have to say. Their views differ significantly from those of Miriam Polster and myself and from those of the "Cleveland School", which Philippson also thinks is "systems" oriented and where for almost 20 years I did my early teaching.

Yontef, (1993) has written the most recent and most comprehensive examination of the role of field theory in Gestalt therapy. Although for him field theory is the indispensable foundation of Gestalt therapy, a "...lodestone that guides the compass of Gestalt therapy" (p. 324) he also says

> We need to evolve a new model, rather than adopting classical or post classical models from physics. Any analysis of Gestalt thinking solely in terms of models of physics is likely to come up short. (p. 369)

Then later he says

> The self concept the Polsters elaborate on is an existing phenomenon and as such is part of the field... When Perls, Hefferline and Goodman state that in health there is very little personality, they are addressing the process of attachment to an old image rather than the current field reality. That is quite consistent with the Polsters' emphasis on the importance of expanded I-boundaries. (p. 375)

Yontef recognizes that the concept of I-boundaries represents a co-ordination between the continual summation of personal inner experience and the continuing impactful connections which the person has with the world. He differs with us on other issues, but the key point is not whether we agree on everything or not but that there is a *commonality* between us, out of which *differences* evolve.

Latner, (1983) is another writer who has addressed the question of field theory in Gestalt therapy and who has preceded

Philippson in placing Miriam Polster and me, as well as the Cleveland School, in the camp of systems theory. Latner's positions, as Philippson's, are more exacting than Yontef's. Nevertheless, Latner seems to recognize the veil which stands between him and his wish to transpose field theory into psychological application. His intuition tells him clearly that the world of people can be better described from a field perspective than from what he thinks of as our mechanistic ways. But he also observes that he has "not done an adequate job of conveying just what it is to see the world from the perspective of field theory." (p. 84) But that is what must be done.

The heart of the difficulty in conveying such a world is that people, physics theory notwithstanding, generally differentiate entities from each other. If we were to speak of people as variations in the density of matter, we would be bypassing the essence of people. The human reflex to differentiate is unavoidable when we speak of the person who is in contact with other people and who is aware of the world outside himself or even within himself. The existence of these differentiations is not a contradiction of field theory; differentiations are the *experience* of people, a part of the field. These experiences, interconnected with each other as they are, form into the patterns which holistically-oriented therapists, including me, are trying to translate into necessarily human terms.

However, though Latner differs strongly with what he sees as a departure from field theory by Miriam Polster and me, he also says (p.81) in describing our approach: "I want to emphasize its roots and assumptions, and to distinguish it from *another way of thinking* about Gestalt therapy." One may infer that he is not questioning, as Philippson does, whether we are still operating from a Gestalt frame of reference. *A Population of Selves* is in fact devoted to elaborating the Gestalt frame of reference: in it, I extend the concept of contact, as already proposed in more general terms by PHG; I expand and clarified the role of introjection in therapy, already proposed in more narrow terms in PHG; I spell out—in greater detail and with greater personal recognitions—how the self becomes formed (already proposed in PHG in less concrete terms); and I urge a new view of the merger of self and community, already proposed implicitly in PHG's concern with the organism/environment relationship.

2. *Philippson believes that I emphasize the role playing layer, and PHG emphasizes the impasse.*

I am guessing that he means that I try to help people out of their stuckness before they have, themselves, first realized their stuckness fully. To Perls, (1970, p.20) "role playing" is an *as if* or phony adaptation that falsifies one's own real ways of behaving. As a therapist, I exercise discernment as to whether any patient's expressions are only a flimsily based attempt to do the "right thing" through mistaken adaptation—role playing—or whether these expressions or feelings fit their own movement through their lives, serving their own needs and style. In my writing, I've emphasized that therapy rides on what our patients have already said or done and builds the therapeutic movement on the patient's own directionalism.

Perhaps Phillipson thinks my incorporation of the healthy aspects of introjection would contribute to "role playing." My illustrations of actual therapy experiences try to show that, with the best perceptions I can muster, I face people with their actual realities. Some might even think of me as tough minded. But it is also true that the experiences I face people with often include favorable experiences, which for one reason or another may have been excluded from their repertoire. If a person doesn't know how intelligent they are or how generous or how beautiful, I think they are best off knowing it and I don't mind telling them.

This kind of intervention represents a Gestalt oriented homage to good quality contact. I further think attention to *movement* is as important as attention to *stuckness* and that in any person's life the two should be intertwined, not dichotomized.

This improvement of the sense of movement, as for example in the concept of the awareness continuum, has always been important to Gestalt therapy as it would necessarily be in all therapies.

3. *Philippson contrasts me with PHG by saying that I introduce new, more humane introjects rather than an awareness of introjects and their assimilation or rejection.*

As I mentioned above, if a new truth is a humane truth, proffered by kindness or admiration or other positive reactions, I have no objection to offering it. For me, the humane is not a trick to delude people into thinking things are better than they are. The issue is not *whether* someone is introjecting but *what* they introject and *how* it fits into a sense of the wholeness of being— and the *directionalism* their life takes on. That applies to the pleasurable as well as the painful truths.

Philippson's sense of the humane quality of introjects implies that the therapist may be too helpful, interfering with the self-discovery of the patient. I think that is an important question, and calls for sensitive therapeutic judgment. But help should not be viewed categorically as interfering with self-discovery; indeed, help may often accelerate it. It sometimes serves the requirement for good quality contact to respond to specific needs of patients— by offering a better word to describe their experience or giving a warning about trouble the therapist sees them getting into or telling a story to offer hospitality to their stories. To me this seems to be a reflection of the partnership which therapy represents. One of the first things I was taught in Gestalt therapy is to go beyond Freud's concept of the ambiguous therapist. In the final analysis, we are there to be helpful, even though it may not always be evident how we may best do that. It will be great raw material for cartoonists when a Gestalt therapist's desire to be helpful to a person who explicitly comes for help would be considered counter-Gestalt.

As to the question of awareness: I give attention to awarenesses of all kinds, including introjections. I simply do not *insist* on awareness. It is a powerful and valuable tool, which I describe at some length in my book, showing among other things its relationship to Perls' concept of concentration, a powerful "antidote to avoidance" (Perls 1947, p. 8) Perls' almost hypnotic use of awareness was a great advance in what I refer to as the focus revolution. In my writings and teachings, I have recognized the ability to focus as a key factor in Gestalt therapy. This high focus is especially evident in the work of Robine (1996), who describes a therapeutic process in which he sensitively guides his patient's imagery in a series of awarenesses, evoking new realization and direction. Though Robine is also strongly PHG oriented, his work as a Gestalt therapist is altogether harmonious with my own position, and could have served well as a case example of the effects of sequential concentration.

But Gestalt therapy is more than a search for awareness. Some patients do better by improving their contact than they do with high focus on awareness. Or they may do better with experiments than with awareness. Contact, awareness and experiment are an interwoven set of procedural options, and how these are interwoven depends on both the needs of particular patients and the repertoire and style of the therapist (who may be more skillful with one than the others). Some time ago, I described (Polster, 1966) one of the attributes of Gestalt therapy to be its range of concepts and noted that this range permitted the development in its adherents of a personal repertoire and style. I believe that Gestalt therapy has overplayed the continual importance of awareness. Awareness is often a natural accompaniment of action and does not always call for special focus. In fact, excessive concern with awareness may slow down a therapy which is proceeding fluidly and validly through the natural engagement between the therapist and the patient, a testament to the effects of good quality contact rather than awareness.

4. *Philippson contrasts my encouragement of the client to fit in with his/her community with the choice to be a separate, individuated person.*

This is not an either/or dimension. There is a great surge within humans to belong but there is also a wide variety of options, including individuated ways of belonging, as well as the choice for separateness. The sweep of a person's life and the directions which they themselves are seeking are the primary foundations of the proposals I set forth in *A Population of Selves*. In that book, I propose an expansion of psychotherapeutic methodology to include the forces of the community when I say

> Communal magnetism is a fact of life. When we, in psychotherapy, derogate the unruly process of creating new formats for people to congregate and attend to common psychological concerns, they will still be compelled to congregate, and our abdication will leave the field to others. They will surely fill it in their own ways, often in ways alien to our (psychotherapists') beliefs. (Polster, 1996, p. 197)

5. *Philippson calls my view of the self an internal identification and contrasts this with the self as polar relational process.*

My concept of the self builds on three basic Perlsian positions. These three principles are:
1) The principle of "neurotic splitting" (alienation among the parts of the person) and "the coming creative integration of the split", as described in PHG (p. 240)
2) The anthropomorphic inclinations of the mind, represented ingeniously in Perls' topdog and underdog. These metaphors take a set of *characteristics* of the person and

transform them into person-like *characters*. Where I have gone beyond Perls is that instead of limiting the splits within the person to the topdog and underdog, I have extended the concept of splits. I expand on the topdog and underdog split to include more specific and personal sets of characteristics and characters. I feel it is important to look beyond simple polarities so as to encompass the much more complex set of experiences and characteristics of which all people are composed.

3) The principle of synthesis, which I have expanded from the original Perlsian view of synthesis as a fusion of the alienated parts. I've written

> *However important this form of synthesis is*, I want to propose a point/counterpoint interrelationship as a new slant on synthesis, different from the fusion that Perls advocated...(one) characterized not by fusion but by the retention of dissonant selves, each one continuing to play out its own original quality within the diversity of the person's voices. (Italics added) (Polster, 1996, p. 15)

It is possible to conclude from this that I don't care whether the person's selves change. I do, but change sometimes resides in a re-integration of seemingly incompatible dissonance. In other words, one may be stubborn *and* accommodating. Even though the person may not change one or the other characteristic, one might nevertheless integrate these contradictory qualities into a sense of a whole person, who is sometimes stubborn and sometimes accommodating. This point/counterpoint synthesis is not *instead* of the fusion concept but what I find to be a common sense *addition* to it.

I don's see anything incompatible with PHG in these expansions. Rather it is Perls' introductions of these aspects of human personality upon which my concept is built. I think it is enough for us contemporary theorists to honor Perls' first words as foundational rather than to think he has already had the last word 45-50 years ago.

Philippson also feels I use the concept of selves where PHG uses the concept of personality to encompass what I have described as the formation of self. What PHG said (p. 382) is

> The Personality is the system of attitudes assumed in interpersonal relations; is the assumption of what *is*, serving as the ground on which one could explain one's behavior, if the explanation were asked for. (Italics mine)

My concept of selves expands PHG's concept of personality formation rather than negates it, as it fleshes out the concept and gives it a life it never had in the original brief reference. We don't have to use the same language to be on the same team.

6. *Philippson thinks that for me awareness is primarily self awareness, while in PHG awareness is primarily about contact with the environment.*

Here is a quote from *A Population of* Selves, which may help to clarify my views about attention to the environment as well as to inner experience. I said

> The concern with the superficiality/depth dimension is a key requirement in the search for experience that matters. Whatever is going on always takes place in a larger, unmanifested, depth inviting context, including both the unconscious and all the other experiences that might be available. We Gestalt therapists call this the *ground* within which all immediate experience is always positioned. Depth is commonly understood to exist when experiences are highly significant or strongly felt or very clever, or very obscure. The depth to which I am pointing, however, is the depth one achieves by relating any awareness to whatever context is accessible for that awareness. In a sense, depth is the

undoing of the isolation of any single event from others that matter. (Polster 1996, p. 204)

As this statement shows, I see *self*-awareness as a profoundly important part of existence, as would PHG, but that I also position awareness of the world outside ourselves as crucial, always affecting our self-awareness, always interwoven with the awareness of otherness.

In closing, it is plain to me that there are significant differences among Gestalt therapists and that if we want to be a coherent union of people, we must also have a common ground supporting these differences. I have tried to show the relationship between the common ground provided in PHG and the differences represented in my work. I believe these differences are not only compatible with PHG but also expand Gestalt therapy, setting new proportions in the relationship of humanity to technology, content to process, contact to awareness, and actual therapeutic method to abstract theorizing. In supporting these, and fresh perspectives contributed by other writers, I call attention to this observation from PHG

...what is selected and assimilated is always novel; the organism persists by assimilating the novel by change and growth... What is pervasive, always the same, or indifferent is not an object of contact.

In this spirit, I invite Gestalt therapists everywhere to join, not in agreement, but in appreciation of the dissonance which helps to keep us all listening carefully, aware that nothing is to be taken for granted when tuning into the complex web of phenomena we are trying to synthesize.

In Memory of Carl Rogers: Great Men Cast Great Shadows

Erving Polster

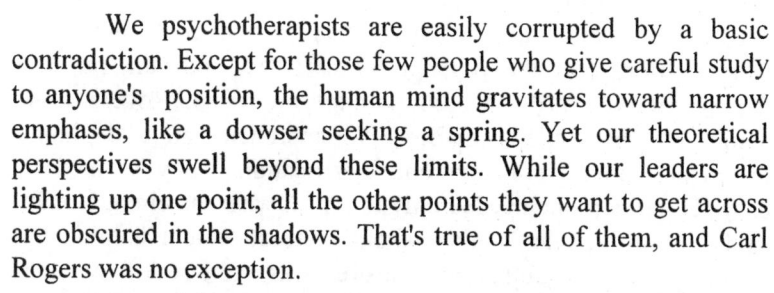

We psychotherapists are easily corrupted by a basic contradiction. Except for those few people who give careful study to anyone's position, the human mind gravitates toward narrow emphases, like a dowser seeking a spring. Yet our theoretical perspectives swell beyond these limits. While our leaders are lighting up one point, all the other points they want to get across are obscured in the shadows. That's true of all of them, and Carl Rogers was no exception.

One of the great psychologist-communicators of our age, he was nevertheless a victim as well as a creator of this dilemma, giving special emphasis as well as receiving it. Some examples: When he emphasized his special techniques, reflection and clarification, about which I shall say more later, many of his readers lost sight of the sensitivity needed to use these techniques. When he emphasized congruence between inner experience and outer expression, the empathy which would turn the congruence into an interpersonal event, was overshadowed. When he emphasized simple experience, the importance of understanding receded.

Rogers had good company. Freud, for another, when emphasizing interpretation, blurred face-value experience; when emphasizing free association, side-tracked the importance of conversation; when emphasizing transference, set actual relationships into the shadows. For clear communicators special emphasis is compelling and for Freud and Rogers, the however's, and if-onlys of their positions, often present, were given less prominence. Their readers in any case, would glean special emphasis whether or not Rogers or Freud intended them to because they are also captivated by simplicity. By the time the resulting distortions became fixed, both Freud and Rogers said they would be neither Freudians nor Rogerians.

Since we are all fated to speak lopsidedly and to be heard with biased emphases, I would like to flesh out these inevitable contrasts by pointing out some of the specific interplay of light and shadow which Rogers created. His greatest early fame—mid-1940s—came with his challenge to the psychoanalytic hegemony and this challenge was only dimly prophetic of the changes that were to transform the psychoanalytic basics into the populist therapy of the third force in psychology. When Rogers came along, his then-called non-directive approach had two simple technical planks, reflection and clarification. They seemed so easy. To reflect, one needed only to repeat what the client already said; to clarify, one would elaborate the statement helping the client to get a more full sense of his remarks and where they might be heading. That's all the therapist had to do, as many applied the method.

In an age accustomed to a complex interpretive mode, requiring almost mind reading powers, the simplicity of these procedures was both eye-opening and tempting, even though many objectors thought Rogers to be merely naive. The value of these techniques was backed up, though, not only by a rationale but also by extensive research which took special advantage of the then new technology of tape recording. The techniques consequently received great attention and Rogers himself rued the day they were born, but he need not have felt so embarrassed as he did. In his rudimentary way, he was cutting through the abstruse and though he was surely not recommending these practical techniques to be used mechanically, as they often were, he was unwittingly unveiling a new age of therapeutic technology. Soon there were others, Perls and the Group Dynamics people developed a whole body of techniques, which for years has powered diversity and innovation in psychotherapy. Encounter group exercises, the empty chair, biofeedback, hypnosis, Reichian exercises, Gestalt experiments: they are all part of the expanding repertoire of techniques, of which Rogers' innovation was only a hint.

For Rogers, however, the brightness of his technical innovations was dimmed for two reasons. First, they were badly misused. He said (in the Journal of Humanistic Psychology Vol. 127, No. 1, 1987) "Reflection of feeling can be taught as a cognitive skill...Genuine sensitive empathy, with all its intensity and personal involvement cannot be so taught...I wince at the phrase reflection of feeling." Whenever I saw Rogers therapeutic work, he was in deep concentration and fascinated with everything his clients said. He fully recognized the mysteries, dangers, deprivations, loves and adventures of the people with whom he worked. He has said,

> "I hear the words, the thoughts, the feeling tones, the personal meaning, even the meaning that is below the conscious intent of the speaker. Sometimes, too, in a message which superficially is not very important, I hear a deep human cry that lies buried and unknown far below the surface of the person." (Rogers, 1980).

Be that as it may, Rogers always felt plagued by the professional impression that the early techniques were superficial and best used by people who didn't know how to do any better and he came to shun the techniques which had placed more important messages into the shadows of his theoretical emphasis.

Not only did Rogers think his techniques were upstaging what he believed to be more crucial elements of his methodology—empathy, prizing, congruence, inherent growth surge—but a second dimming factor is that the presumed superficiality of the techniques also obscured some of their effect on what was to become the core of therapeutic concerns for the next forty-five years. Three of these landmark implications were those which pointed to: 1) awareness as a central force in living, 2) experience as a strong counterpoint to the then-prevalent preoccupation with the meaning of experience and 3) the here-and-now as life's major reality dimension. Each of these developments contributed mightily but, as I shall point out, their brightness left other important psychological concerns in the shadows.

First, as to awareness: reflection and clarification were instruments for amplifying anything that the client said or did. Though the centrality of awareness was more explicitly accented by Fritz Perls shortly after Rogers' techniques were described, they both helped move psychotherapy beyond searching for insight into realizing that everything people did was worthy of accent. In a sense, giving a potential for notice to all experience democratized the events of life, giving them all a voice rather than giving primary value only to those special moments of psychoanalytic insight. Once giving notice to the statements people continuingly make, it became apparent to Rogers that these recognitions, re-encompassed into the self, would become springboards for the natural movement toward growth, inherent in all people. The therapist, following the patient's trail of experience would be led to where the patient needed to go. One could also make the case that refinement in awareness transcended therapy itself, arousing self-awareness in such social groupings as black people, women, students, gay people and other disenfranchised groups. All of these groupings have used their increased awareness to animate themselves to new resolves to confront society with their needs.

The emphasis on awareness required only a short step to concern with the expressions which this awareness would call forth. Recognizing that awareness and expression are inseparable, Rogers applied the term congruence to represent the unification of these two modes of being. When one could correctly give voice to one's insides, this congruence would create trustworthy communication.

Unfortunately, when congruence was featured, it cast into the shadows Rogers' important recommendations for empathy, for positive regard, and for the individual's need for independent growth. The emphasis on congruence has often been taken as license for people to say what is honest and do what is authentic without regard to the consequences, whether in their own lives or in the lives of others. The single issue emphasis serves no better for Rogers' other positions. Comparably, the emphasis on the person's self-propelled growth has often led to neutered leadership by therapists, while the emphasis on empathy and unconditional positive regard will in the hands of many people lead to flabby contact. Clearly, there are contradictions among the various Rogerian emphases and he recognized the trouble by noting that each of his modes will merit their own primacy in differing circumstances (Rogers, 1980, p.100). Consequently there is much room, given any one's preference for one or another of the modes, to place the non-favorite into the shadows. It must be recognized that with light, shadows are inevitable but with shifts in light, what is in the shadows at one time, may receive great illumination at another.

The second implication of early Rogerian technique, was an emphasis on experience over meaning. As I said earlier, his techniques directly refuted the psychoanalytic interpretive mode. He opposed interpretation because it represented an authority over the client, implying the therapist knew the client's experience better than the client did. The unintended consequence of Rogers' position was the belief that understanding and knowledge were not important. For Rogers, however, understanding and knowledge were actually very important, even though he gave disproportionately high emphasis to the process through which the knowledge and understanding came. He opposed slavish homage to the cognitive and wanted to sharpen the flattened experience which otherwise resulted from the heavy attention to meaning. He was also concerned that the primacy given to knowledge and understanding leads to an indoctrination based on the teacher's views rather than allowing each person's experience to lead them to their own views. He believed people would learn best when learning for themselves, rather than through following the instruction of others. This view, taken strictly, as many would take it, would exclude important learning opportunities given the interdependence which is inevitable in people learning from people. Rogers' concern with freedom from indoctrination skewed him away from the cognitive, even though he knew it had to be joined with the affective. Skimming over the cognitive fosters a breakdown in the sense of authorship necessary in the make-up of a good teacher, who has a distinct advantage in knowing what the student should learn. Equality between student and teacher becomes a dubious benefit when the two are actually unequal in knowledge and the teacher is inhibited against using his or hers. Since the cognitive, as well as teacher authority, lost out with Rogers and with a large part of the encounter group culture, one may need a reminder that he was a devoted teacher of the cognitive, at first in his role as a college professor and researcher and later as one who worked to improve formal education—championing student freedom, teacher empathy and direct experience, not for their own sake, but as cornerstones in expanding knowledge.

A third mark of early Rogerian technique was that it favored the here-and-now. Though Rogers never accentuated the present as directly as did Perls, he negated the then-common searches into the past or forays into the future, except as his clients may themselves refer to these time units. The past, in particular had become a fetish because of the mysteries Freud had found them to explain. Rogers was not trying to explain anything, so he had very little need to search the past and he wasn't proposing new behavior so the future did not beckon strongly either. He simply wanted to know and to say what was actually going on, in the here-and-now, though he never put it that way. What this emphasis on the here-and-now did was to help take seriously what each client was actually saying and it also gave a heightened focus to the individual, through by-passing the complex background of their lives. An entire age of our society was impressed. But, in the shadows there have been serious drawbacks, which Rogers recognized. He recently said

> I deplore the present stress on the here-and-now...It seems to me that many of us, and perhaps young people especially, have become victims of the cult of the here-and-now. They want immediate gratification of all their desires...The process of trying to gain ends by hard work and persistence...has lost a lot of the charm that it has in experience. (Rogers, 1987)

All of these implications and others of Rogers early work were directed to the self: recognizing, freeing, and enhancing the individual person. It is for these contributions that Rogers has become revered. Yet, in relatively recent years, that which had also long remained in the shadows of his views emerged into the foreground. At the time of his death, he had already for years been absorbed with the needs of the community, more so than with the needs of individual selfhood. Though he never changed his belief in the primacy of the individual, it was his abiding faith that the uncovering of the individual's worth was the road to creating good community. He recognized the contrasting views all over the world, particularly those in China, which he visited and lauded. In China, he heard the slogan "Fight self—Serve the People" and he proposed an alternative slogan "Be yourself—Serve the People." Pursuing his belief, he sparked the leadership of a group of 800 people in Brazil, tried to humanize educational systems, explored conflicts in South Africa and Ireland, presented his peace views in Russia, and generated a peace conference concerning Central America. At the age of 85, he was still drawing material from the shadows of his views and giving them a clarity and applicability so potentiating that his death caught him in the center of his latest communal actions.

Part III:
The Role of Community

ENCOUNTER IN COMMUNITY

ERVING POLSTER

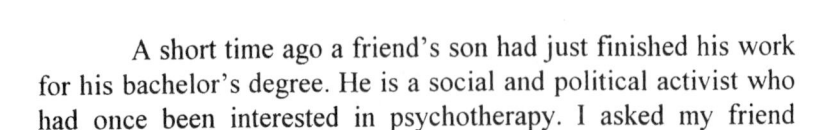

A short time ago a friend's son had just finished his work for his bachelor's degree. He is a social and political activist who had once been interested in psychotherapy. I asked my friend whether her son was going to become a psychotherapist and she said no, he thinks psychotherapy is irrelevant.

The ambiguity of this indictment opened my speculations about what he could have meant. I thought he might, as an activist, just have a point. The speculation I liked best is that the boy is a utopian thinker and he does not sense this kind of thinking among psychotherapists. To be sure, there are some writers close to psychotherapy who have been trying to put Utopia back on the map; but they are few. The ones who first come to my mind are B. F. Skinner, Paul Goodman, and Martin Buber. Although none of them characterize themselves as psychotherapists (though Paul Goodman spent many fruitful years as one), their work has been central to current psychotherapeutic thought.

Skinner's *Walden II*, which fantasies the ideal community, is based upon his principles of learning (Skinner, 1948). In it the hero takes seriously the proposition that what we learn in the laboratory or with individuals can be applied to the cause of living a good life in an actual community. While you or I might differ with certain premises, Skinner's hero at least puts himself to the test of creating the utopian community, thereby opening himself, and presumably Skinner, too, to charges ranging from soft-headed oversimplification to autocratic pomposity.

Paul Goodman, an avowed utopian thinker, wrote a book called *Utopian Essays and Practical Proposals*, in which he presents his views on a wide range of practical problems of our society (Goodman, 1962). He says, "ideas are called utopian when they seem to be useful but they propose a different style, a different procedure, a different kind of motivation from the way people at present do business." He adds that ideas are also called utopian when "the structure and folkways of our society are absurd, but they can no longer be changed. Any hint of changing them disturbs our resignation and arouses anxiety."

Martin Buber wrote *Paths in Utopia* in 1945. In it he traces historical utopian thought as a background for the experiment in Israel of the village commune of Kvuza. He explores the structure of utopianism when he says

> What, at first sight, seems common to Utopias that have passed into the spiritual history of mankind is the fact that they are pictures, and pictures, moreover, of something not actually present but only represented... This 'fantasy' does not float vaguely in the air, it is not driven hither and thither by the wind of caprice, it centers with architectonic firmness on something primary and original which it is its destiny to build; and this primary thing is a wish. The utopian picture is a picture of what 'should be,' and the visionary is one who wishes it to be . . . . What is at work here is the longing for that rightness which, in idea, and which of its very nature cannot be realized in the individual, but only in human community. The vision of 'what should be'—independent though it may sometimes appear of personal will—is yet inseparable from a critical and fundamental relationship to the existing condition of humanity . . . . And what may seem impossible as a concept arouses, as an image, the might of faith, ordains purpose and plan. It does this because it is in league with powers latent n the depths of reality. (Buber, 1958)

Buber blames Marx and his followers for having denounced utopian thinking, which they did from the middle nineteenth century on. He believes this isolated those socialists whose concerns included individualistic and decentralized *social* developments rather than only the centralist *economic* and *political* development favored by the Marxists. Adhering as the Marxists did to powerful centralist control and giving only lip service to the vague hope that at the propitious moment the state would wither away, Buber says they abandoned the indispensable improvisational powers of local communities and the social side of man. For the Marxists social concern and individuality were premature, therefore utopian. For them to have expected political and economic systems, built up because of immediate necessity, to commit suicide at a future propitious moment, and to give way to a socially oriented system, Buber sees as altogether unrealistic and perhaps, one might add, fraudulent, like the rabbit at the dog track. For Buber, social change need not wait for the future, but, indeed, must be an integral part of good community formation.

The Marxist split which Buber describes is also apparent in capitalist society where social needs have also taken a back seat. The varieties of social deprivation are so extensive that their existence is self-evident but the materialistic habits hang on anyway. A breakthrough in methods is needed, methods for establishing a higher priority for the fulfillment of man's social needs. Psychotherapists have found one such method for tackling the problem—the basic encounter group.

For the encounter group to have yielded this promise of swinging powerfully in rhythm with the materialistic needs which have been impelling our society, psychotherapists have had to evolve technical advances over traditional methods. These technical developments have been supported by four primary aspects of contemporary orientation, which are: (1) commonality of people problems, (2) the vectorial nature of people, (3) the characterological view, and (4) the emphasis on interactional dynamics. These considerations take priority now over the formerly preemptive importance of associational introspection, the uncovering of secrets requiring privacy, and the emphasis upon the search for the unconscious.

The first, concern with commonality of people's problems, is well illustrated by Tillich's views about existential anxiety and, later by Bugental's extension of these views. The Tillich-Bugental view is that people have four primary sources of anxiety and four consequent pathological characteristics (Bugental, 1965; Tillich, 1952).

The sources of the underlying anxiety are Tillich's threat of death and fate, the experience of guilt and condemnation, and the confrontation with emptiness and meaninglessness. Bugental adds the threat of loneliness and isolation. The neurotic effects of these anxieties, according to Bugental, are feelings of powerlessness, blame, absurdity, and estrangement. These states are not only commonplace but universal because the rudiments of existence guarantee that we all must be confronted with these basic threats.

A further thrust giving a populist meaning to these concepts is the uncomplicated and untechnical character of the words used to designate the danger and anxiety of life. Compared to the term *castration anxiety*, for example, *powerlessness* can readily be appreciated by unsophisticated persons as immediately relevant to their lives even without expert translation. One does not need to perceive pathology in his life for these anxieties to have meaning.

Powerlessness, in Bugental's terminology, is a result of man's limitations in controlling all the variables of his life. He therefore is not only challenged with death but also with a continued invitation, which he may or may not accept, to take risks. Therefore, the acceptance of the invitation to take a chance becomes a central concern in psychotherapeutic method, particularly in encounter group situations. New technologies evolve out of ideas like these, creating new social situations flowing from the developing view of man. Conceiving of man as a risk-taker rather than as a searcher into the unconscious determines new approaches and changes the entire configuration of our work as psychotherapists.

Blame is another populist concept from the Tillich-Bugental formulation. "Is this my fault?" is a question all people ask themselves. Their concern is with a possible flaw of personality which threatens their identity. Perfection may be a native goal of all people, most of us swallowing society's inculcations about what constitutes perfection and experiencing blame when we fall short of these standards. The alternative possibility is self-actualization according to one's own individual needs. In the encounter group, a part of the new technology is to foster each individual's search for his own needs in relation to the group, setting up a new relativism that freshly challenges those seeking personal fulfillment. It may be said that this has always been the intention of psychotherapy, but in my experience the search has now become more bold and adventurous than previously. It is as though we are beginning to mean what we say and experience what formerly we only hoped for.

The dread of absurdity also arises in the common view especially as the old explanations about the meaning of life usually Judeo-Christian, become less and less convincing. Existentialism has offered a nonreligious orientation to life's nature and man's place in the world and may well be leaning to further articulations which will replace present theological systems. The new views already include the phenomenologically based efforts to recover sensory awareness to encourage and teach bodily movement, to experience living as a present event, to know the nature of our feelings and wishes, to experience choice making, and so on. They fill the gap created by anachronistic morality and social contradictions. These and many other technical formulations of the paths to the recovery of meaning in life are being played out in the encounter movement.

The dread of apartness and estrangement accentuates the fact that we are all finite beings, unjoined to otherness yet needful of contact with otherness. The contact with others is necessary for both survival and fulfillment but is severely impeded through the many prohibitions which people experience. The encounter group is a new medium for altering morality so that people will be freed to make the necessary human contact. Touching and embracing, for example, are commonly acceptable in these groups. Expressing one's anger, boredom, confusion, excitement, love, and so on, are not necessarily evidence of boorishness, evil, ugliness, licentiousness, and so on, as they may well be under the traditional morality.

The second general aspect of contemporary orientation leading to new technical developments comes from Wilhelm Reich. Even before concern with commonality became prominent, he enunciated the importance of character analysis and led us beyond symptomatology. As is well known, the individual's everyday reactions and the details of his style of expression became central in the therapy process. Originally, Reich's interest in character came about only because he believed the removal of characterological barriers was a prerequisite to the care of symptoms. Nevertheless, the general effect was to focus on the individual's function in everyday life. Now, we see that a person who speaks boringly rather than excitingly will diminish his sense of fulfillment. Such characteristics as tenderness, inventiveness, and fluency of language, are all viewed as central to the interactive group process and, indeed, to the individual's personal growth itself. Naturally, the importance of symptomatology is not ignored because symptoms are indeed specifically debilitating and do require attention. Furthermore, the characterology of one age may become the symptomatology of another. For example, the futility experienced by an individual whose work is inexorably wrong for him might be viewed as a symptom currently. Years ago it would not have seemed therapeutically central except as it may have led to pathology. Characterology and symptomatology are inter-related much as the melody and lyrics of a song are. Sometimes one takes precedence over the other. Nowadays the precedence of characterology plays an important technological role in permitting us an increasingly more public development of the encounter group. This is true primarily because it would seem insulting to many independently minded people to come to these groups for the cure of symptoms. The concept of the symptom reflects the isolation of a particular aspect of our lives. This has a self-depreciating effect. The individual dealing with a symptom becomes a less than global enemy.

The third aspect of group process that facilitates its use in community is the view of man as having a vectorial nature. Lewin long ago described the impact of the psychological environment by proposing the concept of vectors to take account of the direction, strength, and point of application of forces affecting the individual. The concept not only described what Lewin believed important for the individual; it also served his need to make descriptive diagrams as in mathematics and physics.

Our needs currently emphasize the raw nature of one's relationship to his environment taking into account the human mechanism and its place as part of the total interplay of social forces which determine the emergence of any described event. The old forms of psychological theorizing were concerned with such factors as morality, neurosis, and the meaning of events. Naturally, we still cannot disregard such inescapable characteristics of living. Nevertheless, now there is a new appreciation of the concepts of power, giving a primary importance to managing or manipulating the power which emanates from the environment. This power threatens the individual in his innermost regions, charging him with the selection or deflection of all forces streaming into his self-experience.

Reflecting the vectorial concern are the forms of anxieties proposed by R. D. Laing (Laing, 1961, 1965). These forms are engulfment, implosion, and petrifaction. Each of these, as we shall see, recognizes the power of the environment to create emphatic current effect. The concepts show appreciation of the emergency nature of ongoing events and take account of the centrality of retaining wholeness in the face of these social forces.

Engulfment, for example, is the loss of autonomy or identity through the development of relationship. One feels the risk of engulfment even when "being understood, in being loved, or even simply in being seen. To be hated may be feared for other reasons but to be hated as such is often less disturbing than to be destroyed, as it is felt, through being engulfed by love." The discovery that one may without succumbing to engulfment become understood and loved is a common phenomenon of the encounter group. The force of one's own identity remains intact even in union and in fact only through union does it become clear to the individual that his emergent nature is not a verification of his already existing identity but is a new nature currently unfolding and currently experienced. This condition creates excitement because unknown emergencies may arise at any moment and one may become newly formed before one's very own eyes and the eyes of other people with whom one is engaged.

Laing describes implosion as the filling of the individual's emptiness with new experience, "like a gas rushing in and obliterating a vacuum." People commonly resist incorporating a new experience. They have a large stake in maintaining their sensation level at an assimilable point. Each individual, knowing he can bear only a finite level of sensation, will be wary about reaching the danger point. If one is to play life safely, one permits only the degree of sensation which stops considerably short of what is actually assimilable. Into this vacuum created by the need to stay safely away from sensation, the implosive force may enter. The individual therefore needs to discover that possible excess of sensation can be discharged, an assurance requiring an atmosphere supporting free expression. The rush, therefore, of new experience may find the individual in panic if free expression is alien to him. However, when free expression is successfully permitted, the sudden rush of crying, laughter, sexual desire, or rage will result in a new sense of completeness. Thus, the individual needs help in the encounter group in transcending his intuitive anxiety about allowing his emptiness to be filled.

Laing's third source of anxiety, petrifaction, is the process of turning a person from a living into a dead thing. The interpersonal process becomes interrupted through habits which turn away the individuality of people and the awareness of the aliveness of present experience. For example, we may categorize an individual rather than describe him. We may pretend to be interested when we are not. We may assume we know what an individual wants before it has become revealed. We may judge others by their clothes or our own needs. In reaction against these depersonalizing forces, the encounter groups become dedicated to live exchange, to discovery of the actual natures of one another, and to the recovery of the senses of autonomy and interrelatedness. To help clarify this process, the following sketch is presented. It was written following an encounter group workshop to describe the group in the process of moving from petrifaction to personal autonomy and a new community feeling.

> People gather around and say we'll stay and know. But at first they do not know how for it seems like one shouldn't. It is dull to be so and each is surprised and relieved when the dullness is broken by a good word that says itself. Such a word is one which is here and says I have read Henry Miller. He says something to me and about me. But you are an assembly line inspector and stodgy and filled up too and how could you be reading so and knowing. I have to live, too, don't you know, and I don't know how out—but in there is something yet. If you can listen to it I can tell it.

> I sit on my simple and play complicated. Simple is I, you, we, they, and now. It plays better than the player. It invades each heart to loosen blood and love and letting. I may. I may talk, look, listen, touch, and jump

and delighted when in one sudden burst it is clear that I am here.

Here in a room with others who are all come to know what new ways there are to know and what the whole world tells of self and being. For it is especially big nowadays to be more—because we have done—and it is not enough.

Soon after the first surprise it is easier to talk from self and to know what sensations of self are. Work is done for this. It is embarrassing to be revealed, but hot and radiant when they are discovered as bending friend who receives all shock and new—without altering into gone.

The days grow and so do they into a warming one of trust, where all could be said and say. They soft each other into life with the flavor of new society.

The fourth factor supporting new modes of encounter is the current focus on interactional dynamics. One method representing this frame of mind is Gestalt therapy. The two primary interrelated principles which determine Gestalt therapy's view of man is that contactfulness and awareness are necessary for optimal function. Through contactfulness, man meets his environment. He confronts it and manipulates it, drawing from it that which he needs for his basic biological sustenance and for the derivative psychological necessities. As Perls, Hefferline, and Goodman have pointed out

> Concern is felt for a present problem, and the excitement mounts toward the coming but as yet unknown solution. The assimilating of novelty occurs in the present moment as it passes into the future. Its result is never merely a rearrangement of the unfinished situations of the organism but a configuration containing a new material from the environment, and therefore different from what could be remembered (or

guessed at), just as the work of an artist becomes unpredictably new to him as he handles the material medium. (Perls, Hefferline & goodman, 1951).

Given contactfulness as a guideline of human function, we might expect that group interactions would be characterized by much interpersonal confrontation. People would reach out to each other in their present situation. They would not be as likely to analyze each other's past developments as to enter into here and now statements and actions. Consequently, the creation of crises and excitement is common. The group becomes an adventure because interactional conflict replaces the older introspections *about* inner conflicts. There is a concerted effort to maximize contactfulness and to identify all possible sources of deflection from contact. The therapist must give specific attention to the characteristic ways barriers to contact are set up. He must see that certain patients look away when talking, ask questions when they mean to make statements, use lengthy introductions to simple observations, compulsively tell both sides of all stories, sit in statue-like positions, use mannerisms and expressions which reflect disinterest, play for sympathy, use submissive words when their tones are hostile, and so on, endlessly. These resistances are approached frontally, in the belief that with their resolution good contact will naturally follow.

Awareness which is reciprocally related to contactfulness is accentuated by phenomenological questions such as what are you feeling, what do you want, and what are you doing. These questions enable people to describe their inner process. Through this accentuation of inner process, excitement is magnified, thereby supporting the strongest interactional possibilities. Awareness is the ground upon which human existence is played out. It forms the support for contactfulness and defines the fulfillment received from the contact operations.

In the foregoing pages, the encounter group has been designated as the transitional experience moving the psychotherapy process into the community at large. In these groups many persons have learned a new depth of personal absorption through full contact with other people, through directed awareness of one's own inner process, and through experimentation with new behaviors. These are the basic ingredients of the new philosophy of encounter and the impact has revealed personal beauty too attractive to be restricted, as in the past, to people willing to be viewed as patients. Becoming aware of the half-filled life through the contrasting fuller experience of encounter group has stimulated the psychological profession to extend its hopes, leaving the private office behind and entering into new fellowship and mutuality with people who are in their accustomed haunts and who are carrying on their familiar functions. The flower is wild and must be appreciated where it lives.

Before proceeding to a description of community exploration, we will now touch base about our readiness for a social psychotherapy, where some of its antecedents are and what the implications are for life in our society.

Many years ago during a discussion with the clergy about the commonalities and differences between psychotherapy and religion, I said teasingly that one of the main differences between the two was that psychotherapists try to put themselves out of business whereas religionists are self-perpetuating. Though I preferred the psychotherapists' attitude at the time, I later came to realize that we have been deluding ourselves through the concept of terminated therapy. We have hoped, if not expected, that after working privately with people for six months or six years, a terminal moment will come and our services will no longer be needed. That this hope is fruitless is now abundantly clear. The expectation of global resolutions ignores the fact that life's most problematic engagements occur repeatedly and we can expect never to be rid of them. Problems centering around death, birth, marriage, loss of job, exclusion from one community or another, expression of self, misunderstandings, new ventures, and so on, are the core of ongoing lives and thus far we as psychotherapists have had no constituted continuity in our relationships with people who live such lives.

The people of religion do involve themselves in these inexorable aspects of living. But they have been operating with severe theological and institutional handicaps and frequently look to the psychological fields to fill the gaps in personal experience fostered by their system. The priority posed in the relationship of man to God has overshadowed the contact between man and man. Psychotherapists have been filling this breach especially recently, by their insights concerning the impactfulness of the encounter. We have known since Freud about the special, even volatile, powers which exist in the psychotherapy encounter. Breuer was frightened when he discovered the intensity of the feelings that his patients developed for him. Freud's discovery of transference acknowledged this intensity. Through this concept, the therapist for many years was able to keep his distance from the fullest potency which developed through the condensed power of the psychotherapy encounter. Over the years we have been learning to accept the intensity of this encounter at its face value. We are now closer to treating it as an authentic interaction revealing the nature of all the people engaged whether in private therapy or in a group situation. The widespread habits of deflection and depersonalization, which have evolved through proliferated politeness, structured grammar, and avoidance of the natural flow of one's own mind, have stored up large quantities of energy. When somebody tells a real truth that is meaningful, pointed, and previously blocked, a room of people becomes enlivened and very deeply absorbed. Because of the extensions in time spent together, there are new opportunities to resolve unfinished situations. This potentiality is increased even though the group impactfulness sometimes comes too fast, even though there may be excessive and unassimilable energy released, and even though the complications of personal interaction may require sorting and interweaving. The power of these experiences may arise through provocative, brash, or hurting interactions, or power may come when a well-timed statement genuinely touches a person. A simple remark like "I think you are a very sensitive man" may bring on tears from a man who has never before been viewed as sensitive. A touch of the hand may bespeak profound acceptance.

With such a power as is inherent in encounter groups, it is only a short step to go beyond the retreat situation into those which normally exist all around us. We already have used encounter methods as a new approach to old consulting requirements. This includes working with education systems, including teachers, administrators, and pupils; industrial executives; religious enclaves and church groups; Synanon; staff development programs; workshops for lay persons; workshops for therapists; and, of course, all this in addition to the expanding use of group therapy methods in working with classical patients. Now we are also becoming emboldened to explore in uncharted community settings where psychotherapists have not only had little prior experience, but deep resistance to participation. One example, among a growing number of them, is my exploration of psychotherapy methods in a public coffee house. A series of coffee house meetings called Encounter was arranged. The meetings were conducted from the stage at regular coffee house evening hours as a part of the public and semicommercial aspect of the enterprise. This particular coffee house was deep in the heart of a Cleveland hippie land. The coffee house was under repeated harassment by the police, partly because of their concern with the possible drug traffic and partly because of supposed disturbances which the coffee house aroused in the neighborhood. We met irregularly, averaging about once every two weeks from July 1967 to March 1968, when the coffee house was destroyed by fire.

These coffee house sessions were set up to explore the encounter possibilities in large community settings. Three main purposes formed the foundation of our engagement. The first was to activate group participation to dramatize the underlying modes of experience that existed in the community. The second was to establish the validity of topic-centeredness within the encounter of therapeutic process. The third was to permit and encourage changes in the attitudes or self-experiences where these were self-defeating.

The first purpose, the activation of group participation, was an attempt to counteract the familiar spectator character of most large group situations. The outsize demands of talking to a crowd of lined-up strangers are familiarly torturous. Large audiences, though they promise magnified liveliness, can also be unmanageably depersonalized. In the art of public communication only the best of us can retain feelings of immediacy or personal effect. The unilateral statement reigns in religion, politics, education, entertainment, and advertising. Little room exists for the working-through process. Religious services are often so stereotyped, repetitive, and irrelevant that one rabbi was able to tell me, half in humor and half in dismay, that some of his most knowledgeable people make excuses to him for having come to the services. One person explains to him that his child happened to be singing in the chorus; another explains he is only interested in a certain speaker; another comes for some special commemorative experience. In politics, strategy transcends all questions of sincerity or immediacy.

Can the encounter group style be assimilated into large groups or even conferences? In the encounter group we learn personal interaction by splitting into smallnesses, no larger a group than would permit everybody the chance to unfold in a way that is personally appreciated. Undoubtedly these opportunities represent a large advance; not so great an advance as to create all we need. The small group is too small a world to live in. In society, since interconnectedness and interdependence are unavoidable, there must be some way of relating to the larger community. Otherwise we invite secrecy, which does characterize current psychotherapy practices, or we become esoteric, spreading bewilderment when we approach the uninitiated. In experiencing the largeness of the community, there is a contagion of spirit which stretches beyond the exclusive workings of the now familiar intimate smallness of the encounter group. We have much to learn about meeting in mass but it is clear that the harmonious presence of many people magnifies our own inner experience and our relatedness to others. This challenge is relevant now wherever responsiveness is minimal.

In the coffee house, conversation and play were the common mode among the customers. That was what they came for. Nevertheless, they needed some activities which could bring the total group together. Usually this would happen through poetry readings, musical performances, and even lectures. These were the only ways they did come together as a united group. The spontaneity of their ordinary dialogue would be interrupted by these spectator experiences. Our wish was to bring the total room together by including spontaneous interaction. Naturally our possibilities were limited by the deliberateness required in starting the encounter session. The proprietor would get on the stage to introduce me and I would explain what we were trying to do. People were permitted to come and go as they pleased or to talk to each other or not. The customers would be different from meeting to meeting, though a core of people would come repeatedly. Naturally, certain disadvantages existed, such as lack of follow-through with people who did not come repeatedly. Some people would leave before resolutions could be reached, but the advantage we gained was that we stayed closer to the real community by making only minimal restrictions and arrangements.

Our first meeting was centered around the topic of hippies and a policeman and illustrates the participating body which emerged in these sessions. People were selected to role-play a hippie and a policeman in conversation. They started out saying very stereotyped words to each other. The policeman wanted the hippie to go out and get a job, quit wearing crazy hairdos and clean up. He described the hippie as being unruly, dangerous, and unappetizing. The hippie, on the other hand, saw the policeman as a brute—cold, lacking understanding, insensitive, unreachable. At first no matter what I would say to them the responses remained stereotyped and cruel. When confronted with the outlandishness of some of his remarks, the policeman at one point was taken aback and began to examine his feelings. He then said that he really had a job to do and could not afford to have much feeling about what he was doing. He just wanted to get it over with. He did not want to have to think about it. Furthermore, he was afraid he might get hurt if he did not stay tough. The hippie did not give any specific recognition to the change in tone of the policeman and continued talking as he had before. When this was called to his attention he recognized that this was true. He recognized that it might now be possible to communicate with the policeman. But he said he did not want to. He wanted the policeman to remain an impossible person against whom he could vent his anger and his superiority. He wanted to continue to be angry and if he could possibly avoid recognizing and accepting the fact that the policeman was different, he would do so. Thus he continued to be adamant and vocal even arousing cheers from the audience when he would get off an especially eloquent line. He was unwittingly making a very important commentary on the nature of conflict, even as it relates to the large social movements, such as black-white confrontation and conflicts between nations. A great force of unexpressed and unsatisfied inner experience builds up and must have its opportunity to emerge. When conditions against which these experiences are directed change and when the expression of inner experience has not been completed, the need to complete the blocked expression remains. One is likely, therefore, to ignore changes in the environment until one's need is completed. The militant blacks have unfinished business and have to release their fury as though no improvements have developed. The variations in timeliness among parties to a conflict cause considerable trouble. One side is resolved, the other is not. Thus, by reacting as though the old conditions were still true, resolutions must be delayed until the party with unfinished business can complete his accumulated need for expression.

In this coffee house session there were about 125 people present. Unlike the ordinary audience, this one actively participated. People began to question the right of the policeman to say that which they felt had no foundation in reality and which they felt illustrated not only his errors of thinking but was also symbolic of the errors in the thinking of society as a whole. As the situation developed, the policeman and the hippie were asked to switch roles. They did this much to the relief of the man who had been playing the policeman. He now suddenly became quite relaxed in the friendly atmosphere. The switch in roles aroused the audience to the dynamics of role-playing and the implications of the barrier-free situation. They also wanted to play roles and several groups of persons did. Soon a communal spirit had developed. There was considerable communication similar to the type one might find in a very large therapy situation. Then, the last person to play the role of the policeman left the stage and went to the rear of the room to arrest the proprietor, confronting him with certain violations which would make him subject to arrest. The proprietor refused to give the policeman full information, standing on his rights to give only his full name. The policeman then told the proprietor that he was under arrest and proceeded to lead him to the door of the coffee house. The proprietor did not go willingly but resisted only a little as he respected and feared the power of the policeman. The people in the audience, however, began to shout "don't let him take him away," leaving their tables to join in a rescue attempt. A wild melee ensued. People were swinging their arms, lifting chairs threateningly, shouting. Anyone entering the coffee house at that moment would have felt certain that a riot was in progress. When the force of their aggression had spent itself and the rescue operation had succeeded, the people returned to their tables. They had a feeling of having yielded to a powerful drama. What had begun as simple role-playing by two people had ended as a most dramatic audience role-playing situation. The community involvement gave a cathartic and poetic line to the expression of 125 people. When all became seated again, there was an air of hushed awe at what had happened. A large group had walked the line between poetry and the reality. Though one could not always tell the difference between the poetry and the reality the individuals in the group, though fully invested, were aware of their perspective and never allowed the dramatic situation to carry them into acts which would have been disharmonious with the existing conditions. Nobody used the situation as an excuse for actual violence. The group discussed the meaning of the experience and the prevailing view was that people were expressing their suppressed aggression against the police—acting out in the role-playing situation what they would like to do in real life, but have felt powerless. This powerlessness resulted, said they, in their feeling of alienation and, furthermore, the opportunity to act the scene out brought them together into a sense of community.

Another illustration of extensive audience involvement was an encounter session on riots and hostility. The topic had been suggested the previous week by the audience and the enthusiasm for it was great. The audience was packed, standing five deep around the room of filled tables. Three people were selected to play roles; one was to play a conservative, another apathy, and the other a Black Muslim. Immediately after the role playing began it became evident that the conservative was playing an extremist role. He was extremely derisive about Negroes. He flung invective about their dirtiness, their animal natures, and their repulsiveness. He accused them of having garbage cans for back yards, of being stupid, lazy, and stinking. He was very persuasively vituperative and insulting. The reaction was very powerful. One Negro rushed up from the back of the room, shouting furiously at the conservative, responding not as a spectator of a stage drama, but as though this invective had been aimed directly at him. Here again it would have been difficult to know whether this was reality or poetry. The atmosphere was electric. It was profoundly absorbing, frightening, and surprising to be sitting in a room where violence could erupt at any moment, yet there was, nevertheless, considerable trust that this would not happen. Indeed, the most volatile of the black people climbed the stage at the end of the session to tell the audience that he loved them despite the anger-making scene. I tried working with the conservative to determine how he felt about getting the kind of reactions he was getting. He became quite confused for a moment because he did not know whether I wanted him to continue role playing or whether he was to tell what his own true feelings were. I asked him to continue role playing but to also tell how he felt and to allow himself the freedom to play the role any way he wanted to. He immediately returned to the original adamant vituperative position, expressing none of his personal reactions to the verbal onslaught which his words had brought on. It became apparent that he was completely inflexible as long as he was playing a role. I explained this process to the audience and to him, the process wherein the people who play roles in the society have lost their freedom, their individuality, and their openness to experiencing the present moment. They wind up with stereotyped, programmed living, experiencing little free choice. This was a dramatic illumination to them. At the next session we continued the same topic but changed the role-playing scene. The audience became very active, many people again presenting their views about racial questions. At one point a young girl called out from the rear of the room, confronting a man playing a liberal suburbanite with his backward ideas. She entered into a heated exchange with him. He asked her whether she would date a Negro boy and she said of course she would. She then went on to describe her happy relationships with Negro boys, seeming quite unself-conscious, unapologetic, and dramatically simple in her statements of freedom of choice irrespective of race. The feeling in the room grew into a feeling of unity and many people described their feelings about race relations. The issue of black power arose. Considerable support for black power was voiced, especially among the Negroes. A climactic moment arrived when a young white man arose and expressed his fury at the black power people because of having been turned away by a Negro group at the anti-Vietnam war demonstrations in New York City. He had come there to join in the march and had wanted to enter with a group of Negroes. They told him they didn't want to have any white man joining them. Thus, he poured out his frustration. The tension in the room grew. Then, after several exchanges, one of the black power adherents stood up on his chair and with what I felt as touching eloquence, tenderly spoke to this man in the crowded audience telling him about the Negro's needs for identification and for self-propulsion. He said he hoped white men would take a path parallel to their own and that they could join together again later. In the meantime, he wanted this man to be patient and recognize the Negro's need for establishing his own identity without white support. The statement had an electric quality. The dangers of violence or vituperation were so great that the contrast created by this man's tenderness and articulateness were a great relief and offered so renewed a perspective on the problem that the audience rested and the session ended.

The second of our purposes was to include topic-centeredness in the encounter situation. Topic-centeredness is frequently excluded from group therapy situations, which focus upon personal experience of the participants and frown upon intellectualism. In some of my therapy groups when an individual brings up topics like the Vietnam war, contemporary architecture, the political structure, current events, teaching techniques, and so on, many people in the groups will protest that these issues are not relevant to their own personal explorations. Actually, nothing is further from the truth. Our lives are tied into external events. As long as we do not depersonalize, we must unite our interests with those of the environmental forces. Indeed, when we have in these groups been able to join personal feeling with discussions of environmental conditions such as the Vietnam war, powerful interactions have developed. One man, after a lengthy discussion of the Vietnam war, said his son might be getting into it and gave his own impassioned view of the conflict, developing real grief about the many deaths and his own deeply felt terror about his son entering it. Psychotherapists, through our theories of personal introspection and our concern with only what is immediately before us, may, in developing group psychotherapy, have cut out the substance of our existences and made our group situations overly stylized and irrelevant. In these coffee house sessions, we have tried to move beyond these limitations and have tried to develop topics as a core around which the encounters emerge. The previous illustrations, though centered around topics, had their most powerful effect as audience dramas. The next illustrations, however, although also involving audience participation, reveal the importance of topic-centeredness in the community encounter. The topic was hippies and straight people.

Arrangements had been made for a group of so-called straight people to attend our session. These people served at another Cleveland coffee house. They were friendly with hippies and respectful but lived well-organized lives, dressed conventionally, lived in familiar family relationships, and worked in continuing jobs. In addition to the invited straight people there were others who just came in. Thus, there were at least as many so-called straight people as there were so-called hippies.

The session started out stiffly but it was not long before one of the hippies confronted the straight people by brazenly accusing them of unwillingness to participate actively. His name was Jack and he became the center of a storm. He was experienced as shoving his stereotypes down the throats of the people present. The straight people did not like it but they were at a disadvantage because they were accustomed to politeness and permissiveness and they were taken aback by the sudden and stark attack. The ball was rolling, though, and a marked polarization developed between the so-called hippies and the so-called straight people. Each side was unhappy to categorize and did not like being called either hippy or straight. The idea that all people are individual and ought to be treated as such was predominant. Nevertheless, in spite of these high-minded attitudes, each side was considerably stereotyped about the other and became very defensive about its own position. Some of the straight people finally became so angry that they left their seats and walked toward Jack and some of the other hippies haranguing them about their refusal to examine them as individual people. They said Jack and his associates were presumptuous. The straight people were especially irate when Jack accused them of coming down to the coffee house to get respite from their dreary lives. Other statements were equally confronting. In the beginning there was little effort to find out about other people's lives. Everybody seemed to know. As the session continued, people within the hippie group began to speak out against Jack's view and to point out that they really cared about the straight people. They did want to make contact on an individual and respectful basis. One hippie girl said they were afraid of the straight people because they were older and because they were really afraid of their own parents. They would like to join their parents but knew they could not. She said her own father would never be caught dead in a place like the coffee house and always refused to have anything to do with her views concerning life. She was glad the straight people had come. This view was echoed by others. They wanted an expansion of their community and an expansion of their opportunity for communicating with people who have made it in society. One girl thought that in hearing the views expressed that the straight people were nothing but old hippies.

The concept of topic-centeredness pervaded all of our sessions just as did the concept of audience participation and drama. A list of the topics includes psychedelic trips, how to experience change, how to create change, hippies and teachers, hippies and schools, sex between the races, how to evade the draft, the meaning of war, getting along without money, the relationship of love and sex, the needs of the coffee house community, hippies and policemen, hippies and straight people, riots and hostility, religion and society, and listening and communication. All of these topics aroused very lively interactions. Frequently these interactions were verbally aggressive. Aggressiveness and directness would almost invariably turn the session into an exciting one. Intellectual discussions invariably toned the room down and resulted in impatience and restlessness. The statement which strongly affected another individual person was the one most likely to pay off in good communication and a sense of unified community.

The third condition underlying our coffee house sessions was the effort to work through problems characteristically expressed by members of the group. One of our sessions dealt with the coffee house people's hang-ups about communicating to people outside of their small groups. There had been a vigorous encounter two weeks earlier about religion. There had been quite a few religionists in the coffee house; some were from an urban ministry program, another group were evangelists who had been asked to come for this night. I introduced the evening by saying we would continue with the topic of religion as we had not finished it the previous time. One of the hippies immediately said that he did not believe in God, thereby dismissing religion altogether. He felt, as I pointed out to him, that God and religion were indispensable to each other and that there was no way to talk about one without talking about the other. He thought it was all a great hoax set up to make people do things they did not want to do and he wanted no part of it. There were echoes of similar sentiment from others in the room. Most of it was deflected and mumbled with an impatience suggesting there really was not much to talk about. Some thoughts about religion were developed which went beyond God and into personal desires, meaningfulness, and so on. One person said his own religion was based on morality rather than God, and that his morality was a morality of self. He said that when he felt that he was doing something "correctly" that he was being moral and religious. This, he believed, had nothing to do with God or the conventional principles of morality. I asked him when he experienced himself doing things correctly, therefore realizing his own religious directions. He said he was doing things correctly right now. As he said this his face rose in a lovely smile, his radiance giving evidence that he did indeed feel that what he was saying was correct and that for him this was an authentically religious experience. In the meantime, one table of about ten hippies was noisy and unwilling to be fully involved in the proceedings. Every once in a while they would engage in perceptive catcalling, making some diminishing remarks about religion but not really engaging with the rest of the room. I became interested in this group. Without their participation it seemed like the discussion would be limited. Furthermore, they were the very people for whom the discussions were intended. Therefore, it was necessary to face up to their disinterest and restlessness.

It was not long before people in the room were beginning to be annoyed with these people. One woman finally arose, loudly remonstrating with them for their refusal to be reached and for their discourtesy. She also wanted to be heard by them. One of them said she was being belligerent and that they did not dig belligerence. The question arose as to whether they would listen to ordinary communication or whether they would respond only to excessive energy.

One man said that these young people had something very special among themselves, great mutual acceptance and deep enjoyment which he felt was a religious expression. Another minister at the other end of the room said he did not think this was very religious at all. He said they were nothing more than a clique refusing to engage with others in society.

After considerable discussion, one of the hippies got up and said, addressing the room in general, "Make it, don't fake it." He said most of the people in the room were not honest and there was no way to have any good communication if people were being phony. This aroused a mountainous rage in me which poured out from the frustrations in communication. I confronted these people with the realities of good communication and the difficulties in communicating beyond one's own restricted clique. They were taking very little responsibility for good contact and I resented their closed system, which threw out potshots every now and then about the worthlessness of whatever did not crack into their system. I left the stage and approached them screaming my words. They now began to listen to my impassioned words about their clique which judges others without listening. When I was done they said to me, "We are not interested in talking about religion, we want to talk about riots." Finally they had said what they were really interested in. Immediately, the room came alive. Somebody referred to whites as honkies. Feelings became aroused and what followed was a familiar encounter session phenomenon of powerful assertiveness in a nonviolent context. This is refreshing because it permits aggressive expression without the usual risks. As we went on the group became more nearly unified than before; not unified in agreement but unified in personal involvement.

Eve's Daughters: The Forbidden Heroism of Women

Miriam Polster

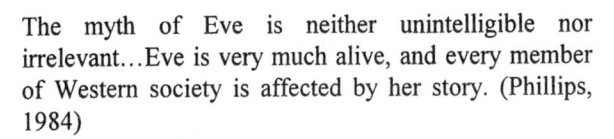

> The myth of Eve is neither unintelligible nor irrelevant...Eve is very much alive, and every member of Western society is affected by her story. (Phillips, 1984)

For centuries, our hero tales have set forth, in dramatic and colorful terms, the cultural ideals and necessities of human times. These tales have provided countless generations of people with models of how to confront and deal effectively with hard times and personal challenges. They still do.

But along the way, and for reasons that make less sense than they once did, our images of heroism have endorsed a persistent model that has left us a legacy of ideals and behaviors that are admired in men, but mistrusted in women.

The predominant image of heroism, immortalized for centuries, has been active: bold, noisy, swift, and physically direct. Boys and men, often to their own discomfort, and sometimes even to their despair, are still admired for this kind of behavior. They have been encouraged to be tough, aggressive, self-confident, and independent—never mind whether or not this actually fits them or the times in which they live.

Correspondingly, girls and women were discouraged from exhibiting such classic heroic behaviors. They were admired for being unaggressive, gentle, submissive, and not self-confident or independent (Bardwick, 1971). Until recently, this is what most people considered normal and healthy behavior in women. Many still do, but ask yourself how healthy such behavior actually is.

The result? Heroism came to be considered an exclusively masculine attribute—one to which men could aspire—and women only if they acted like men. The image of heroism became a grand societal introjection, a massive "should" system. Under this influence, both sexes were provided with standards of "appropriateness."

It seems clear, however, that women (and men, as well) were thereby deprived of behavioral options that might actually be effective and sensible under the circumstances of their individual lives. Their sense of personal choice and competence was reduced. This is a dilemma with which we are only too familiar in psychotherapy.

HEROISM: THE FIRST DOUBLE STANDARD

> Where the apple reddens
> Never Pry—
> Lest we lose our Edens,
> Eve and I.
> —Robert Browning, A Woman's Last Words

The one-sided images that have dominated our ideas of heroism have their early expression in some of our culture's most treasured stories and legends—the Greek and Biblical accounts of the creation of the world. The oldest example of the difference in heroic recognition can be found in the stories of Prometheus and Eve. Both disobeyed the explicit commands of their gods. But although their behaviors were strikingly similar, Prometheus is regarded as a hero, whereas Eve has come down in most accounts as a classic villain.

According to Greek legend, Prometheus made the first man, fashioning him (like the God of Genesis) out of earth and water (Graves, 1982). Zeus, the lord of Mount Olympus, further empowered Prometheus to give his new creature a gift—any gift but fire, which was to remain the exclusive property of the gods.

Prometheus had a special fondness for his offspring and wanted to enrich him as much as he could. Fire seemed the perfect gift, and so Prometheus stole fire from the gods and gave it to the first man. For this, he was punished severely; Zeus had him chained to a rock where a vulture came daily to eat his liver, which, by the way, grew back nightly, thus extending his cruel (and certainly unusual) punishment even further (Bulfinch, 1979).

Prometheus' gift, as in most mythological themes, was a metaphor. His gift of fire was an assertion of his wish that his creature dominate all the other animals. It also symbolized one step along the way in humankind's increasing control of the dangerous natural elements that threatened human survival. Not only could fire create light in the darkness, but it also could transmute raw and unformed matter into a useful form. Prometheus' gift forged an ambitious connection between human aspiration and divine mastery. Although his gift proved to be a mixed blessing, generating its own burdens, his generosity was esteemed as a noble and beneficial act.

What about Eve?

One tradition tells us how the wily serpent nudged Eve against the forbidden tree and thereby proved to her that she would not die from just *touching* it (as Jehovah had warned). But this was just the opening salvo in his sales pitch. The serpent went further and argued that this proved that she could, therefore, also *eat* of the fruit of that tree—and not die (Graves & Patai, 1966). The benefit of that snack, the serpent promised, would be that the day she ate of the fruit of the tree, her eyes would "be opened" and she would be "as God, knowing good and evil." As with

Prometheus, Eve aspired to a capacity that was explicitly limited to divinity. But this time the suggestion came from a disreputable source and was directed toward a gullible and naïve subject.

Eve was enterprising. She found the serpent's message irresistible: Imagine, a privilege reserved for divinity also might be appropriate for human purposes. Like Prometheus, she was ambitious, and like Prometheus, she was punished for her defiance. But the similarity ends there.

Prometheus suffered in a "manly" fashion. He suffered alone, and he did not lie or try to pin the blame on anyone else. Once punished he endured his agony admirably. He became the subject of poetry, music, and paintings, all which extolled him. Eve, on the other hand, has been portrayed as evasive and unadmirable. She has been held responsible for evoking all the pain and toil that her descendants have endured ever since.

But let us take another look. Actually, Eve's act of disobedience admitted her—and all of us, whether or not we want it—into a previously forbidden territory of awareness, the knowledge of good and evil. Because of Eve, we all live in a world where personal consciousness underlies individual decision, where personal responsibility replaced docile obedience to divine authority. Like Prometheus' gift of energy and power, Eve's legacy ensured that, through our own energy, we are now to be held responsible for the consequences, happy as well as tragic, of our own actions.

Most parents welcome the development of curiosity, judgment, and conscience in their children. The curiosity of children and their increasing ability to ask useful questions mark their progress in becoming intelligent, reasonable, and self-determining members of society. The elementary questions of childhood, and the responses to these questions, serve as the basis for the moral and ethical standards of adulthood. As psychotherapists, we consider the development and support of these qualities essential to healthy self-governance.

Eve was unwilling to live innocently under protective restrictions, submissive to a divine but unexplained command that assured her status forever as the protected child of a benevolent but not-to-be-questioned father. Her surge into maturity grew naturally from her curiosity and liveliness of mind. She, like Prometheus, had aspirations that distinguished her from less complicated creatures — animals for whom knowledge and choice were dominated by instinctual species-specific needs and controlled, therefore, almost exclusively by instinct. The knowledge of good and evil is a source of energy and power, like fire, and brings with it the inevitable need to develop judgment, deliberation, and conscience.

The legacy of Prometheus is still with us, even though our generation has gone far beyond the simple fire power of our mythological ancestors. We have escalated this energy into creative and life-supporting activities that Prometheus could not have dreamed of, but we have learned, to our dismay, that it also can carry within it a destructive power that our ancestors thought only gods possessed. The issue now is whether or not we can develop the wisdom to control this force.

The legacy of Eve is also still with us. Unwilling to live in a Paradise where she could not direct her own thoughts and behavior, her example has resounded throughout history in other troublesome human demands for appropriate participation and self-governance. The American colonists and the French peasantry made the same claim centuries later. Less than 100 years after that, woman suffragists asserted their right to vote on the laws and legislators that in large part determined their way of life. Eve's legacy reverberates in every woman's assertion that it is her birthright to make informed decisions about the conduct of her own life and of the world in which she lives.

Eve's dilemma also is repeated in the predicament that many modern women experience. Few women today would be willing to submit to an imposed innocence, nor would they believe that such a prerequisite would carry the promise of a Paradise in which it is worthwhile to live. Hungry for the full exercise of their intelligence and energy, modern women are asking disturbing questions and making troublesome demands. Their struggles lead women out of a distant and mythic Paradise into a real world of struggle—and achievement.

THE FUNCTIONS AND ATTRIBUTES OF HEROISM

> Without heroes, we're all plain people and don't know how far we can go. (Bernard Malamud, *The Natural*)

The search for heroes begins in our childhood and continues for a lifetime. As children, we knew pretty early who our heroes were; we found them in our families and in our fairy tales. Later, as adolescents and adults, we peered beyond the limits of our accustomed selves and found heroes in other times, other places, and sometimes other worlds. The concept of heroism nourished a constant and important hunger. It connected us with eternal and central human concerns.

The image of the hero endures because it serves a basic human need. It appears in different forms, with different voices and different actions. At its best, our admiration for heroes represents the human desire to resolve, even for a moment, the inconsistencies and injustices that every person experiences or witnesses. Heroism links the events and challenges of the commonplace actions, when behavior often seems dictated by reflex or habit, and reminds us of the lasting concerns and aspirations that have animated the human spirit for centuries. The hero dramatically transforms noble impulse into appropriate action, and for that moment, the kaleidoscopic pieces of human experience fall into place.

In its earliest form, the heroic image was a persuasive way to assure the continued survival of the community, be it family, clan, or tribe. In primitive times, a definition of heroism based on strength, speed, and the physical ability to overpower an adversary was essential to survival. Introspection would be, at best, a leisure activity, not useful in dangerous conditions.

Today, however, thoughtful men and women are questioning whether or not the classic stereotype continues to offer a viable promise of survival in our complicated universe. Mark Gerzon (1982), for example, suggests that we now have a choice of heroes but that they must be heroes of a different kind, since today we *all* live on the battlefield. John Kegan (1987), too, eloquently points out the risks that inhere in our antiquated concept of heroic leadership. He argues that we live in a "postheroic" age, and that this is no time for our leaders to play Alexander the Great.

If we think of Eve as a hero like Prometheus, instead of as a disreputable sinner, her behavior becomes a challenging legacy instead of a taint. Eve's Biblical name, Hahweh, means "the mother of us all" (Phillips, 1984). So we live in the world she left us—no Paradise to be sure. We pick up where she left off. Her struggles preceded ours, but they still are relevant to ours, and even more important, her heroism adds a woman's dimension to the heroic image.

Once we move beyond the archaic heroic stereotypes, it is apparent that heroes are more numerous than we thought. Such an abundance of heroes, fully perceived and appreciated, provides a range of heroic characteristics that are shared by women and men. The power of the heroic image to encourage and inspire is not lost; it is actually enlarged. For the individual, the sense of personal heroism can make the difference between feeling like a victim of immutable influences and feeling like a person who has a hand in shaping the events of her or his own life.

WOMEN'S HEROISM

What distinguishes the heroism of women in particular? Let us single out two elements, connection and fairness or responsibility, although there are more. These particular characteristics add breadth and dimension to the more traditional images we have inherited. Perhaps, if we can assimilate them into our present images, it will make the heroic attitude more reachable for contemporary men, as well as for women.

Connection

Gilligan, Lyons, and Hamner (1990) point out how the sense of connection shapes much of women's adolescence. Tannen (1990), too, has shown how the sense of connection pervades women's language. It is also a rich source of their heroism. Women's heroism is more likely to be marked by a sense of personal connection to other people with whom they feel a strong bond of kinship. This kinship may be familial, it may be neighborly, or it may be a link with other people with whom they feel they share a plight.

Much of women's heroism is directed by a strong sense of "the other." Their political involvement, for example, often begins in fighting for or opposing issues at a *grass-roots* level, in circumstances that move them or their loved ones personally, with characters with problems with which they can identify. From these beginnings, they move on. Many women who later worked for women's suffrage, for example, actually cut their political teeth on the abolitionist cause.

Remember the persistent vigil of the mothers and wives of political victims in South America? Under the windows of the dictators, they carried photographs of their husbands, sons, and daughters who had disappeared. These individual pictures cohered like tiles in a mosaic—each one adding its share of protest against the oppressor.

Sophia Bracy Harris and her sister were the first black children to go to an all-white high school in Wetumpka, Ala., in 1965. Her home was bombed, and she lived daily with the ostracism and scorn of both students and faculty. Years later, inspired by that early experience, she organized the Black Woman's Leadership and Economic Development Project to help black women get off of welfare and out of dead-end jobs. She remembered the anguish of her own high school days and wanted to help others to move beyond their pain. She said, "I'm not taking struggle. Struggle is OK. It's the pain that is wrong" (from *Mother Jones Magazine*, January 1988).

From their beginnings with personal projects, women moved on to founding local institutions to care for the sick, the needy, and those too young or too weak to care for themselves. Now women are moving on even further, to more global issues, generalizing from individual cases into powerful statements that dramatize larger concerns. The women who were active in political campaigns, either for specific causes or as workers for someone else's candidacy, have progressed in increasing numbers to become candidates themselves.

Fairness or Responsibility

In a ground-breaking study, Carol Gilligan (1982) inquired into the basis on which women and men make their moral judgments. She observed that men seem more likely to base such judgments on a principle of "fairness," while the judgments of women more often rest on the basis of "responsibility."

"Fairness" implies a set of rules or a code (either articulated or implicit) that determines what behaviors may be justifiable under certain circumstances. Furthermore, it then establishes precedents that are to regulate subsequent interactions. The concept of fairness assumes the existence of a rational and orderly world.

The problem is that, all too often, fairness is an ethic that is invoked to govern the dealings between supposed equals. While this is admirable in theory, it may be a failure in practice, because this equality rests uneasily on an exclusionary system of eligibility. Some individuals, although subject to a system's rules, have been powerless in formulating them. Continuing debates about the need for separate *but* equal criteria for school curricula, funds, and teaching staff, and about quota systems that some people claim create new ills to take the place of those they were set up to correct, are examples of the riddles that remain to be unraveled in the name of fairness.

How one woman combined a sense of fairness and a heroic sense of connection is exemplified by the legal battle of Beulah Mae Donald against the Mobile, Ala., Klansmen who murdered and lynched her son Michael. The trial was dramatic, with a tearful witness-stand apology from one of the defendants and a forgiving response from Ms. Donald. When the trial was over, the jury had awarded her a sum of money that led to the Klan's having to turn over to her the deed to its headquarters building. To her, the money was unimportant, as she had lived on little money all her life. What was important to her was that it had been proved that Michael had done no wrong (reported in the *New York Times*, November 1, 1987).

"Responsibility" is less devoted to calculating equality or regulating evenhanded transactions. Considerations about responsibility hinge instead on a scale of relationship, continuity, and circumstantial complexity. The dominant values here are interpersonal. They center around human costs rather than statistical values that are figured in percentages and precedents.

There is no doubt that the principle of fairness regulates many important human affairs. It seems clear, however, that these principles may not always be adequate to deal with much that matters deeply to many people. No sensible argument would try to establish which of the two values is superior. But moral judgments strongly influence the heroic response. *Heroism, after all, is idealism in action.*

The classic heroic images that have lasted throughout centuries still animate the heroic attitude. Cleared of traditional stereotypes, they can reflect the influence of women's heroism, enriching the heroic possibilities for men as well as women. Let us consider four basic attributes of heroism, essential values that animate the heroic attitude and that are served by heroes of either sex.

FOUR BASIC FUNCTIONS AND ATTRIBUTES OF HEROISM

First: Respect for Human Life

The single outstanding and lasting example of heroic behavior is when one person risks her or his life to save another's. And women are well represented in those efforts. Uli Dericksen, the purser on a plane that was involved in a 1985 hijacking, is credited with saving the lives of the plane's passengers. One survivor said, "She put her body between blows and took blows herself. I think there would have been many more killings, perhaps an entire planeload, if it had not been for Uli." And what did Ms. Dericksen herself say? "Fortunately or unfortunately, I was the purser on that flight, and I did my job" (from the *New York Times*, July 7, 1985).

Harriet Tubman, an ex-slave, risked her own life every time she went back to the pre-Civil War South to lead caravans of other slaves northward to freedom. Some people called her the Moses of her people; others compared her to Joan of Arc. One abolitionist said she deserved "to be placed first on the list of American heroines" (from the *New Yorker*, March 25, 1985).

Respect for human life takes other forms as well. Valuing life also can mean preserving or maintaining the dignity with which a life must be lived, often against overwhelming odds.

Many of the chores that women have performed through the years have been simple services that supported the dignity and welfare of the people in their care. Women often have been in the forefront of efforts to obtain humane treatment for undervalued or silent victims of an indifferent society. Feeding, clothing, and keeping people clean, and insuring them a decent place in which to sleep, are very humble tasks, but think of how quickly a life deteriorates when these basic needs go unattended.

Florence Nightingale, to use a familiar example, rebelled at the prospect of the conventional life that a genteel Englishwoman of her time was destined to lead. She chose instead to walk the grimy corridors of army hospitals miles away from her homeland. If you picture for a moment what that actually meant, you can get a measure of her heroism. She was much more than our image of her, prim in a lace collar. She challenged the appalling hospital care that was as devastating for injured soldiers as their experience on the battlefield. She established training standards for nurses that reformed the entire profession and, in doing so, reformed what had been a slatternly occupation and made it an acceptable way for respectable women to earn their living—thereby insuring the dignity of even more lives.

Less familiar, but chillingly instructive, if you have read any of the accounts of life in a German concentration camp, you will remember how dehumanizing and deadly it was to be deprived of the simple ability to keep clean (Des Pres, 1976). Even in less malevolent settings, research, for example, on the epidemic of foreclosures on farms that had been in a family for generations has suggested that the farm wife is the family bulwark: "If she remains strong," a journal article says, "the family stays together. If she crumbles, the family will probably dissolve" (APA, 1986).

Ultimately, respect for the dignity and value of a human life also rests on and enriches the respect for one's own worth. The ability to tolerate remarkable hardship, to persevere in the face of discouraging odds, to create and then take heart from dedication to a cause are often quietly personal behaviors. We are privileged as therapists to be admitted into the private world of heroic struggle and victory where the cast of characters may consist of only one person and a small group of intimates. But the heroic spirit is clearly there.

One woman, confronted with her imminent death, wrote notes from the bed she knew that she would never leave to all who were dear to her—acknowledging their importance in her life and her importance in theirs.

The story told by a social worker who works with AIDS patients provides us with another example. One afternoon, after a young patient had died, she and his brother shaved and dressed him neatly before his mother came to see him. To do this was not included in her job, but it was included in her sense of humanity. She spoke simply about her purposes in doing this. She felt that his mother had been through so much that she should be spared at least some last pain, and she wanted to insure for the young man some of the dignity he deserved.

Second: The Sense of Choice and Personal Effectiveness

The hero sees herself as a potential force for change; an unhappy circumstance is not merely to be endured. She identifies a need to change and not only works toward that goal personally, but often mobilizes others to move against common problems.

Beverly Carl, a lawyer and a professor at Southern Methodist University, filed a class-action complaint against the university because of the bias she felt they exercised against all women in "hiring, promotion, retention, compensation and appointment to prestigious posts." In an out-of-court settlement, the school agreed to adjust the salaries of four women professors, complete an affirmative-action plan, and "correct some inequities in pay and working conditions for the custodial staff" (from *Dallas Life Magazine*, March 23, 1986). As a result, Ms. Carl received many phone calls from women in various other occupations who felt that they, too, were being discriminated against and wanted to know what they could do for themselves.

Betty Washington single-handedly recruited and organized her neighbors for a citizen's watch program to rid the neighborhood of drug dealing and crime. Her open opposition made her a prime target, vulnerable to reprisal from those whose income she was threatening. Here is how a modern hero talks: "Either you speak out and take the risk, or you die in the cesspool" (from *Newsweek*, July 6, 1987).

The sense of agency, of one's personal effectiveness at correcting a wrong or of supplementing an omission, is often awakened and supported in therapy. This sense of choice, restored in therapy, can make a crucial difference in whether or not people feel that they are living their own lives or merely following a well-worn path with no sense of individuality or appetite.

One young woman with whom I worked is a teacher at a nursing college. Dismayed at the insensitivity of the student nurses (and some more experienced nurses, as well), she challenged the standard curriculum that had not been changed for years. She organized a series of lectures during which people who had suffered from a debilitating injury or disease described their shame and anger at being treated as objects with no contribution to make to their own rehabilitative treatment. She designed these sessions to include dialogue between the nurses and the speakers, and these exchanges were found to make a visible difference in the nurses' attitudes toward, and subsequent interactions with, their patients.

Third: The Original perspective

The relationship between the hero and the established order of things is fluid; she perceives, within the established order of things-as-they-are, things-as-they-could-be. This can be a risky vision, since questioning the validity of well-established assumptions may result in scorn, isolation, and ostracism for the troublesome questioner.

Professor Robin West of the Law School of the University of Maryland, for example, suggested a drastic revision of some of the assumptions that underlie legal decision making. She defined what she called "gender injuries": the pain felt "only by women from injuries experienced only by women," and presented the woman's perspective as crucially important in legal judgments (from the *Los Angeles Times*, October 7, 1988).

Anna Quindlen discussed the implications of having women serve in the armed forces. She saw beyond the image of women soldiers into women as-anything-they-can-be. She said

> But those of us who have been first woman something-or-other, who have done the jobs they said we couldn't do, know there's another way to move things along. Just do it. Just find a way to argue the case, to perform the surgery, to cover the war, and then everyone will know that it can be done. (from the *New York Times*, January 7, 1990).

I remember working with a woman who was chief administrator of a large church. As she sat in on organizational meetings over the years, she began to realize that what she wanted was not to be a member of the support staff, but to be the *minister*. For her, this was a revolutionary awareness, upsetting all the things she had learned as a girl, from her parents and from her ministers, about what her "proper place" was. It would involve years of study, taking her away from her husband and children and requiring *them* to assume many of the domestic responsibilities she had carried (along with her job). This was yet another separation from the familiar introjections about the responsibility of wives and mothers. She went through months of painful deliberation before she could even bring up the idea and her struggle with it to her family.

Fourth: Physical and Mental Courage

Heroic action requires courage, both physical and mental, and is not put off by the prospect of personal cost. The traditional hero almost inevitably risked death, injury, or humiliation. In our sensationalistic age, the defiance of these disasters remains the stereotypical hallmark of heroism.

But this is too easy. In disregarding personal conflict or welfare, the hero, it is true, may *appear* to court death, when actually she either considers the risk of death or loss to be less important than her purpose, or she may be so intent that she overlooks it entirely.

Heroic courage is often more than simply physical strength. It involves persistence and focus and the stamina to tolerate demanding situations. The hero may calculate the personal cost of following a different drummer or of espousing an unpopular cause or opposing a popular one—she is not deterred.

In moments of crisis or opportunity, the mental courage of the hero is often stunningly efficient. Her perceptions are sharpened rather than dulled. Her behavior is on target, specific; she is aware of, but not restricted by, circumstance. She identifies the essentials and responds to them directly.

Carolina Maria de Jesus wrote about her life in a Brazilian slum. At one point, a reporter happened to overhear her berating the men who were beating some children, threatening to include them in her "book," the diary she was writing of life in the *favela*, the slums of Sao Paolo. The reporter asked her permission to publish excerpts of her diary in his newspaper—and they created a sensation. Maria wrote: "The politicians knew that I am a poetess. And that a poet will even face death when he sees his people oppressed" (Moffat & Painter, 1975).

An increased recognition of "female" heroism—rooted in human connection and responsibility, but sharing the timeless qualities that have been recognized for centuries—expands and enriches the heroic image. The heroic image becomes relevant to humble settings, as well as to the grand stage. Such recognition seems particularly valuable in an age when merely striving to be stronger or faster than one's adversary could be suicidal.

THE HEROIC ATTITUDE AND THERAPY

> One must think like a hero to behave like a merely decent human being. (May Sarton)

Much has been written about the hero's journey and the significance that a personal sense of heroism could have in the lives of people who might not ordinarily think of themselves as heroes. Clearly, many people look to eternal heroic examples as a way of inspiring a perspective that they lack in the day-to-day practicalities of their lives. The books and articles that link contemporary life themes to the tales of ageless gods, goddesses, and heroes all are responding to people's need to make sense of the rush of experience that threatens to engulf them, like Alice in Wonderland, who finds herself, much to her surprise, swimming in a pool of her own tears.

The people who come to a therapist's office are often so embedded in their problems that nothing seems farther from their needs than a call to heroism. Even so, I would suggest that, among other complications, they are stuck with an archaic image of heroism that prevents them from seeing how a personal concept of heroism might be relevant to their dilemmas. The hackneyed image of heroism has disqualified what they *could* do, because it is not what they have been taught that they *should* do. They are stuck, unable to conceive of another course. To counter these unnourishing introjections, they must construe for themselves a new and individual definition of heroism. And often, in therapy, this is what happens.

Let me give you some examples from therapy of the heroic attitude: the hero's respect for the dignity and value of human life, the heroic sense of personal choice and effectiveness, the originality of the heroic perspective, and the physical and mental courage that supports heroic decision.

One woman agonized in therapy for a long time before she finally chose to become pregnant again after two devastating experiences. She had nursed an infant son through his illness until his death from a brain tumor. In her next pregnancy, she had had to have a painful late abortion because the fetus had died in utero. Nevertheless, after much anguish, she decided to try once again. Even after the birth of this healthy child, she still anxiously counted the days until the baby had lived beyond the short lifetime of her first child. But she said she was glad that she did it.

Another young woman suffered from a debilitating and chronic disease. While she was working toward her doctorate (a draining process under the best of conditions), she kept a detailed record of the phases of her disease and its response to the various prescribed medications she was taking to control it. Her hope was that such data, recorded properly by an informed person, might ultimately prove to be valuable in the eventual conquest of the disease. Refusing to be a victim, she hoped to seek a grant so that she herself might conduct research on her disease.

A well-established top executive in a national firm that had recently changed top management staff was dissatisfied with her life. She found the new style of management abrasive and inhumane. There was no doubt that she was well respected and could easily adopt, and even influence, the management philosophy. Unmarried, she had no financial support other than her own income. She had been reared in a conservative family that believed that once you had found your economic niche, you *stayed there.* As she talked, though, it became clear that she did not want to stay. She realized that she didn't want what she called "another career quest." She knew the routine; you complete one quest and right away you just start on another one. After considerable personal turmoil, she quit her job, set up a strict budget for herself, and took off with no guarantees to create a way of life she wanted to live and to find a place in which to live it.

> The urge to heroism is natural, and to admit it honest. For everyone to admit it would probably release such pent-up force as to be devastating to societies as they are now. (Becker, 1973)

Although these examples from therapy all involved women, they represent *human* heroism, heroism that moves beyond the flamboyant images that crowd our newspapers, magazines, television news broadcasts, and movie screens. Such heroism is plentiful, but we have not accorded it proper notice, and thus the influence that it could have on our lives and on our communities.

CONCLUSIONS

These days, we must be less willing than our myth-making ancestors to picture our heroes as part-human, part-divine. Superman notwithstanding, we must make distinctions between fantasy and actuality. We must get smarter at looking for substantial heroes who are within our reach—heroes who live in the same world that we do and who share our vulnerabilities. In emphasizing the humanity of our heroes, we also emphasize their relevance to our own humanity. The heroic image is invaluable when our admiration inspires us to look at our own lives with an eye to the heroic possibilities.

Heroes are all around us, more numerous than we thought. Heroism is also more diverse. Not limited to the dramatic, quick-thinking, life-saving deed, human heroism also animates the active voices that are raised in schools, courtrooms, legislatures, and hospitals. It inspires the heroism that occurs at the negotiating table, as well as at the kitchen table; in the lawyer's office, as well as in the nursery; at the judge's bench, as well as at the bedside; in Congress, as well as at PTA meetings; and at the controls of powerful machinery, as well as at the stove. Women and men belong in all of these settings and more.

I remember a young woman, facing her own death, who clung tenaciously to life until she felt she had fulfilled her responsibilities to her young sons. I heard not a word of complaint about the debilitating treatment, about the monstrous surgery she underwent to get a few more months of life, about the implacable, discouraging progress of her disease. When someone called her "indomitable," she could accept it, but to be called a hero was hard for her to assimilate.

"What's in a name?" Shakespeare's Juliet asks. I think a name brings with it recognition, dignity, inspiration, and permanence, among other things. And all these are lost when heroes who differ from the familiar images are deprived of their rightful titles. A stereotyped view of heroism limits both women and men because they are arbitrarily compelled to surrender half of their potential range of actions in order to conform to archaic formulas.

These are essential qualities that pervade the range of heroic possibilities. As therapists, we have the opportunity, as well as the responsibility, to recognize heroism in its many everyday guises, and to call it by its proper name. Each individual, by seeing the substance of heroism in herself or himself, can develop a view of her or his own life, a heroic attitude, that can transform human hopes into human achievement.

Individuality and Communality

Erving Polster

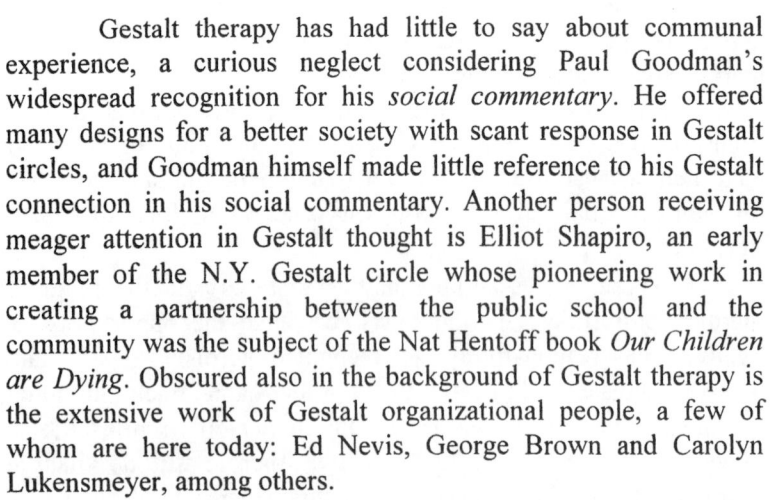

Gestalt therapy has had little to say about communal experience, a curious neglect considering Paul Goodman's widespread recognition for his *social commentary*. He offered many designs for a better society with scant response in Gestalt circles, and Goodman himself made little reference to his Gestalt connection in his social commentary. Another person receiving meager attention in Gestalt thought is Elliot Shapiro, an early member of the N.Y. Gestalt circle whose pioneering work in creating a partnership between the public school and the community was the subject of the Nat Hentoff book *Our Children are Dying*. Obscured also in the background of Gestalt therapy is the extensive work of Gestalt organizational people, a few of whom are here today: Ed Nevis, George Brown and Carolyn Lukensmeyer, among others.

One way to understand this neglect is to recognize that Goodman, Shapiro and the organizational workers were dealing with the community in its everyday function—the secular, so to speak. This secular focus stood in sharp counterpoint to the therapeutic focus, most commonly directed to the individual or the small group. Without spelling out the details of difference between the secular and the therapeutic, the secular attends to the hour to hour, day to day events of the world and the therapeutic focuses on a time away from that world, set apart for purposes of self-exploration. There is little doubt that the secular is the force which counts most in the lives lived by most people. It is in the secular sphere where we take account of food, shelter, government, information, productivity, economics, politics—even the Boston Red Sox! The question to be addressed is how to encompass our Gestalt secularists, like Goodman, Shapiro and the organizational workers so as to extend our voice into the community at large. First, let's look at the barriers represented by Gestalt therapy's historical emphasis on the individual, then on some options for adapting Gestalt therapy principles to the community at large.

This Gestalt therapy emphasis on individuality is recently showing signs of change. This conference—especially the attention to Paul Goodman and the scheduling of this symposium—is one example but over the years our concern with individuality has overshadowed any attention to the communal. This skewed perspective was influenced by distortions of the Gestalt understanding of, first, figure/ground and, second, of health/pathology. First, a quick look at figure and ground, which our theory says are in constant flux. Indeed, most of the time the relationship between figure and ground is so fluid that it would be difficult to say definitively what is figure and what is ground. Contrast this Gestalt fundamental, however, with Fritz Perls, when in his *Gestalt Therapy Verbatim*, he declared

> The discipline is simply to understand the words *now* and *how*, and to bracket off and put aside anything that is not contained in the words *now* and *how*. (Perls, 1969)

To bracket off and put aside anything beyond now and how is *his* vote, a mighty one, for figure, and by implication a vote for the individual. It was joined by other aphoristic approximations. The so-called Gestalt prayer is only one representation of this elevation of individuality. Another is the almost reverent homage given to personal choice and responsibility in a world where many people experience much less choice, as for example in breathing polluted air, than the philosophers say they have. Still another is the view of aloneness as a natural and healthy state. Of course, each person needs to encompass aloneness, yet in spite of the partial truth in all these glorifications of the individual, it is not news that people are also innately gregarious and that for many of us aloneness can be a damnable experience. Further, since Gestalt therapy esteems the contact function as a natural human mandate, it would seem consonant to see the agony of aloneness as a failure of gregariousness and to foster, even construct, communities in which this aloneness would be dissolved in an abundance of contact opportunities. Emphasizing the *health* of aloneness for those who *hunger* for contact, one might as well be Marie Antoinette telling people to eat cake.

An aspect of the health/pathology dimension is the Gestalt treatment of *introjection* and *confluence*, both of which are key processes in community formation and both of which have been largely pathologized. Introjection includes the codes which compel people to be as the community wants them to be. These ordained orientations form a light from above, a guidance for communal function. Unfortunately, as we all know, these guidelines may also clash with contradictory individual needs and sometimes drive people crazy. Similarly, confluence adds to the sense of communality by creating connections among people, a shared identity, requiring each person to accommodate their individual purposes to the coordinations required in communal formation.

For a psychological price—sometimes prohibitively high and at other times an excellent bargain—these two counterforces to individuality, introjection and confluence, contribute to a sense of belonging, to a promise of being more fully and readily understood, to an easy access to substantive support, to an established and consistent sense of self and most compellingly to a hospitality to the generic gregariousness of people. Yet, though Gestalt therapy, broadly interpreted, is neutral on the health or unhealth of introjection and confluence, they are almost invariably spoken of in pejorative terms, with distrust of community a natural consequence. Have you ever heard anyone admire how beautifully one has introjected? Or express happiness about fruitful confluence? Of course, there is some merit to this wariness since both of these processes are indeed major threats to individuality. But, conversely, a monopoly of individuality is also a threat to the communal. Whichever way our priorities go, we risk getting them wrong and getting either individuality or communality hobbled in the process. Right or wrong, though, we have been dealt a hand from which we have to play both cards.

Over twenty years ago I played the communal card by taking a look at the middle ground between the secular and the therapeutic. I reported some of these explorations at that time, then I dropped them and haven't written on this theme until now. In quick summary, since there isn't time now to go into the details, I did four separate things. The first thing I did was to get out of my private office to conduct public sessions in a coffee house during its regular evening hours, exploring themes of immediate concern to the coffee house community. Second, I explored the relationship between religious worship and psychotherapy by setting up prayer groups in a temple, where, in co-leadership with the temple's rabbi, we extracted personal meaningfulness from the prayers, exploring how gratitude or awe or sacrifice or other prayerful concerns appeared in the everyday life of the congregants. Similarly, I set up a worship and human relations exploration in Oberlin's Graduate School of Theology. Third, I introduced large group communal sessions into the Gestalt Institute of Cleveland, in which I was joined later by Ed Nevis. Under a subsequent succession of leaders, Sonia Nevis, Sandra Leon and Joseph Zinker, these sessions continue to this day, some twenty-five years later, under the current leadership of Donna Rumenik. Fourth, at Case Western Reserve, I co-taught courses in large group design with my wife, Miriam, showing how large groups could deal with important thematic issues in the lives of all the participants. At the same time, I worked with other large groups such as an incoming freshman class; in co-leadership with Joseph Zinker, a large student meeting at Kent State University, examining the aftermath of the infamous shooting of Vietnam War protesters; in coordination with Cynthia Harris and others, the combined faculty and student body of a small Midwestern college; under the coordination of Paul Frisch and the American Academy of Psychotherapists, a large group meeting exploring the problems of an impoverished African-American community near New York City; and in co-leadership with Miriam, the student body of a boarding school.

Since my absence from these activities, I have no inside view of the process but it is clear that expansions of communal orientation with psychotherapy overtones have continued over the years. For example, self-help groups are mushrooming. They address specific problems, such as gambling, child abuse, co-dependency and obesity. Richard Higgins, a writer for the Boston Globe, reported two years ago that there were 200 types of twelve-step recovery groups and he also said that each week they attracted 15 million American to 500,000 meetings. People have obviously been drawn to join with those people with whom they have some common identity to address the core issues which bother them. Not only to these groups emanate a communal feeling, tapping into a generic hunger for bondedness but many of them do it without professional leadership, thus multiplying the availability of such communal opportunities.

These groups are usually small but another therapeutic offshoot is the large group innovations of people like Jacob Moreno, Elizabeth Kubler-Ross and Jean Houston, each of whom in their own distinctly different ways has inspired powerful large group experiences. More widely organized and marketed but also widely scorned by therapists was the work of EST, which caught fire some years ago and the style of which is currently discernible in a new group called the Forum. I think EST confirmed Gestalt fears about introjection and confluence. They used procedures already familiar to Gestalt therapists: directed visualization, the accentuation of simple awareness, the featuring of the paradoxical theory of change, meaning one recognizes and accepts "what is" in order to, as the EST people said, "get it" and also the creation of safe emergencies. These groups were very austere and they enhanced receptivity to the leaders' messages through the heavy induction of introjection and confluence. Some of the messages were the dictatorial tones of the leaders, isolation from the outside world and from each other, repetition of themes, inducing fatigue, and spotlighting communal example. While this authoritarian force exploited the natural introjective and confluent reflexes and resembles brainwashing, it would be a short step to *honor* the interpersonal *resonances* and *responsiveness* of introjection and confluence, each of which has a continuing interplay with the individual freedom of the participant. Kindness, free choice, compelling themes, contact vibrancy, fitting experiments, laughter, music, poetry, continuity of meetings and the community, inspirational talks, relationship to the larger community, including nation and universe: all of these may by experienced within the introjective and confluent processes.

We all introject. Through the quality of spontaneous receptivity, introjection is a fundamental venue of learning. As I have written more extensively in a recent paper, introjection is not an isolated phenomenon and should be viewed together with other functions for shaping experiences, specifically contact, configuration and tailoring. Since introjection is so central, a continuing psychological force, we must ask not only *whether* introjection occurs but also *what* is being introjected, *how* the message is infused and what is being *done* with it. Because some of the EST messages did indeed have merit, the process had widespread effects including many laudatory testimonials. In spite of obvious alienations, there the EST people were—doing much of what psychotherapists generally support; bringing people together in mutual psychological exploration, fostering open communication, helping to find relief from shame and other sources of personal paralysis and guiding people to get clear about what they want and what they are doing in this often incomprehensible, lonely and disheartening world. When large groups such as these have unacceptable values and methods, we must distinguish the *abuses* of the process from the *process*. If we want to damn the abuses, must we also damn the need?

Communal magnetism is a fact of life. When we, in psychotherapy, shun the unruly process of creating new formats for people to congregate and to attend to common psychological concerns, they will still be humanly compelled to congregate and our abdication will leave the field to others. They will surely fill it in their own ways, often in ways alien to our beliefs. Why not create our own voice?

BEYOND ONE TO ONE

MIRIAM POLSTER

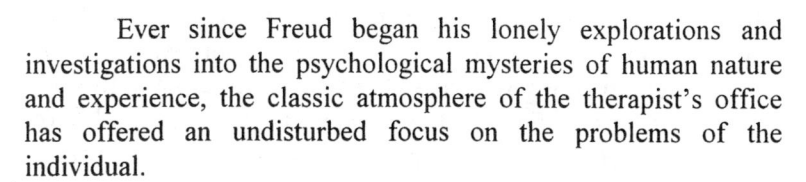

Ever since Freud began his lonely explorations and investigations into the psychological mysteries of human nature and experience, the classic atmosphere of the therapist's office has offered an undisturbed focus on the problems of the individual.

But ghosts from the past and troublesome people from the present keep intruding into this supposedly private setting. It became clearer to Freud's therapeutic heirs that it might be therapeutically fruitful to invite these influential but absent presences into the actual therapeutic meeting. So we began dealing with numbers larger than the original one-to-one. We invited the spouse into the office and began doing couples' therapy. We invited different members of the household and began doing family therapy. We invited other troubled individuals into the office and began doing group therapy. And once we began doing that, we let the whole cat out of the bag and began working with organizations, classrooms, and large groups learning to acquire one desirable trait or to dissolve another destructive one (Wuthnow, 1994). Gestalt therapy also had its origins, classically enough, in individual work. Frederick Perls was, after all, a product of the psychoanalytic tradition of Germany in the twenties and thirties. But Perls was also influenced by other theorists of that time and place. They were trying to understand individual behavior as embedded in and reactive to the behavioral field in which it occurred, rather than as drawing its energy from purely instinctual and internal struggles. Field theorists, like Kurt Goldstein and Kurt Lewin, who were also influential in Germany at that time, inspired Perls to propose the therapeutic necessity of understanding the behavior of any individual as a response to or interaction with the environment in which that person functioned. This interaction, which could be rich and fruitful or awkward and unsatisfying, he called "contact".

Interestingly enough, Perls himself was not particularly interested in, or adept at, working with *groups*. Although he is known for his teaching demonstrations of therapeutic work with individuals within a large group, he only rarely recognized the group as a presence in the work. He might sometimes ask the person he was working with to address the group or an individual as representing specific outside influences in that person's life or perhaps representing a general public presence. He might (much more rarely) permit someone in the group to respond or offer a personal perspective. Perls' work, even in this setting, was clearly that of the one-to-one therapist/patient interaction, in front of a group but not *within* it. Even so, the public nature of such work was in itself a profound influence. It moved out of the privacy of the original therapeutic scene and increased the range of how personal issues could be openly dealt with.

GESTALT THERAPY IN GROUPS

Obviously, the possibilities for contact are enhanced in any therapy group; there are many people present, each of them with a particular history and set of needs, each with a personal style of response, communication and presence. So it is not surprising that several Gestalt therapists have described how attention to some basic Gestalt therapy principles, such as contact, awareness and experiment, is central when working with groups (Feder and Ronall, 1994; Polster and Polster, 1973; Rosenblatt, 1989, to list only a few).

The purpose of any theory of therapy, whether the focus is on the individual or the group, is to define the data and the desired outcome of therapeutic work. As is to be expected, Gestalt group therapy views the quality of the *contact* between the individual and the group as a major criterion. Good contact in turn rests on the individual's *supported awareness* of herself, of the other people who may be present, and of the relevant environmental conditions. Awareness is arousing and can move into fulfilling contact, or it can be inaccurate or disruptive and unwelcome.

The individual's awareness must include the other people in her group and by implication the other people in her life. What is she aware of in observing or interacting with them? Is she flexible and versatile enough to alter the interaction with the other person so as to enrich the interaction between them—to do this without losing what it is she wants to say or do, but tailoring it to connect more sensitively with the other person? Does he expect to be listened to or does his manner tell you that he has already decided that nobody will take him seriously, or that they are only pretending to be interested as a matter of form and so he restricts his speech to a superficial, pro-forma delivery?

One man had a habit of letting the end of his sentences just trail off, as if even he had lost interest in what he was saying. I asked him to continue talking, but to add the phrase, "...and I *really* mean that!" at the end of his sentences. He began to enjoy what he was doing, putting more animation into his speech. His sentences ended energetically, keeping the rest of the group fully interested until he finished talking.

Contrary to its reputation as a simple "here and now" therapy, the goals in a Gestalt group, as in other therapy groups, involve an equal respect for process and content. The group members are talking about aspects of their lives that concern, disturb or baffle them and leave them feeling perplexed and uneasy. So, although we honor the importance of the individual's contactful relationship to her present environment (in this case, the group), we also remember that her environment is also composed of her personal history as well as her current experience.

Her contactful style within the group is influenced not only by the actual events in that particular group but also by the events that have preceded the group meetings and the events that continue to happen in between group sessions. There is much important experience there. We cannot know her well until we hear her story. But the story itself is not enough. It is not only whether she tells us the story but also *how* she tells it—and how we *listen*. The corollary of how pungently the individual group member speaks is how the group members look, listen and take seriously what other group members do or say. Their awareness of her as well as their awareness of their reaction are the other half of the person's story.

One woman in an ongoing therapy group was asked, in a perfunctory show of politeness, how she had enjoyed the weekend conference she had just returned from. Her response matched the question; it was a bright, chipper answer. But another woman in the group was listening sharply and didn't buy it. She observed that the answer felt "gift-wrapped", like a bright package, revealing nothing. The first woman, responding to this new tone, wryly told a different tale. She brushed aside the bangs that covered her forehead and revealed a neat bandage. She then told how she had bumped her head on the sharp corner of a table at the first session and had to go to an emergency room to have it stitched up. It had pained her for the rest of the weekend. Quite a different story. All this because the other woman in the group had been listening and looking—and was unwilling to settle for the pretty answer.

The leader in a Gestalt group is alert to these contradictions. She aims at heightening both the individual's experience and the poignancy and directness of the interaction between members. The quality of the contact between Gestalt group members rests on their willingness and ability to see and comment on what they see. So the Gestalt leader watches for opportunities where differences or similarities between individual group members and others can be noted and discussed. In the interaction between group members the leader focuses on how they deal with similarity or difference once it is observed. Are they alienated by difference or interested in it? How might the differences between members offer a sense of options? Does a perceived similarity become too much like a big cloak that assumes a confluent identity beyond what may actually be justified?

All of these complexities occur within a group—as they do outside the group—and the hope is that experience within the group will have relevance beyond the walls of the office. There are limits, however. Interactions and experiments within the group setting are not to be taken as scripts or dress rehearsals to be put to use indiscriminately. Within the Gestalt group there are options that a person might *not* have available in everyday circumstances or might not think of, or dare to do. There is time and opportunity for a level of individual exploration and group participation that is possible precisely because of the special circumstances.

The Gestalt experiment, the "safe emergency", offers the individual the opportunity to explore beyond the personal contact boundaries that have become restrictive and habitual. The person learns the difference between feeling *exposed* and the developing sense of the possibilities in simply being *visible*. The internal struggle between personal polarities, or characters in a life situation, or in a dream can be brought into the open by having the individual carry on a dialogue between them, with himself playing both parts. Or this may take the form of enacting a metaphor the person has used in describing himself or some person in his life, or a personal predicament, or a circumstance or relationship that plagues him. Using other group members like this loosens his control and risks having other people play their roles in a style that may not be exactly as he conceived them. But it adds an element of surprise that provides a juicy energy to the individual work.

One woman, for example, who was just beginning to be politically active, was feeling uncertain about how to arrange the seating at a table for eight prospective volunteers that she was sponsoring (as an unpracticed but idealistic novice) in support of a political candidate. So she cast seven group members as these particular people and told them what kind of personalities they had, and what some of their interests would be. She then seated herself in a circle among them and listened to the conversation, exercising her options to re-seat them when it became apparent that it was an unsuitable pairing. She discovered that she actually had a better sense of how to do it, and furthermore that she *liked* being influential.

Even when silent, the group is there. In addition to the sense that they might participate in the drama of another member's life, the group *witnesses* what happens and provides a sense of continuity and breadth. It is a microcosm of possibilities, with a tacit sense of good will. This good will is not cheaply or casually given. Some of it is accorded simply through the acknowledgment that the group members all want to do something better. Some of it comes from the assurance of continuity and the accumulation of joint experience.

Some of it also comes from simply learning how other people may work through to resolution. This can encourage another person to create his own way of confronting his dilemma, emulating not the particular solution but the courage and inventiveness that it took to *find* that solution. Even so, much of the good will comes from the engagement with struggle, with confusion, and with not being intimidated by uncertainty.

As with all good experience, the benefits of these therapy groups were clearly too good to remain limited to the private therapeutic setting—more and more people sought ways to extend the relevance of what they had learned.

SUPPORT GROUPS

An issue of a bi-monthly referral directory of groups meeting in San Diego listed psychotherapy groups for men and/or women dealing with bereavement, sexuality, overeating, sexual or substance abuse, and other themes of human dissatisfaction. Common issues concerned communcation, intimacy, assertiveness and power, as well as specific diseases or caretaking roles in dealing with disease or disability in relatives. These groups are meeting a widespread need; recent research reveals that "At present, four out of every ten Americans belong to a small group that meets regularly..." (Wuthnow, 1994).

These groups are communities in miniature, formed to meet individual need in the company of one's fellows. For a person who is intimidated by the larger scene, they reduce communal interaction into smaller numbers and encourage people to speak of their personal concerns, sometimes in a group identified by a shared problem. Although there is a danger that a theme-oriented group may move too quickly into a sense of intimacy and identity, reducing individual people to their common symptom, nevertheless theme-oriented groups have proved highly effective in battling a variety of debilitating physical and emotional problems including insomnia, breast cancer and learning disabilities. There may be some evidence that the *lack* of an identified group may also be injurious. Jonathan Shay, for example, argues that the unavailability of the opportunity to mourn *communally* in the Vietnam War may well have been an important casual factor in the development of Post-Traumatic Stress Disorder (Shay, 1994).

Many of us have had the experience of seeing someone realize that a shameful secret that they had concealed for years—while dealing in isolation with the fear that they alone were crazy—disappears when they speak of it in a group of attentive listeners. I remember the response of a group of veterans in a VA hospital when one profoundly depressed man revealed, after weeks of silence, that his suicide attempt was a reaction to being rejected by a woman he was in love with. They understood how he felt and sympathized, but they could also keep alive a sense of his being able, eventually, to find the courage to love again.

Most importantly, groups can provide a transitional setting where its members learn how they might participate in the community that bustles outside the therapeutic meeting room. Satisfying engagement in the larger, more impersonal community calls for a personal balance between commonality and uniqueness. Many people are in support groups because they find this balance difficult to achieve and need the intermediation of a support group. A good group, like a good community, offers a mixture of support and independence.

The problem is not new. Over forty years ago Erich Fromm described the personality packaging some people go through in order to fit into their societies (Fromm, 1955). All too often in a larger society an individual makes an uneasy bargain where one characteristic is allowed to predominate and casts another quality into the shadows. So one individual is great at blending in, like a social chameleon, but finds that any sense of his individual difference is unwelcome and sometimes even frightening. Others may feel uneasy in groups, they see themselves as "loners" who risk their singular integrity when they become group members.

Many of the groups that "four out of ten" people belong to are perfectly in sync with our mobile society. The continuity they promise is the continuity of a negotiable relationship not unlike a pre-marital contract where the conditions for ending the relationship are all spelled out—*right from the beginning.* The underlying agreement is that the group is important but *temporary*; any member may quit as long as he or she gives a week's notice in order to "reach closure" properly. Just what a mobile society needs—disposable relationships.

Even so, they offer at least a partial solution to a feeling of social isolation in the light of American society's increasing reliance on technological contact. The group is *there*, physically present instead of on the other end of the Internet or as a flickering message on the screen of someone's computer.

The remnants of original community rest like artifacts just below the surface of everyday life. Fewer and fewer of us live in the city where we were born. We raise our children in circumstances where their intimates are friends, and family is too often a group of people you meet after a long trip and on special occasions. Sometimes family is the other half of the original parental scene with whom contact has been regulated in a courtroom. Comic movies adore these situations and send them to us around holiday time so we can laugh at ourselves for a change. Our old folk seldom live nearby and the richness of personal history as described in the tales of our elders is frequently relegated to a few impatient moments at a family gathering, or the taped reminiscences of an arranged interview. Some of us have closet shelves stacked with boxes of photographs of family members—many of whom we cannot identify.

These historical communities hover on the fringes of individual work and exert their influences from the distance of time and geography. Their customs may sometimes hinder the ability to find a contemporary community. For example, take a child who has been raised by a harsh and begrudging parent, perfectionistic and critical. He learns as an adult in therapy how to resolve the destructive introjects and construct a more accurate self-portrait. The appropriate therapeutic question is, "what next?" How does this person who has, in therapy, finally reduced the allegiance to a toxic community identify where to go, what companions and associates fit his present sense of self?

There are two forms of group experience that can be useful at this stage. One is the familiar group therapy setting that we have already referred to where the protocol is expanded beyond the one-to-one interaction of individual therapy but the emphasis still remains primarily therapeutic and the purpose is to come up with the resolution of personal difficulties.

Other groups can be designed to deal with specific situational needs, like a large group design for the entire incoming freshman class of a school, or an introductory session integrating new church members within an established religious congregation. The group forms temporarily to incorporate individuals into an ongoing system or to provide entry and companionship for those people coming into a strange new experience.

Other group possibilities come from the identification of common causes or activities. Many communal efforts rely on and encourage affiliation; they welcome members because they need impressive numbers in order to speak with a weightier voice. These groups are likely to be focused on issues of political governance and community self-regulation. They may have a temporary focus, on a particular issue, but often they have a renewable sense of concern that gives the group a sense of history of past accomplishments and a sense of a future as it continues to focus on recurring issues.

It is not outside the proper sphere of psychotherapy to explore what personal talents and interests a patient has that might lead him into connections with like-minded people. Such abilities may lead into a fresh sense of engagement with one's environment. They may lead to membership on voluntary citizen committees. Many such groups offer the promise of continuity and shared experience because they continue to identify new endeavors that engage them beyond the original purpose.

In social action groups that are formed to reach certain social or political aims, there is much to learn and practice in the give-and-take that persuasion and advocacy require. Argument must always leave room for further talk and eventual resolution. Eshtain calls this the basic "civility" that is an essential component of a "democratic disposition" (Eshtain, 1995).

Other groups coalesce around a common stage of life or a shared interest. Some of these groups are formed out of a deep-felt need to obtain and share information that pertains to a very specific aspect of their lives. They may be physically close, like the Texas group of 125 laid-off employees of a downsizing move at IBM. They meet regularly at a local church and discuss their individual reactions to their dismissal that have ranged from depression over the loss to pride in their newly discovered sense of self-reliance. One man observed that he had discovered that he had more time to volunteer and to "give back to the community."

The need for community can sometimes transcend physical distance—or even psychological substance. Smithsonian Magazine devoted an article to some of the off-beat societies that actually get together only rarely but still provide a sort of sense of community (Watson, 1995). The author introduces the topic by observing, "It's not what you do that counts, it's what you *belong to.*" Members keep in touch through correspondence or periodic conventions. Eligibility for membership is simple, ranging all the way from having the same name (the Jim Smith Society), the same activity (National Organization of Mall Walkers), or the same predicament (Edsel owners). We all know people who belong to a bird-watchers group, a photography association, a race-walking group, a biking or hiking group.

BEYOND ONE-TO-ONE

Many of the television programs we watch reflect societal trends. We can almost trace our values and experiences through the way they change. Some of the early programs celebrated the centrality of family connections, like *Father Knows Best, Ozzie and Harriet,* or *The Beverly Hillbillies.* Even explorations of prejudice were peopled by relatives and neighbors. Rmember *All in the Family*?

Even so, there were notable exceptions that leaned into the future. The opening shot of the old *Mary Tyler Moore* program showed her at the wheel of her car, driving into her new adopted city. Her parents almost never were referred to and rarely even made an appearance. The program centered on the comedic value of colleagues and friends. The popularity of her show may well have recognized the growing concerns of an audience of working women, no longer connected with family and "belonging to a group" consisting of co-workers and friends. It spawned *Lou Grant*—where a previously comedic character became a serious big-city journalist with professional associates. These settings are now commonplace as sitcoms deal with how people associate with co-workers; *Murphy Brown, ER, LA Law, Designing Women,* or with friends; *Ellen, Friends, Seinfeld.*

To be sure, many of the TV programs are still the same-old same-old. But there is a refreshing influence in some of the new programming. *ER* and *LA Law*, for example, take seriously the complexities of relationships when both persons work hard at what they do and pay for it in terms of exhaustion and disillusion. *Frasier* strikes a little closer to home for us. It deals, comedically of course, with the anonymous distress that causes people to seek advice via the telephone and also with troublesome but vital family relationships. *Mad About You* takes a two-career marriage, adds some troublesome siblings and in-laws, a dog, difficult neighbors, and a temperamental janitor.

We have a lot to learn from comedy. *Seinfeld* has a cast of eccentric friends. These people are all portrayed as having troublesome, outrageous characteristics. They lie, they do disgraceful things and then compound the situation by offering incredible justifications for their misdeeds. Obviously, these traits support the comedic intent—we would hardly tolerate them in real life. But here's the point: despite these shenanigans, these people, wonder of wonders, *continue* the relationship. Even the most egregious interactions do not seriously disrupt the friendship. They don't expect perfection from their friends or from themselves. We could learn something from them.

In 1938, not too distant in time from Perls' formulations of Gestalt therapy, Henry Murray was formulating his theory of "personology" with an intense focus on individual motivation. He listed twenty needs that he felt motivated and organized individual behavior. Here is how Murray describes four of them

> 1) *Affiliation*: To draw near and enjoyably cooperate or reciprocate with an allied other (an other who resembles the subject or who likes the subject). To please and win the affection of a cathected object. To adhere and remain loyal to a friend.
>
> 2) *Nurturance*: To give sympathy and gratify the needs of a helpless object: an infant or any object that is weak, disabled, tired, inexperienced, infirm, defeated, humiliated, lonely, dejected, sick, mentally confused. To assist an object in danger. To feed, help, support, console, protect, comfort, nurse, heal.
>
> 3) *Exhibition*: To make an impression. To be seen and heard, to excite, amaze, fascinate, entertain, shock, intrigue, amuse, or entice others.
>
> 4) *Succorance*: To have one's needs gratified by the sympathetic aid of an allied object. To be nursed, supported, sustained, surrounded, protected, loved, advised, guided, indulged, forgiven, consoled. To remain close to a devoted protector. To always have a supporter. (Hall and Lindzey, 1978)

These are needs that can only be met in community. They represent the behaviors that reveal the individual's need for a personal, interactive sense of community. It is important to notice that they are *reciprocal* needs—not only to receive, but also to give.

Daniel Goleman has recently introduced a human capacity that he calls "emotional intelligence" (Goleman, 1995). He observes—as we all have noticed at one time or another—that a high IQ alone cannot explain why some individuals prosper and others bungle. He proposes two behaviors, physiologically based but still amenable to change, that comprise emotional intelligence. They are "the ability to control impulse", and "empathy". To these abilities he links two moral attitudes: "self-restraint and compassion". Goleman also talks about the centrality of self-awareness, of managing one's emotions and of handling difficult relationships.

He offers some recommendations for teaching these behaviors to our children and shows how groups that sound like a combination between teaching and psychotherapy can ameliorate destructive behavior in children who may otherwise be headed for trouble. What do these programs teach? Through class discussion and specific exercises, these children learn how to recognize their own and another's feelings; how to cooperate in a group solution; how to resolve conflict, and how to think of alternate solutions to a disagreement, to name a few.

Here, I propose, is where group therapy and our current batch of sitcoms meet. An improbable development, but stay with me a moment. *Seinfeld*'s friends are clearly an exasperating bunch. They come up with a series of improbable explanations and convoluted interpretations that get them into more trouble than the original dilemma they were invented to resolve. But these behaviors are absorbed into the basic premise that the relationship is never seriously ruptured. It may flounder, they may holler at each other, but the continuity of their friendship is never in doubt. There is an underlying attitude of hopeful persistence and a willingness to deal with interpersonal troubles that prevents rupture.

The steadfast assurance of a reliable source of community support which was previously based on family and neighborhood took on new forms as a consequence of our love affair with individualism. We have gone through the invulnerability of the rugged loner, who rides into town, eliminates the villain's threats, and then rides out again, like a *deus ex machina* on horseback. Many people are becoming aware of the consequences of this kind of solitary function and saying it won't do. The recent trend of successful career people opting out of the rat-race and either simplifying their lives, or becoming their own bosses and being in charge of their own schedules is too broad a trend to overlook.

The skills that Goleman describes are very similar to the behaviors we emphasize in groups. But these skills have a value beyond enabling a person to deal with his or her individual environment. These skills are important in *building* a particular personal community. They are central in learning how to enter the already existing communities that our mobility may plunk us into. These abilities must be transferable beyond therapy and support groups into the communities where people spend the hours and minutes of their lives, with the people who are important to them, and who will be there for a predictable time to come.

Individual therapy is invaluable. It helps us achieve a perspective on troublesome aspects of our lives. But it risks maintaining too narrow a focus compared to the wide-angle life we live with our daily companions and co-workers. Group therapy is an intermediate step between close attention to exclusively individual concerns and finding one's place in the traffic jams of a broader community.

The one-to-one therapeutic style emphasizes the importance of attention to individual needs for resolution, expression, and self-sufficiency. Transposing this attitude to group work—and further understanding its relevance to the larger community—can release some important societal implications that the individual members of the group can apply to their lives outside the therapy group.

CONCLUSION

Most of what we are as individuals is defined and shaped by our encounters with "otherness". How we relate to all the similar and dissimilar others who intersect our daily life greatly influences how appetitive and comfortable we feel in these incessant interactions. The sense of uniqueness that challenges and defines every individual requires a personal and communal etiquette of participation and interaction.

One of the most basic sources of interpersonal difficulty is how communities deal with individual difference. The attempt to muzzle disagreement, whether it results in shouting down a speaker in a public forum, blocking a person's access to medical treatment, a threatened filibuster in a legislative chamber, or a political assassination, is not only hateful, it doesn't work. Objection and difference exist, like it or not.

The opposite, dealing with similarity, is also worth looking at. Friendship and affiliation cannot require absolute agreement, they cannot depend on an uneasily imposed sense of shared identity. People must learn how to remain in the same group while tolerating variation, perhaps even finding difference a fertile ground for creativity. When a person feels alienated or angry does he become more articulate or less, more or less loud? How well does he listen to another's response and find ways for clarification or a useful combination of shared purpose?

How can we teach patience, in a harried world where the tempo feels always like a fast march? Patience, when a person listens carefully to what another is saying rather than simply waiting impatiently for him to finish so that she can have her say again. How can we teach how to distinguish between the persistence that moves toward resolution or the fixity that prevents progress?

We must learn, as professionals who deal with difference and conflict, that it is important to work against an indiscriminate sanctification of individuality that allows one individual to label as an "enemy" a person with whom she differs or whose behavior she disapproves of. This kind of linguistic escalation begins with words but all too often ends in violence. We must learn how to argue with mutual respect. We must learn to continue, not by merely repeating the same old arguments but by restating them, possibly including some insights from the other side.

Remember, some of the skills that are learned and practiced in a group may be even more useful as we move beyond one-to-one into the casual encounters where the rules of communication are not always spelled out. Contact under these less structured conditions must be durable enough to be maintained through episodes of poor or frustrating interaction with other people.

It is easy for us to feel the common purpose of a community under special circumstances, when we are engaged in a war or in launching a national space program; these are vast events and we respond with a kind of almost reflexive enthusiasm that we may have thought we lost. With on-the-spot media coverage of these events we can feel a whole nation collectively hold its breath until an endangered space mission returns to earth.

These moments are compelling, but we cannot hang a life on such incidents. Most of our lives are spent in simple communal interactions with other ordinary people. Nothing special. That's the point. We have to learn how to interact in the "not special" moments. We have so many of them.

It's Only the Most Recent Year of the Woman

Miriam Polster

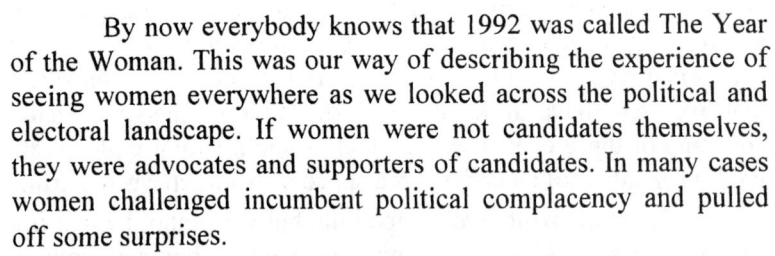

By now everybody knows that 1992 was called The Year of the Woman. This was our way of describing the experience of seeing women everywhere as we looked across the political and electoral landscape. If women were not candidates themselves, they were advocates and supporters of candidates. In many cases women challenged incumbent political complacency and pulled off some surprises.

Women's articulate appearance in these previously limited activities testifies to the range of their concerns and does indeed demonstrate how far they have come. But even "The Year of..." reveals a chronic dilemma. Too many people still remain undecided about which "Woman" we're talking about: Hillary or Barbara, Murphy Brown or Donna Reed, the woman who stayed home with the kids or the one who went off to help earn enough money to feed and clothe them, the woman who struggles privately to keep a family together or the one who has become a public voice on behalf of these families.

Now, after the election, we see women who carry briefcases as easily as shopping bags, who wield a gavel as easily as a rolling pin, who call a business meeting to order as easily as they comfort a crying child. We see women on television in state legislatures, in the Senate and the House, and as Presidential appointees to his cabinet or advisory councils. We see women invited to televised nationwide teach-ins and town meetings, speaking out about their concerns, addressing political issues and proposing possible approaches to our nation's ailments.

We are conditioned to accept easily that one of the most eloquent speakers was a woman advocating prenatal and preventive medical childcare who argued with passion and intelligence, as she has for years, for more governmental attention to the poverty and deprivation that stunt the development of an alarming percentage of our nation's children. Tradition has conditioned us to believe that was fitting—a "woman's concern, after all. But the real surprise (for too many people perhaps) was how many other women spoke knowledgeably and persuasively on topics that have historically been less associated with women's concerns—about flexible worktime, the prudent use of energy and other natural resources, training and retraining workers in a technologically evolving world, the wise use of business loans, and the revitalization of our judicial system.

Our chronic ambiguity about the "proper" place of women has had a long history in American affairs. Women's leadership has traveled a difficult and sometimes circuitous road.

From the beginning, when the colonists first set foot on fertile but unwelcoming land, women have played an essential but paradoxical role. Not only were women scarce in colonial times, but the new land required all of the settlers to work hard. And women worked as hard as the men. Women made many of the domestic articles needed for their homes and families; many of them were competent butchers, silversmiths, upholsterers. They learned many other trades through apprenticeship, often as assistants within their own family trades. Even so, women's place in colonial times was anonymous and subordinate, limited to supportive activities for the men of their families but politically and educationally irrelevant.

The same curious position of women as valuable allies in hazardous times and circumstances continued into the territorial expansion and homesteading that went on in the years after the arrival of the colonists. The courage and durability of the women who confronted the harsh, unfriendly welcome of the prairies and the big sky country matched that of their men. Even more than that we learn, as we read from their diaries and journals, about their sense of joy and exhilaration as they overcame the hardships and learned to love the rough beauty of their new land.

But women's indomitability and inventiveness went beyond that challenge. The same womanly spirit of enterprise and involvement grew into activities that went beyond simple survival—into women's leadership in the essential public dedication to community that men were either disinterested in or too busy to identify.

In the settlements and towns that resulted from the original movements westward, women began to emerge from their private homes into their larger communities. They did this organically, by extending their homemaking and caretaking skills to the needs of their growing and increasingly complex neighborhoods. Moving beyond the four walls of their own houses, they began to develop and establish the life-supportive services that their communities required. Women founded and funded schools, hospitals and agencies to care for the orphaned, the disabled and the needy—all the institutions that elevate and concern a community when it is free to rise above preoccupation with simple subsistence needs.

Still later, in the Industrial Revolution, the leadership of American women took another turn. At the onset of this new age, men were still centrally important in farming. Young, unmarried women, on the other hand, could be spared periodically according to the seasons. So it was women (and regrettably, children, since they too were more available for work in the factories) who initially powered the industrial age. Nevertheless, faithful to the patriarchal spirit of the times, the young women who went to work in the New England textile mills, for example, were not allowed to fend for themselves in the towns where they worked. They were housed protectively in communal boarding houses—but with unforeseen and powerful consequences.

Gathered together under one roof these women began, naturally enough, to talk with each other about some of the common grievances they had about their work. And from these informal exchanges grew concerted efforts aimed at improving working conditions and wages, and forming simple labor organizations. The mill owners, quick to catch on, promptly abolished the construction of any new boarding houses and the young women, forced to find individual housing with private families, were thus dispersed throughout the mill towns. Once women had entered the labor movement, though, their influence was central. One of the most active groups in arguing for and securing better working conditions were the female workers in a women's specialty—the shirtwaistmakers' union.

Historically, many women developed their political backbone on someone else's cause and then later discovered how to use that backbone for purposes of their own. The Abolitionist movement, for example, attracted many women who worked tirelessly for the emancipation of slaves. But working for the abolition of slavery turned out to be a kind of training program for later political engagement. Women learned how to conduct campaigns, how to get signatures on petitions, where and to whom to send those petitions when they were completed, and how to argue persuasively and publicly for their cause. When that cause was won, the emancipation turned out to have been reciprocal. The women realized that they could indeed alter the Constitution. Although the founding fathers had constitutionally denied women the vote, these women wanted a voice in all the political and judicial decisions that governed their own lives—and so the Suffragist movement was born.

Now, as we have seen, women have moved beyond the original vision of the Suffragists to become candidates themselves. And to do this they have become even more canny politically—and more self-supportive. In the past, women candidates were notoriously under-funded but in the recent election their campaign coffers benefited mightily from unique fundraising techniques, the "small potatoes" approach, that women had practiced for years in support of charitable purposes. This past year, small personal contributions from many individuals countered the traditional blockbuster contributions from the powerful few. And these contributions resulted in the vigorous and often successful campaigns of women candidates—novices and experienced hands alike.

What the Most Recent Year of the Woman has to teach is that, if women are to be more than obediently governed, we must all recognize that the opportunity to lead is anywhere that women care passionately about their lives and the lives of others. The women who preceded us have taught us that. They moved beyond what was formally or informally defined as their proper station and claimed their relevance to all the activities of their communities and of their country. Women are citizens who must remember that leadership begins right where we all live. Whatever happens in this country is our business.

But like the wisdom Eve purchased, the cost is high. Women must be informed participants in their own governance. Unlike Eve, we never did live in Paradise. But instead of being a curse this may actually have given us an advantage. Our knowledge was not magically bestowed. We have had generations of brave women teaching us what leadership requires and what it takes to exercise it.

It takes vision. The homesteading women saw beyond the crude settlements to the kind of communities that they wanted for themselves and their children. For them, their challenging circumstance was a jumping-off place into a future that moved beyond present need into a fuller vision of humanity. They were not given a Garden of Eden, they had to work for it. We have to nourish this combination of vision and energy in ourselves and our children. We have to nourish the ability to see past things-as-they-are, into things-as-they-could-be.

It takes courage—the willingness, if need be, to go first and to support an unpopular stand against entrenched opposition or just the simple inertia of the status quo. This is the kind of courage shown, for example, by the woman who confronted the callous domination of a one-industry textile town in order to win better working conditions for herself and her neighbors.

It takes a sense of affiliation—the ability to see oneself in another person's place, the awareness that often we are speaking for more than ourselves and that our hopes typify the lives and hopes of others who may not yet know how to put their own aspirations into words. Women who work with battered wives and abused children, women who work for the education of teenage mothers, are often women who have either emerged from their own tragedies and are helping other women to do that too—or they are women whose compassion allows them to put themselves in the place of the less fortunate women.

It takes the will to know—to identify the issues in order to ask pertinent questions. Women need to know what has been tried so that we can recognize ineffectual directions and explore others. When we know more about the leadership within and around us we are better able to identify the leaders we want to elevate to the next level.

Most of all it takes a sense of agency. There is work to be done and women must see themselves as agents who can make things happen. From the women who argue that they belong on the battlefields fighting for their country, to the grandmothers who organize patrols of their dangerous neighborhoods, they are all asserting their willingness to do what they see needs to be done.

Certainly some of our fundamental human aims have not changed all that much. But what has changed is that women have begun to see that their community is global, not simply bounde d by the four walls of household familiarity. Women must speak about issues that had formerly been considered men's concerns, adding their voices and their perspectives to traditional thought. We, men and women alike, need to talk with each other, to confront difference and disagreement, to learn what can be gained from different points of view—and to arrive at new harmonies and solutions.

This Most Recent Year of the Woman told us that leadership is a ladder that each of us can put our foot on, wherever we live, in the decisions big and small that shape our daily lives. Leadership is not out there, it resides in each of us right from the beginning. We must assert our own right to it, we must nurture it in our children, we must value and support it when we can in a neighbor or friend.

So it is that this past electoral year was not the Year of the Woman. It was only the most recent year of the woman. Let us look forward to the next years.

Coda

WHAT'S NEW?

MIRIAM POLSTER

A long time ago I was asked what I wanted to be like when I got to be an old woman. I answered that, after years of being a considerate and well-mannered person, I would like to become an old curmudgeon in tennis shoes and with a cane which I would use to poke young people and exhort them to "Shape up!"

Well, the tennis shoes and the cane remain future equipment so far, but the curmudgeonly attitude has begun to settle in. I notice it most when I'm asked about what's new in Gestalt therapy by people whose acquaintance with it is fairly recent.

Gestalt therapy is in its middle years, younger than the pioneer theories of psychotherapy but no longer an impudent upstart protesting the stodginess of its older relatives. It is a theory which can no longer be wished away or dismissed as a fad. It is a blend of clinical exigencies and philosophical insight, of learning theory and psychotherapeutic technique, of psychological inquiry into the nature of experience and one person's simple concern with another. Mastering the principles of Gestalt therapy supports the possibilities for lively contact—un-selfconscious and spontaneous.

Every theory and its practitioners have to strike a fertile balance between the basic principles and philosophy and the fresh insights that result from a vital connection to contemporary needs and circumstances. If fidelity to the initial outlook is ignored or twisted to meet a current vogue, the theory loses its integrity and becomes indistinguishable from other "eclectic" theories. On the other hand, if it clings too rigidly to the original formulations of its founders theory becomes an orthodoxy whose followers devote most of their energy to identifying heretics and claiming exclusive authority over definitions and deviations from the true faith.

Recently, at an American Psychological Association convention, I sat in on a seminar which dealt with Otto Rank and his therapy with artists. As you know, Rank's concepts have had a profound influence on the formulations of Gestalt therapy. One of the speakers quoted Rank as saying that he needed a new theory whenever he met a new patient. Now, of course he didn't mean that he started all over again each time. What he was saying was that he wanted to keep himself free to respond to the novel invitation that each unknown individual implicitly presented to him. This same opportunity confronts us.

What's new?
Ladies and gentlemen, I'm glad you asked.

The patient is new.

References

APA. (1986). *Monitor*, June. American Psychological Association.

Bardwick, J. (1971). *Psychology of Women*. New York: Harper & Row.

Beck, A. (1979). *Cognitive Therapy and the Emotional Disorders*. New York: NAL Dutton.

Beck, A. (1991). Cognitive Therapy: A 30 Year Perspective. *American psychologist*, April, 1991.

Becker, E. (1973). *The Denial of Death*. New York: Free Press.

Beisser, A. (1970). The Paradoxical Theory of Change. In Fagan, J., and Sheperd, L. (Eds.), *Gestalt Therapy Now*. Palo Alto: Science and Behavior Books.

Berlin, I. (1996). *The Sense of Reality*. New York: Farrar, Strauss, and Giroux.

Bohm, D. (1982) *Wholeness and the Implicate Order*. London: Routledge, Kegan & Paul.

Buber, M. (1958). *Paths in Utopia*. Boston: Beacon Press.

Bugental, J. F. T. (1965). *The Search for Authenticity*. New York: Holt.

Bulfinch, T. (1979) *Myths of Greece and Rome*. Compiled by Brian Holme. New York: Viking Penguin.

Cary, J. (1961). *Art and Reality*. New Yok: Doubleday.

Corsini, R. (1957). *Methods of Group Psychotherapy*. New York: McGraw-Hill.

Davanloo, H. (1980). Trial therapy. In H. Davanloo (Ed.), *Short Term Therapy*. Northvale, NJ: Jason Aronson.

de Assis, M. (1990). *Epitaph of a Small Winner.* New York: Noonday Press.

Des Pres, T. (1976). *The Survivor.* New York: Oxford University Press.

Dreiser, T. (1900) *Sister Carrie.* New York: Harper.

Eisely, L. (1975). *All the strange hours.* New York: Scribner's.

Eliot, T.S. (1943). *Four Quartets.* New York: Harcourt, Brace.

Erickson, M., and Rossi, E. (1979). *Hypnotherapy: An Exploratory Casebook.* New York: Irvington.

Eshtain, J. (1995). *Democracy on Trial.* New York: Basic Books.

Feder, B. and Ronall, R. (1994). *Beyond the Hot Seat.* Highland, NY: The Gestalt Journal Press.

Fromm, E. (1955). *The Sane Society.* New York: Holt, Rinehart and Winston.

Gerzon, M. (1982). *A Choice of Heroes.* Boston: Houghton Mifflin.

Gilligan, C. (1982). *In a Different Voice.* Cambridge, MA: Harvard University Press.

Gilligan, C., Lyons, N. and Hammer, T. (1990). *Making Connections.* Cambridge, MA: Harvard University Press.

Goleman, Daniel. (1995). *Emotional Intelligence.* New York: Bantam.

Goodman, P. (1962). *Utopian Essays and Practical Proposals.* New York: Random House.

Goodman, P. (1971). *Speaking and Language: Defence of Poetry.* New York: Random House.

Graves, R. (1982). *The Greek Myths 1.* Middlesex, England: Penguin.

Graves, R. and Patai, R. (1966). *Hebrew Myths: The Book of Genesis.* New York: McGraw-Hill.

Greenberg, L. and Pavaios. (1997). Integrating "Being" and "Doing" in Working with Shame. *Gestalt Review*. 1:271-274.

Hall, C. and Lindzey, G. (1978). *Theories of Personality*. 2nd Edition. New York: John Wiley and Sons.

Hazzard, S. (1982). New York Times Book Review, November 14.

Heidegger, M. (1962). *Basic Writings: Being and Time*. New York: Harper Collins.

Heidegger, M. (1962) *Being and Time*. New York: Harper Collins.

Heidegger, M. (1993). The Origin of the Work of Art. In: *Martin Heidegger: Basic Writings*, Krell, D. (Ed.). New York: Harper Collins.

Howard, M. (1982). New York Times Book Review, April 25.

Hunt, J. (1964). Concerning the Impact of Group Psychotherapy on Psychology. *International Journal of Group Psychotherapy*, 14, 3-31.

Jacabowitz, T. (1985, January 23). Letter to the editor. *New York Times Magazine*.

James, H. (1914). *Notes to Novelists*. J.M. Dent & Sons, Ltd.: London

Johnson, D. (1985). Review of *Austin and Mabel* by Polly Longworth. New York Times Book Review, March 4, 1985.

Kegan, J. (1987). *The Mask of Command*. New York: Viking.

Kierkegaard, S. (1948). *Purity of Heart is to Will One Thing*. New York: Harper.

Kozinski, J. (1977). Interviewed by Gail Sheehy, *Psychology Today*.

Krell, D. (Ed.). (1993). *Martin Heidegger: Basic Writings*. New York: Harper Collins.

Laing, R. D. (1965) *The Divided Self*. London: Penguin Books.

Laing, R.D. (1961) *The Self and Others*. London: Tavistock.

Latner, J. (1983) This is the Speed of Light. *The Gestalt Journal*, 6(2).

Lowith, K. (1993). The Political Implications of Heidegger's Existentialism. In: *The Heidegger Controversy*, Wolin, R. (Ed.). Cambridge, MA: MIT Press.

Marrow, (1969). *The Practical Theorist: The Life and Work of Kurt Lewin*. New York: Basic Books

Miller, J (1972). *Theory of Fiction, Henry James*. Lincoln, Nebraska: University of Nebraska Press.

Moffat, M. and Painter, C. (Eds.). (1975). *Revelations: The Diaries of Women*. New York: Vintage.

Mowrer, O. (1964). *The New Group Psychotherapy*. Princeton, NJ: D. Van Nostrand.

O'Connor, F. (1974). The nature and aim of fiction. In J. Hersey (Ed.), *The Writer's Craft*. New York: Alfred A. Knopf.

Nietszche, F. (1967). *The Birth of Tragedy*. New York: Vintage.

Nietszche, F. (1989). *Beyond Good and Evil*. New York: Vintage.

Perls, F. (1947). *Ego, Hunger and Aggression*. London: George Allen and Unwin, Lmt.

Perls, F. (1970). Four Lectures. In *Gestalt Therapy Now*, Fagan, J. and Shepherd, I. (Eds.). Palo Alto: Science and Behavior Books.

Perls, F. (1969). *Gestalt Therapy Verbatim*. Moab, Utah: Real People Press.

Perls, F., Hefferline, R., and Goodman, P. (1951). *Gestalt Therapy*. New York: Julian Press.

Perls, L. (1976). Comments on the New Directions. In Smith, E. (Ed.); *The Growing Edge of Gestalt Therapy*. New York: Bruner/Mazel.

Philippson, P. (1996). A Population of Gestalt Therapies. *British Gestalt Journal*, 5(1).

Phillips, J. (1984). *Eve: The History of an Idea.* San Francisco: Harper & Row.

Polster, E. (1966). A Contemporary Psychotherapy. *Psychotherapy: Theory, Research and Practice*, 3(1).

Polster, E. (1987). *Every Person's Life is Worth a Novel.* New York: Norton.

Polster, E. (1990). Introduction to the Revised Edition of James Simkin's *Gestalt Therapy Mini-lectures.* Highland, NY: Gestalt Journal Press.

Polster, E. (1995). *A Population of Selves.* San Francisco: Jossey-Bass.

Polster, E. & Polster, M. (1973). *Gestalt Therapy Integrated.* New York: Brunner/Mazel.

Proust, M. (1924). *Remembrance of things past.* New York: Random House.

Reich, W. (1949). *Character Analysis.* New York: Orgone Institute Press.

Rogers, C. (1980). A Way of Being. Boston: Houghton Mifflin.

Rogers, C. (1987). In *The Evolution of Psychotherapy.* Zeig, J. (Ed.). New York: Brunner/Mazel.

Robine, J.M. (1996). The Unknown Carried in Relationship. *British Gestalt Journal*, 5(1).

Rosenblatt, D. (1989). *Opening Doors.* Highland, NY: The Gestalt Journal Press.

Sartre, J.P. (1964). *Nausea.* New York: New Directions. (Original work published 1938)

Schachtel, E. (1959). *Metamorphosis.* New York: Basic Books,

Schwartz, L. (1983). *Disturbances in the Field.* New York: Harper & Row.

Shahn, B. (1957). *The Shape of Content.* New York: Vintage Books.

Shay, J. (1994). *Achilles in Vietnam.* New York" Touchstone.

Skinner, B. F. (1948). *Walden II.* New York: Macmillan.

Steiner, G. (1989). *Martin Heidegger.* Chicago: University of Chicago Press.

Tanner, D. (1990). *You Just Don't Understand.* New York: Morrow.

Tillich, P. (1952). *The Courage to Be.* New Haven: Yale University Press.

Watson, B. (1995). *Smithsonian Magazine*, v.26, No.1, April.

Watts, A. (1964), A psychedelic experience: Fact or fantasy. In D. Solor (Ed.), *LSD, the consciousness expanding drug.* New York: Putnam.

Weber, R. (1982). The Physicist and the Mystic: A Conversation with David Bohm. In *The Holographic Paradigm*, Ken Wilbur (Ed.). Boulder: Shambala

Wilbur, K. (1982). Reflections on the New Age Paradigm. In *The Holograph Paradigm*, Ken Wilbur (Ed.). Boulder: Shambala

Wolin, R. (1993). *The Heidegger Controversy.* Cambridge, MA: MIT Press.

Wuthnow, R. (1994). *Sharing the Journey.* New York" Free Press.

Yontef, G. (1993). *Awareness, Dialogue & Process.* Highland, NY: The Gestalt Journal Press.

Zinker, J. (1977). Creative Process in Gestalt Therapy. New York: Brunner/Mazel.

ABOUT THE AUTHORS

Erving Polster (Ph.D. Case Western Reserve University, 1950) is Director of the Gestalt Training Center-San Diego. He is also Clinical Professor in the Department of Psychiatry, School of Medicine, University of California, San Diego. Erv is co-author, with his wife, Miriam, of an important text in Gestalt therapy, *Gestalt Therapy Integrated* (Vintage, 1973). He also has written *Every Person's Life is Worth a Novel* (W.W. Norton, 1987), in which he spells out the therapeutic applicability of the kinship between the novelist and the psychotherapist. His most recent book is *A Population of Selves* (Jossey-Bass, 1995) presents a theory of the self which coordinates the concept of wholeness with the concept of personal splitting, and narrows the gap between theoretical principles and therapeutic practice.

Erv conducted the first locally led workshops at the Gestalt Institute of Cleveland in 1956, and was its first faculty chairman until 1973, when he and Miriam moved to San Diego.

Miriam Polster (Ph.D. Case Western Reserve University, 1967) is Co-Director of the Gestalt Training Center-San Diego. She is also Associate Clinical Professor in the Department of Psychiatry, School of Medicine, University of California, San Diego. She has taught psychology at the Cleveland Institute of Art, Case Western Reserve University and Cleveland State University.

Miriam is co-author, with Erv, of *Gestalt Therapy Integrated*. She has also written *Eve's Daughters: The Forbidden Heroism of Women* (Jossey-Bass, 1992), in which she enunciated some general characteristics of heroism, showing how cultural perspectives have excluded the particular kinds of heroism which women have commonly exercised. She examined prospects for cultural change should the personal qualities evident in the excluded examples of women's heroism be expanded to include the neglected heroism of women.

Together, the Polsters formed the Gestalt Training Center-San Diego, where for the last 25 years they have been teaching Gestalt therapy. Their work is widely known, and for many years people from all over the world have been coming to San Diego to work with them in their training programs.